PERFORMANCE OR COMPLIANCE?

Performance or Compliance?

Performance Audit and Public Management in Five Countries

Christopher Pollitt, Xavier Girre
Jeremy Lonsdale, Robert Mul
Hilkka Summa, Marit Waerness

OXFORD
UNIVERSITY PRESS

OXFORD
UNIVERSITY PRESS

Great Clarendon Street, Oxford OX2 6DP
Oxford University Press is a department of the University of Oxford.
It furthers the University's objective of excellence in research, scholarship,
and education by publishing worldwide in

Oxford New York

Athens Auckland Bangkok Bogotá Buenos Aires Calcutta
Cape Town Chennai Dar es Salaam Delhi Florence Hong Kong Istanbul
Karachi Kuala Lumpur Madrid Melbourne Mexico City Mumbai
Nairobi Paris São Paulo Singapore Taipei Tokyo Toronto Warsaw
and associated companies in Berlin Ibadan

Oxford is a registered trade mark of Oxford University Press
in the UK and certain other countries

Published in the United States
by Oxford University Press Inc., New York

First published 1999

British Library Cataloguing in Publication Data
Data available

Library of Congress Cataloging in Publication Data
Performance or compliance? : performance audit and public management
in five countries / Christopher Pollitt . . . [et al.].
p. cm.
Includes bibliographical references.
1. Administrative agencies—Europe, Western—Management—Auditing.
2. Executive departments—Europe, Western—Management—Auditing.
I. Pollitt, Christopher.
JN94.A63P47 1999 352.3′094—dc21 99-25365
ISBN 0-19-829600-2 (hardbound)

1 3 5 7 9 10 8 6 4 2

Typeset by Graphicraft Limited, Hong Kong
Printed in Great Britain
on acid-free paper by
Bookcraft (Bath) Limited
Midsomer Norton, Somerset

Preface

Performance audit involves assessing whether government policies, programmes, and institutions are well managed and are being run economically, efficiently, and effectively. This is a task of potentially great significance—at a practical level for citizens, and at a more abstract level for the health and vitality of democratic governance. In historical terms it is, in many senses, a relatively new procedure, one that has been adopted by many but not all EU member states. These aspects alone may be regarded as sufficient to justify our adding this book to the world's library shelves. Nevertheless, we seek the reader's indulgence to say something more about our aims, who 'we' are, and how (and with whose help) we have put this text together.

With respect to the book's *raison d'être*, we argue, first, that performance audits, as carried out by the Supreme Audit Institutions of individual countries, are actually and/or potentially activities of high democratic significance, as well as holding out the promise of helping to improve the functioning of government. Second, we point out that the number of publications offering sustained, independent analysis of the audit process is rather small. Third, we suggest that there are good reasons to explore the connections between performance auditing and public-sector management reform.

Performance audit is important because, in principle, it offers a means by which the citizens of democratic states may be offered independent reassurance as to the economy, efficiency, effectiveness, and good management of the programmes pursued by their governments. Over the last two decades most national audit offices (or 'Supreme Audit Institutions', as they collectively term themselves—hereafter SAIs) have devoted considerable energy and resources to the development and refinement of performance audit. Performance audit has, in effect, become a new instrument in the armoury of many SAIs—it has been added to a portfolio of other activities which usually includes more traditional forms of financial or regularity audit. In the following chapters we discuss what performance audit is and what its development trends have been.

Despite the centrality of SAIs in the legislative or executive machinery of most democratic states, the amount of academic attention that has been devoted to them has been modest. Only recently has the corpus of published work exceeded what a determined scholar could read in a single week. In contrast to the performance audit work of SAIs, the attempts of governments to modernize, streamline, and 'downsize' their administrative apparatuses have attracted the attention of many authors. A considerable academic and practitioner literature has grown, discussing the virtues and vices of privatization, corporatization, agentification, performance management, results budgeting, citizens' charters, total quality management, re-engineering, and a number of other managerial innovations. Yet—ostensibly at least—most of these reforms have been concerned with the very same things with which performance audit is supposed to be concerned: economy, efficiency, effectiveness, and good management. So in principle there should be some connection between them. The nature of this connection will be one main focus for our analysis.

The reader may well be suspicious of a book with six authors. Will it turn out to be anything more than a loose collection of disparate ideas and preoccupations, bound together more by the covers than by any intellectual coherence? While the proof of the pudding must ultimately lie in the eating, we can at least assure readers that this book is the product of a single project, a close and friendly collaboration between all six of us during which extensive efforts have been made to achieve coherence and continuity in our approach. Over a two-and-a-half-year period we have met regularly as a team and intensively reviewed each other's drafts as well as the overall structure of the book. This is a single work, not an edited collection.

As to who we are, there are at least two common denominators: first (obviously), we share a common interest in performance audit; second, we have all, at times in our careers, been public servants. Beyond that, there is considerable diversity. Four of us have been employed full time by our respective SAIs but two have not. Several among us have held or currently hold academic posts. We comprise one Frenchman working in France, one Dutchman working in the Netherlands, one Englishman working in England, one Englishman currently based at a Flemish university, one Finnish woman working for the European Commission, and one Norwegian woman employed by the Swedish National Agency for Higher Education. Brief biographies appear at the front of the book.

Collectively and individually, we have received a great deal of assistance with our project, and without that help this book could not have been written. The assistance has taken various forms. Access, time, and/or some financial support have been generously given by the SAIs covered by our study—the Dutch Algemene Rekenkamer, the French Cour des Comptes, the British National Audit Office, the Swedish Riksrevisionsverket, and the Finnish Valtiontalouden tarkastusvirasto. The European Court of Auditors has also been very helpful. Of course, none of these institutions bears any responsibility whatsoever for our interpretations: this has been an independent and essentially academic study, and we the authors are fully responsible for the concepts and argumentation of which it consists. As befits an academic study, we draw attention to issues, choices, and consequences but leave to others the business of making recommendations or passing judgements.

In addition to the SAIs themselves, various of us owe thanks to a range of other institutions which have granted us time or money to pursue this work. In this context, we wish to mention the Swedish National Agency for Higher Education (Marit Waerness) and the Finnish Ministry of Finance and the European Commission (Hilkka Summa). Finally, as project co-ordinator, Christopher Pollitt was dependent upon a grant from the UK [illegible] facilities provided by the Department of Government at [illegible] Public Management Centre at Katholieke Universiteit Leuven.

Beyond this, the book has been designed to be self-explanatory. We hope that it will be of interest to those public servants and media professionals who work for or regularly deal with SAIs, but we also hope that we succeed in infecting many researchers and students with our own curiosity concerning performance audit, public management reform, the relation between them, and—most significant of all—the implications of all these elements in combination for the democratic process itself.

C. P.
X. G.
J. L.
R. M.
H. S.
M. W.

Leuven, Paris, London, the Hague, Brussels, Stockholm
August 1998

Contents

Notes on Contributors

XAVIER GIRRE Manager (*conseiller*) at the Cour des Comptes in Paris. Has been involved in audits of major public firms, diplomatic services, and various bodies in the defence sector. Graduated from the Ecole Nationale d'Administration in 1995. Also an Assistant Professor in Economy at the Institut d'Etudes Politiques de Paris. Author of a report on the taxation of household assets (*Conseil des impôts*, 1997).

JEREMY LONSDALE Audit manager at the National Audit Office, London, working on value-for-money studies. Qualified accountant (CIPFA). Editor and co-author of the NAO's 1996 publication *State Audit in the European Union*.

ROBERT MUL Formerly head of the Algemene Rekenkamer's section on justice. In the autumn of 1998 moved to become the first director of Rekenkamer Rotterdam. Author of several academic and professional articles in the audit field.

CHRISTOPHER POLLITT Began working life as a Whitehall civil servant. Subsequently became an academic and consultant. Professor of Government at Brunel University, London, 1990–8; now Professor of Public Management, Erasmus University, Rotterdam. Consultant to the OECD, EU Commission, and other public organizations. Author of many books and articles on public management.

HILKKA SUMMA Head of Evaluation Sector, Directorate General for Budgets, European Commission. Formerly a counsellor at the Public Management Department of the Finnish Ministry of Finance, and a Professor of Political Science at the University of Helsinki. Author and editor of a number of academic publications in politics and public management.

MARIT WAERNESS Formerly worked for the Financial Management Department of the Riksrevisionsverket in Stockholm. Has also worked for the Swedish National Agency for Higher Education. In 1999 moved to the Norwegian Statskonsult, Oslo. Researcher and author in the field of public management reform.

CIPFA	Chartered Institute of Public Finance and Accountancy (UK)
DAS	*Déclaration d'assurance*/Statement of Assurance (EU)
C&AG	Comptroller and Auditor General (UK)
EFQM	European Foundation for Quality Management
GAO	General Accounting Office (USA)
INTOSAI	International Organization of Supreme Audit Institutions
MTMs	market-type mechanisms
NPM	new public management
NAO	National Audit Office (UK)
PAC	Public Accounts Committee (UK)
PFI	Private Finance Initiative (UK)
PRP	performance-related pay
RRV	Riksrevisionsverket (Sweden)
SAIs	supreme audit institutions
TQM	total quality management
VTV	Valtiontalouden tarkastusvirasto (Finland)
VFM	value for money
ZBOs	Zelfstandig bestuursorgaan (Netherlands)

1

Performance Audit and Public Management Reform

CHRISTOPHER POLLITT AND HILKKA SUMMA

In God we trust, all others we audit

University of Vermont 1997, p. 79

1.1 Audit, Performance Audit, and Public Management Reform

Audit is one of the oldest and most venerable state functions. The French Cour des Comptes traces its origins back to 1318; the UK National Audit Office cites 1314 as the date of its first manifestation; the Dutch Algemene Rekenkamer finds ancestors as running back to 1386. State audit thus long preceded the emergence of modern forms of democratic government. However, state audit offices have made many adaptations in the course of their long history, and during the nineteenth and twentieth centuries they fashioned a crucial role for themselves within the machinery of democratic accountability.

On this kind of historical scale, performance audit is a very recent activity. Although more or less plausible claims can be made for the existence of performance audit-like activities back to the 1960s—or even considerably earlier (Dewar 1985)—performance audit as a large-scale, self-consciously distinct practice dates mainly since the late 1970s. Performance audit represents a modern variant of audit—not the only one but, as we shall demonstrate, a challenging and fascinating one. It is distinctive to state audit and does not have a close counterpart in private-sector, commercial audit.

Over almost exactly the same period as performance audit has emerged as a distinct form of audit, the governments of Western Europe, North America, and Australasia have embarked upon extensive programmes of public management reform. These have aimed at modernizing, streamlining, and in some cases minimizing the whole of the state apparatus. Although the details of these reform programmes have varied considerably between one country and another, most of them have given a central place to the themes of decentralization and performance management (Hood 1996a; OECD 1995; 1997b; Pollitt *et al.* 1997a; Pollitt 1998). This has entailed a widespread rethinking of the balance between the autonomy and the control of public organizations. It has generated a search for mechanisms and incentives that will help realize these new management ideas in practice.

Prima facie, it appears highly probable that there is a connection between these two phenomena: on the one hand the growth of performance audit, and on the other the search for a new solution to the ancient governmental problem of giving autonomy yet retaining control. Yet there seems to have been little systematic investigation of what the nature of this interaction might be. One of our ambitions is to fill this gap. We begin, in the next chapter, by looking at the boundaries and definitions of performance audit, and then move directly (in Chapter 3) to describe the patterns of management reform in the five countries that form the basis for our comparisons: France, Finland, the Netherlands, Sweden, and the UK. This provides the context against which later chapters can tease out the connections between the development of performance audit and the forces of management change.

If the official descriptions are anything to go by, performance audit is not just a technical tool. It does not at all correspond to the traditional image of auditing as a process centred on 'checking the books' in order to see that they have been accurately and properly kept. Performance audit has a more ambitious manifesto. Its practitioners declare that they are seeking to establish whether public policies or programmes or projects or organizations have been (or are being) conducted with due regard to economy, efficiency, effectiveness, and good management practice. It thus brings together, in a potent new combination, the older tradition of 'audit' with a much more recent focus on 'performance'. The exact terms within which audit bodies undertake this activity (and what they call it, and how it is combined with their other activities) vary from country to country and over time. So we should not rush to say exactly what 'it' is or isn't, but rather should problematize and explore the concept. This is a task we embark upon in the next chapter. In that chapter we will also take a brief look at some of the many other uses to which the term 'audit' has recently been put, a diversification of meaning and practice that recently led one academic to write an ambitious text entitled *The Audit Society* (Power 1997). For the moment, however, it will suffice to say that sets of practices termed (in English) 'performance audit' or 'value-for-money studies' have become central activities for an increasingly powerful group of organizations—Supreme Audit Institutions (SAIs). In most democratic countries, the SAI is located near the heart of the apparatus of the state. Potentially, therefore, performance audit should be of considerable political and democratic significance. It is practised by powerful, independent institutions and is presented as a mode of investigation aimed at establishing whether, at what cost, and to what degree the policies, programmes, and projects of government are working.

Given these general characteristics, one might expect that the considerable community of scholars working in subjects such as political science, public administration, public management, and public finance and accountancy would have generated a large literature about performance audit. Surprisingly, this is not the case. One may speculate on the reasons why SAIs and, within them, performance audit have suffered relative neglect as compared with, say, various aspects of public management reform.

Several reasons for the apparent disparity of interest in (on the one hand) performance audit and (on the other) public management reform suggest themselves. To begin with, public management reform has been led—or at least fronted—by politicians, for whom it is natural to make public claims that what they are doing is innovative, valuable, and successful. Furthermore, such change has generated its own supporting 'industry', including various kinds of consultant who have (equally naturally) taken every opportunity to propel such reforms even higher up political and administrative agendas. By contrast, SAIs are single institutions—and generally rather sober ones. The bulk of their work appears to be technical and detailed and they take some pains to stand clear of party political controversy. Typically, supreme audit institutions are mentioned briefly in general textbooks which describe the institutions of government in a given country, but few books or articles have been written specifically about them. (In the UK Normanton, 1966, was a rare exception, and for France Descheemaeker, 1992, was similarly unusual.) The USA, though not part of the present study, was perhaps something of an exception to this general neglect, with a certain amount of analytical literature focusing upon the General Accounting Office (most notably Mosher 1979). Only in the last few years has the trickle of journal articles and booklets begun to gather some momentum (e.g. Barzelay 1996, 1997; Bowerman 1994; Leeuw 1996; Lovell 1996; Pollitt and Summa 1997b, 1998; Power 1995; 1997). In the past, SAIs seldom went out of their way to publicize themselves—it is only in the last decade that most of them have begun to produce booklets and brochures for popular consumption, or to deal proactively with the mass media. Some are still cautious in these respects (Pollitt and Summa 1997a).

Finally, there is, of course, a difference of scale. Public management reform has swept across entire public sectors, affecting ministries, executive agencies, quangos, local authorities, and other kinds of public body. SAIs, by contrast, are single organizations, seldom employing more than a few hundred staff. Thus, changes in what auditors do simply do not appear to be as important or newsworthy as changes that (potentially or otherwise) affect the work of tens or hundreds of thousands of public officials, and which may impact directly on citizens' use of public services.

Even if the above considerations go some way towards explaining the relative lack of media and scholarly attention given to the development of performance audit, that does not mean that such activities are insignificant. On the contrary—and as we shall show—performance audit has become (in terms of resources) the largest single activity for some SAIs and an important part of the work of all the SAIs in this study. This is a relatively recent development. Although the definition of performance audit is less than straightforward, it is probably accurate to say that, allowing for some earlier, partial precedents, its emergence as a distinct and mainstream activity dates mainly from the late 1970s and 1980s. Thus, over the last two decades, a number of SAIs have invested a considerable proportion of their resources in developing a relatively new area of activity, one that is directly focused on those issues of performance that have themselves become such a central focus of concern for modern governments.

While governments have declared themselves to be intensely concerned with the 'three Es' (economy, efficiency, and effectiveness) at the same time as SAIs have been developing performance audit as a way of investigating those same three Es, the connection between these two lines of activity has not been as straightforward as might at first appear. Of course, some impacts are fairly obvious. For example, a recent UK National Audit Office handbook acknowledges that performance audit has had to respond to the fact that: 'Two thirds of government business is now carried out by agencies, outputs and delivery are more important than inputs, and there is much greater involvement of the private sector in the delivery of publicly funded programmes' (National Audit Office 1997c, Introduction). This is an example of a direct influence, running from public management reform to performance audit. However, the whole picture is considerably more complicated, with direct and indirect influences running in both directions. Chapter 4 identifies and illustrates these multiple connections.

1.2 The Nature of this Study

The absence of much previous scholarly work made our task both easier and more difficult. As researchers, it was easier for us in the sense that, unlike the situation that obtains for more popular research topics, relatively little investigation was required before we began to get the feeling that we were breaking fresh ground. The reverse side of this advantage, however, was that we found that little work had been done for us. Establishing a reasonably robust set of categories and concepts that would hold across the five countries in our study itself involved an extensive debate, attended by a number of unforeseen complications. The collection of data within these categories was also laborious; we were seldom in the happy position of being able to stand directly on the shoulders of other scholars who had gone before and 'done the spade work'. One very useful text describing the work of all the European Union (EU) SAIs appeared just as we were beginning our own project (NAO 1996a), and this gave us a firmer foundation than we would otherwise have had. Nevertheless, we were not able to answer all the questions we would have liked to address and we are very conscious that our answers to some of those we did tackle are hedged about with caveats and qualifications. To take one example, although we probed the issue of the impacts and influences of performance audit quite vigorously (Chapter 10), in the end we were able to say less about these aspects than we would ideally have wished.

Making (we hope) due allowance for all these various considerations, the project that emerged was one that sought to answer—at least in a preliminary way—each of the following questions:

1. What *is* performance audit, as practised by the SAIs in our study?
2. What have been the main trends in the development of performance audit since the mid-1980s?
3. What have been the interactions between performance audit and the public management reforms which have, to greater or lesser degree, affected most OECD countries over the same period?
4. What is the nature of the performance auditor's craft?
5. What methods are used in performance audit?
6. What criteria are applied within performance audits?
7. What kind of 'products' are generated by performance audit?
8. How is performance audit work presented, to what audiences, and with what discernible effects?
9. What changes have there been in respect of each of the above, over the last ten to fifteen years?

Our empirical basis for addressing these questions has been a study of the performance audit work carried out within five European SAIs: the Dutch Algemene Rekenkamer (AR), the French Cour des Comptes (the Cour), the UK National Audit Office (NAO), the Swedish Riksrevisionsverket (RRV), and the Finnish Valtiontalouden tarkastusvirasto (VTV). Although our set of SAIs cannot in any way be regarded as a statistical sample, it is at least representative of the four main types of SAI identified in the most authoritative recent survey of state audit in the EU (NAO 1996a):

1. the 'court' with a judicial function (represented in our set by the Cour);
2. the audit office headed by an Auditor General within the structure of executive government (such as the RRV and the VTV);
3. the audit office headed by an Auditor General located outside the executive (e.g. the UK NAO, reporting to the Parliamentary Public Accounts Committee);
4. the collegiate body without a judicial function (e.g. the Algemene Rekenkamer).

These constitutionally different formats do seem to exercise some influence over the ways in which SAIs present and regard themselves (Pollitt and Summa 1997a). However, all the SAIs in our set are substantially engaged in activities that could reasonably be described as performance audit, so, in that sense at least, it seems legitimate to compare them.

Our aim has therefore been to study the practice of performance audit and relate it to contemporary developments in public management. We have investigated the 'state of the art' of performance audit and explored its links with the processes of management reform. In empirical terms, we have had twin foci. First, we have gathered material about public management reform in each country—this describes the context in which SAIs have developed performance audit (Chapter 3). Much of this has necessarily been secondary data, though some of it derives from other recent work by members of our team (e.g. Pollitt and Summa 1997c; Pollitt *et al.* 1997a, b). Second, in relation to the performance audit side of the relationship, we have conducted extensive primary research. Our main focus has been on the performance audit report (or study, or decision) and on the process that leads up to that report/study/decision. Some other recent work, though conceptually sophisticated, has been limited by its reliance on a more general type of evidence (OECD 1996; Barzelay 1997). We would contend that the acid test of what performance audit 'is', or is capable of, may lie more in the bedrock of individual audits than in the superstructure of what SAIs say about performance audit in general, although both types of evidence are, of course, useful in their own right.

We have therefore counted, categorized, and read a large number of audit reports. In practical terms, these seemed the least unsatisfactory unit for comparative analysis. They had the advantage of being concrete, discrete, and the basis for a number of recording systems within SAIs themselves. Unfortunately, however, they also carried some disadvantages. First, not all SAIs distinguish between performance audit reports and other types of report (and, among our five SAIs, the Cour does not lay the same emphasis on the centrality of public reports as do the others). Second, not all performance audit reports are in the public domain (again, the Cour publishes only a fraction of its work, though this fraction is increasing). Third, there are other important performance audit 'products' apart from individual reports. For example, some performance audit work by the NAO takes the form of unpublished reports to departments rather than reports to the Parliamentary Public Accounts Committee (though some of these documents do get published later). The bulk of the Cour's work on *bonne gestion* (good management) takes place in the form of unpublished communications with the audited bodies and the ministries, often at ministerial level. Fourth, there is very considerable variation both between and within performance audit reports. They come in different shapes and sizes in different countries, and even within the corpus of a single SAI such reports may be long or short, expensive or cheap, very broad or quite narrow in scope, etc. Indeed, these variations are one of the features we describe and comment upon. Finally, it should be pointed out that choosing a different unit of analysis would likely have yielded different insights, but at the same time, and by the same token, would probably have concealed or obscured some of the features that our focus on reports has illuminated. For example, we have encountered some difficulty in analysing the *methods* used in performance audit, partly (though not entirely) because some reports use a variety of methods within a single study while others say virtually nothing about which methods may have been adopted.

Our treatment of the time dimension requires some explanation. Ideally, we might have attempted to take a long and continuous retrospective view. Thus, we might have considered the balance of work within SAIs well before performance audit work became as prominent as it is today, and then moved forward towards the present describing the pattern of change from year to year. In practice, there were two barriers to adopting this approach. First, gaps in the data begin to appear as we went further back in time. Second, our team simply did not have the time and resources available to analyse the vast amount of documentation that such a strategy would have confronted us with. Our compromise was to look intensively at two periods of activity for each of our five SAIs. The most recent period was 1993–5 inclusive. We attempted to identify every performance audit report published during those three years, and then analysed a sample of them. We also examined a second, earlier, period, also of three years, but varying slightly from one SAI to another so as to capture what we suspected had been important shifts of policy and practice. The periods selected were all in the mid or late 1980s and, again, we attempted to identify every performance audit report that had been published. We were thus able to compare the two periods.

In addition to this basic investigation of performance audit reports, we consulted SAI Handbooks and other explanatory literature. We also conducted a number of interviews with senior audit staff in each of the five SAIs. We used these interviews partly to validate some of the findings and interpretations we had drawn from our study of reports and other documentation, and partly to explore in depth some of the questions which that documentary work had stimulated. Our methods are described in greater detail in Appendix 1.

The basic logic and method of our research is summarized in Figure 1.1. In this figure the central sequence of boxes (4–10) represents the process of performance audit, beginning with the selection of a topic to audit (e.g. defence contracts; quality of service in national museums; strengths and weaknesses of a privatization process) and running through to the production of the final report or judgement (box 10). To a considerable extent, the plan of the book will mirror this sequence, moving from the types of topic selected (Chapter 5) through the choice of criteria (Chapter 6), the craft skills employed (Chapter 7), the methods applied (Chapter 8), the nature of the final products (Chapter 9), and the impacts of the work (Chapter 10). However, the figure also depicts other, broader influences which can affect the process of performance audit. These include the exact constitutional position and powers of the particular audit organization, the skills available to the

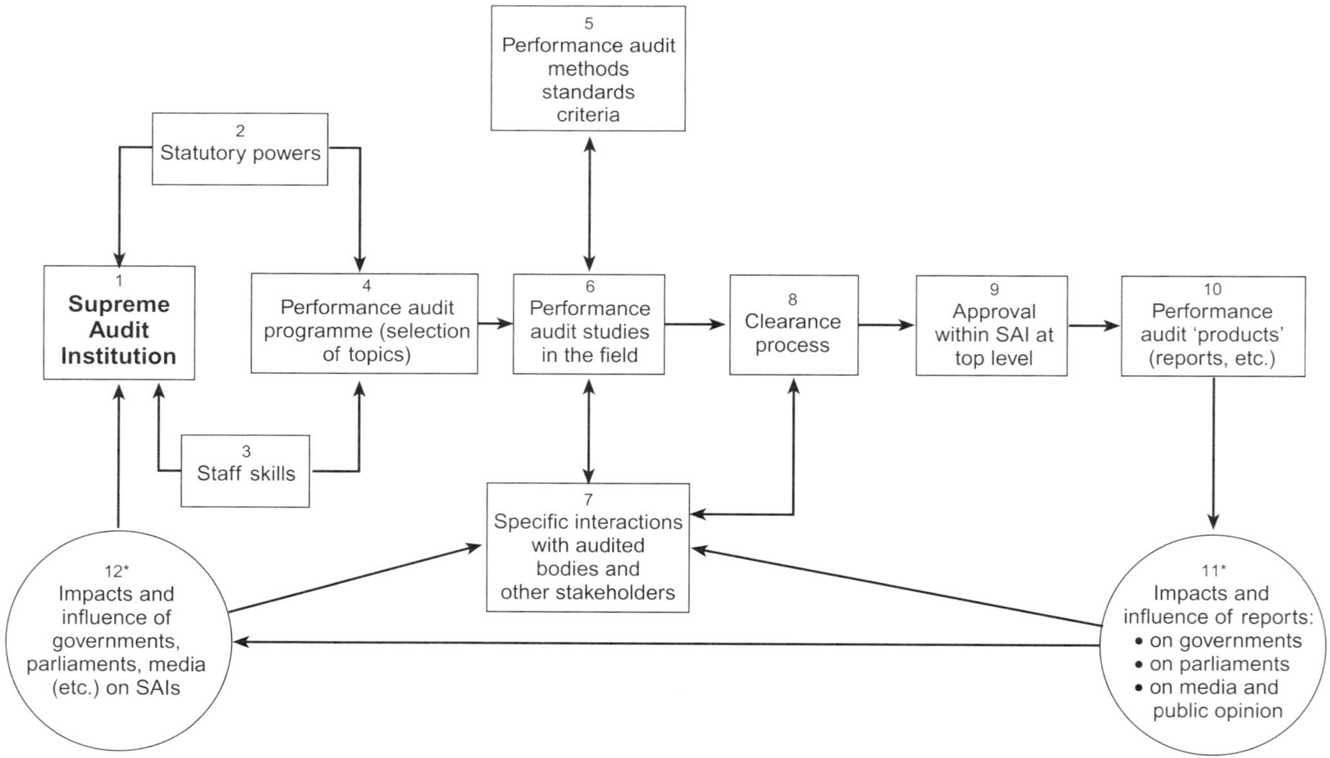

FIGURE 1.1 The process of performance audit

Note: The links between performance audit and public management reform may influence many steps in this process, but especially steps 11 (where an audit report may stimulate a specific reform) and 12 (where government, by carrying through reforms that affect the audit institutions or their audit fields, may directly influence steps 1, 2, 4, 5, 6, and 7). These links are addressed in Chapter 4.

organization, and trends and preoccupations in the wider political environment (boxes 1–3 and 11 and 12). Furthermore, it is necessary to take account of the general standards applying to performance audit work (box 5) and to the specific interactions with audited bodies that almost invariably take place during performance auditing (box 7). All these larger, contextual influences are referred to throughout the book, but most especially in the early and final chapters, i.e. 2–4 and 10 and 11.

1.3 The Input–Output Model

It should be noted that, by adopting this framework, broad and flexible though it may be, we have already taken up a particular perspective. This might be described as an 'input–output' (or 'production process') perspective. It envisages performance audits as a process in which certain inputs (organizational authority, auditors' skills, etc.), are deliberately combined, using a defined process (fieldcraft, techniques, approval within the audit body) with the aim of producing a specific 'product' or 'output' (e.g. a public report). Let us hasten to acknowledge that this is far from the only legitimate perspective on audit. However, it is one that suits our purposes well, partly because it is a perspective that is increasingly adopted by some SAIs themselves and partly because it is appropriate to an analysis that seeks to interrogate the connections between performance audit and public management reform. A great deal of the public management reform that has swept over most of the OECD world has to do with privileging what is essentially an input–output model of management. 'Performance management' and the focus on the 'three Es' are themselves constituted from an input–ouput discourse in which targets have to be set, efficiency and effectiveness have to be measured, and public organizations are supposed to shift from input-based systems of control towards 'results-steering' (OECD 1997b). This is a discourse and conceptual framework which has been insistently advanced by many governments, and which is represented in Figure 1.2.

Note that, while a large proportion of the daily discussions that take place in public management (and performance audit) are confined to the shaded area (inputs/activities/outputs) of figure 1.2, these organizational elements take on their full meanings only when connected to the 'outside world' in the form of the socioeconomic needs which originally gave rise to the existence of an activity, and the outcomes of that activity, in terms of meeting or not meeting that need. Note also that, while economy and efficiency may be measured without going outside the organization or programme (shaded area), effectiveness is different. An assessment of effectiveness demands an investigation of outcomes, and outcomes which, by definition, take place in the world beyond the organization or programme. More detailed discussion and definitions of these concepts will be offered later, especially in Chapter 6.

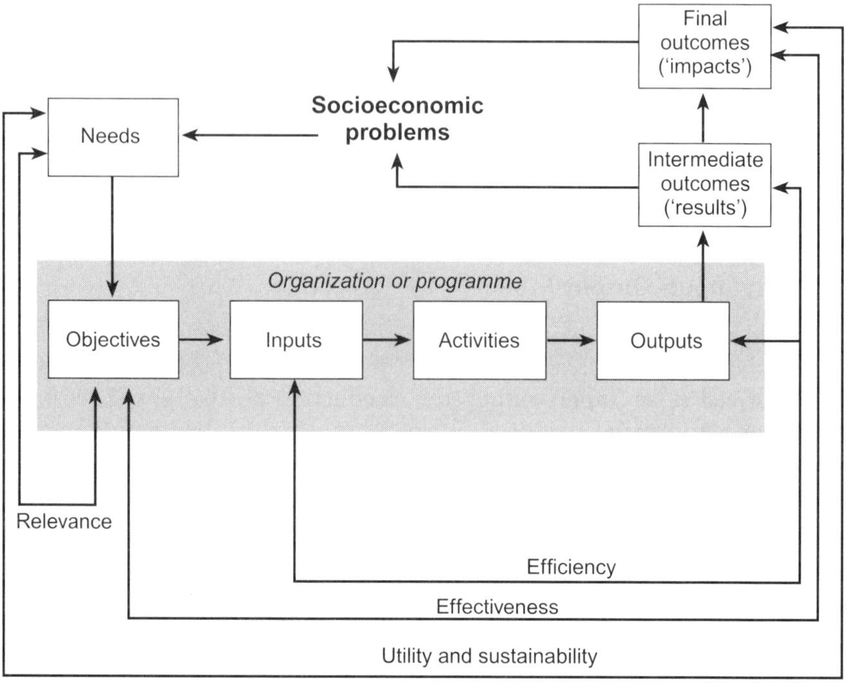

FIGURE 1.2 The input–output model

Thus, this input–output model provides both a template for public management reform and a discourse within which performance audits are supposed to be conducted. Whether it also offers an adequate framework for the assessment of the performance audit work of SAIs themselves is an interesting question, upon which we will reflect at various points in the book.

In conclusion, we should say that, although this work is certainly not intended to be prescriptive, we have nevertheless thought it appropriate, in the final chapter, to set out an agenda for discussion. Drawing from our descriptions and analyses, we have identified a number of issues likely to shape the future development of performance audit. In effect, these constitute a set of strategic choices, with significant implications for the roles of SAIs. Some of these issues could be clarified by further research. All of them could benefit from wider and deeper debate. Just as politics is too important to be left to the politicians, the activities of our Supreme Audit Institutions are too important to be left exclusively to auditors.

2

Definitions and Frameworks

Hilkka Summa

2.1 The Scope of this Chapter

Supreme Audit Institutions, while proud of their independence and autonomous position in the structures of government, are nevertheless part of the overall developments in the public sectors in their respective countries. A wave of reforms which can be characterized as being oriented towards improving public performance has swept over a number of European countries, and at the same time performance audit has become an object of attention in several European SAIs. Some of them have established distinct performance audit functions, others have oriented some of their regular audit work towards performance-oriented approaches. Within the professional audit community, efforts have been made to develop methodologies and to define a proper role and scope for performance-oriented audit work. In some countries, performance audit has been included into the mandate of the SAI only fairly recently and is considered as a widening of the traditional mandate of the institution; in others it has been an accepted part of the SAI's repertoire for some decades. Nevertheless, performance audit is usually considered as a more 'modern' form of audit compared with the more 'traditional' financial or compliance audit.

The question 'what is performance audit?' can be answered in many ways. First of all, one may compare the different definitions suggested for performance audit, and try to synthesize them into a coherent and covering depiction. It is also possible to answer the question by clarifying the distinction between performance audit and other related activities, such as financial or compliance audit, inspection, or programme evaluation. These conceptual considerations will be the focus of the next section of this chapter.

Besides definitional and conceptual specifications, performance audit can also be described through the mandates and organizational frameworks that define the performance audit work done in different SAIs. In Section 2.3 we will look at when and how performance audit has been included in the mandates of each of our five SAIs, how performance audit is organized in them, and what part it plays in their overall agenda.

A third, different, way of answering the question 'what is performance audit?' is simply by looking at what different SAIs do when they say they are conducting performance audits. Still another is by looking at the purposes and the motivations on the basis of which performance audits are done. These, in turn, can be expected to be reflected in the methods and criteria that are used in audits. These empirical questions will be studied in the later chapters of this book.

2.2 What is Performance Audit? Distinctions from Neighbouring Concepts

Definitions

Instead of attempting a conceptual elaboration of the 'correct' meaning of performance audit, the idea here is to discuss some well-known definitions, and to map their frontiers with some neighbouring concepts. On a general level, there seems to be a quite clear professional consensus about a broad meaning of performance audit: it is understood as being a form of audit that is focused on the efficiency and effectiveness, or value-for-money aspects of public activities. Yet, on the other hand, there is a lot of discussion and even controversy about what part performance audit should play in the changing government structures and systems of accountability, what role it should have in the efforts to improve performance in the public sector, and how it relates to other review and feedback activities in the public sector. Distinctions are requested, on the one hand in relation to programme and policy evaluation and on the other to more traditional forms of audit. Some have even denied that performance audit is a form of audit (Barzelay 1996; see below). Yet, even if there is some controversy about the proper role and scope for performance audit in the field of state audit, most European SAIs do recognize the concept and have no problem in classifying some part of their work under this heading.

The most widely accepted definitions connect performance auditing with the review of the 'three Es'—the economy, efficiency, and effectiveness of public bodies or programmes. The International Organization of Supreme Audit Institutions (INTOSAI) states that performance auditing embraces

— audit of the economy of administrative activities in accordance with sound administrative principles and practices, and management policies;
— audit of the efficiency of utilisation of human, financial and other resources, including examination of information systems, performance measures and monitoring arrangements, and procedures followed by audited entities for remedying identified deficiencies; and
— audit of the effectiveness of performance in relation to the achievement of the objectives of the audited entity, and audit of the actual impact of activities compared with the intended impact. (INTOSAI 1992, p. 19)

Quite similarly, the US government auditing standards (GAO 1994) identify performance audit as a concern with the 'three E's' of government organizations, programmes, or activities: the General Accounting Office

(GAO) definition states that performance audits include economy and efficiency and programme audits. 'Programme audit' in this definition is further described as a concern with effectiveness, with the achievement of desired results, and with compliance to applicable laws and regulations. The UK National Audit Office's conception of performance audit resembles the above-mentioned two definitions, even if the term used by NAO is 'value-for-money audit'. A NAO brochure states that 'our value for money investigations evaluate the economy, efficiency and effectiveness achieved in major fields of revenue and expenditure and in the management of resources' (NAO *c.* 1987, p. 9).

It should be noticed that the INTOSAI definition (and many others) actually refers to *more* than the 'three Es': it also speaks of 'sound administrative principles', 'good management', and 'remedying deficiencies'. These other issues are, as we shall see later, an important element in the criteria and bases of judgement for the SAI, and, however their content may finally be specified, they are a central part of the work of SAIs.

The resemblance of these 'official' definitions of performance audit reflects, of course, a fairly intense international professional cooperation between SAIs, and a willingness to reach common standards for auditing, including the newer field of performance auditing. Yet, in spite of this apparent professional consensus on the general features and orientation of performance audit, there is a discussion going on about what performance audit 'really is' and what should be its proper role in the control and accountability arrangements of modern government. In 1995 the Public Management Committee of the OECD organized a conference among representatives from government audit institutions and experts involved in public management reform, to discuss the possible contribution of performance audit to the modernization and performance improvement in government. The discussions showed that, even if performance auditing is seen as an important aspect of accountability and a potential contributor to performance improvement, there is no particular uniformity of approach to this part of the work of the Supreme Audit Institutions of the member states (OECD 1996). It should be added that there are also considerable differences in the practice of financial audit in different European countries (see NAO 1996a).

The question 'what is performance audit?' is posed several times in the articles of the 1996 report from the OECD conference. One of the answers given (Barzelay 1996, p. 19) is somewhat disturbing: that performance audit is a misnomer because it is not a type of audit at all, and it does not share the essential features of 'traditional' audit. According to this view, performance audit is an evaluative activity of a particular sort whose name happens to include the word 'auditing'—a word that is misplaced because the goals and the modes of working in 'actual' audit and performance audit differ in crucial aspects. The work that is actually done in performance auditing is inspection and evaluation of aspects of programmes or organizations, whereas in traditional audit the core activity is verifying information. Barzelay's conclusion is that an essential difference between performance audit and traditional audit is the role of these two types of auditor: the business of a performance auditor is to *exercise judgement*, while the essence of the traditional auditor's job is to *verify*—not an evaluative activity at all.

In a subsequent article, Barzelay takes this line of argument further. He appears to drop the idea that performance audits can be thought of as 'inspections' and insists instead that: 'performance audits are not a type of audit; they are evaluations' (Barzelay 1997, p. 237). Again, this assertion is based on the argument that 'real' audit is verification and that performance audit, by contrast, 'entails making or reviewing instrumental judgements' (Barzelay 1997, p. 241). In arriving at these definitions (the article also proposes that a majority of evaluators may not be doing 'real' evaluation), Barzelay claims he is identifying the 'various idealised cognitive models that together characterise the concept' (p. 237).

It is hard to see how the professional community of auditors could agree with this reasoning, and there are also academic grounds for treating it cautiously. First, the traditional core of audit work may also be seen as a judgemental activity: Giving a 'true and fair statement' obviously requires an exercise of judgement, as does a statement that a set of accounts are 'in compliance' with requirements. Second, as we shall see later, notions of compliance—or, at least, of conformance to standards of good practice—play an important part in many performance audits. Third, it is not entirely clear that there yet *is* a single set of 'idealized cognitive models' underlying the use of the term 'performance audit'. Rather, as Barzelay himself observes, 'a process of demarcating a new domain of bureaucratic activity is underway' (1997, p. 235). That is, the vocabulary and practices of performance audit are evolving, and it seems premature to fix on a single, stipulative definition, however subtle. Finally, it might be said that there is just a whiff of academic hubris about an analysis which insists that, despite what they say about their activities, many auditors are not doing audit, but evaluation, while many evaluators are not doing evaluation, but audit!

Nevertheless, it is true that, in order to specify the role and meaning of performance audit, some distinctions have to be made between it and other related concepts and activities. Not only is there a line to be drawn between performance audit and 'traditional' audit (even if it can be questioned which type of audit is more 'traditional'), there is also a distinction to be made between performance audit and other types of evaluative and review activities, such as the monitoring of performance and (programme) evaluation. Another thing worth noting when trying to delimit the proper 'niche' for performance audit is that the discussion on performance audit is almost entirely limited to the context of *public audit*, and is almost never mentioned in the context of private-sector audit. Thus, the differences between public and private audit are also relevant for defining the meaning of performance audit.

Financial audit and performance audit

The INTOSAI auditing standards state that the 'full scope of government audit includes *regularity* and *performance audit*' (INTOSAI 1992, pp. 18–19). Financial audit is not mentioned in the standard as a category of audit. According to the standard, regulatory audit embraces:

(a) attestation of financial accountability of accountable entities which involves examination of financial records and expressions of the auditor's opinion of these;
(b) attestation of financial accountability of the government as a whole;
(c) audit of financial systems and transactions, including an evaluation of compliance with applicable statutes and regulations;
(d) audit of internal control and internal audit functions;
(e) audit of the probity and propriety of administrative decisions taken within the audited entity;
(f) reporting of any other matters arising from or relating to the audit that the SAI considers should be disclosed. (INTOSAI 1992: 18–19)

This description emphasizes *attestation* as a main activity in regularity audit, which is a clear difference from the definition of performance audit. Even if it is hard to find a similar, widely approved, single definition of financial audit, it seems to us that this term can be used as a rough equivalent of the INTOSAI definition of regulatory audit.

Although the definitions of performance audit and financial or regulatory audit differ, the line between these two types of audit is not always clear, particularly if you look at the audit practices in various SAIs. Different types of audit activity can be distinguished also within the category of financial audit, some of which are close to performance audit, others not. For instance, the judicial task of giving discharge for an accountant on the basis of an audit of his accounts (a central task for the Cour des Comptes) has nothing to do with assessment of performance, whereas the audit of financial management systems (which often is a part of a traditional financial audit) is in a sense close to assessing management performance.

Examples from our sample of SAIs show that it is difficult to draw a line between performance audit and financial audit which would be consistent across SAIs with different traditions and practices. For instance, the Cour usually includes both aspects of audit in its inquiries (see later). In the Riksrevisionsverket (RRV) in Sweden, audit of performance information is conducted by performance auditors and financial auditors jointly, whereas in the Valtiontalouden tarkastusvirasto (VTV) in Finland the same task is understood to be in the territory of financial audit. Also, some NAO value-for-money reports focus on quite narrow questions of regularity and propriety.

In many SAIs, performance audit and financial or regularity audit differ in the way they are managed: the traditional model of financial audit consists of a repeated annual cycle of 'checking the books', while performance audit is usually carried out as an individually tailored project. For instance, in the VTV financial audit is understood as 'annual audit of accounts', the result of which is a short and fairly formal auditor's statement on the correctness of the accounts, including a commentary on whether adequate performance information has been presented in the annual report. Financial audits are carried out in a standardized way for every government body every year; performance audits, on the contrary, vary in their scope, length, and focus.

Another feature that distinguishes performance audit from the traditional financial audit model is obviously its lower level of standardization, both as to methods and content. There is a tradition guiding financial audits with well established standardized procedures, and most SAIs have manuals for conducting them. Performance audit is much more difficult to standardize as each performance audit tends to be a project on its own which has to be designed individually. Nevertheless, some SAIs have produced performance audit manuals to help this process along (e.g. Algemene Rekenkamer 1998; NAO 1997a, c).

Performance audit and evaluation

In the methodological development of performance audit, a number of SAIs have turned to specialists in other fields, including programme and policy evaluation, to see if the approaches and methodologies used there could be transferred to the field of audit. Some have seen performance audit as being closely related to evaluation—both being viewed as external forms of analysis and assessment (Leeuw 1996)—whereas others have doubted whether evaluation and audit can really come close together in the context of an SAI (Pollitt and Summa 1997a, c, 1998).

With the rise of 'performance audit' over the last fifteen to twenty years, one interpretation would be that the overall balance of the work of Supreme Audit Institutions has shifted towards a more evaluative stance. Indeed, measured by the crude indicator of numbers of analytical studies produced per annum, some SAIs could now be thought of as the most prolific evaluative institutions in their states. Certainly auditors in some countries (particularly the Netherlands, Sweden, the UK, and the USA) are showing an explicit interest in evaluation, and have, for example, played an important role in the creation of the new European Evaluation Society. Also, the international organization of SAIs (INTOSAI) has put a discussion on this topic on its agenda, hosting since 1992 a working group on evaluation which, at the time of writing, is chaired by the *premier président* of the Cour des Comptes. Some commentators go so far as envisaging a new twenty-first-century 'inter-discipline' combining the best features of audit and evaluation (Leeuw 1996, p. 59).

However, we would argue for a more cautious interpretation of the developing relationship between SAIs and evaluation. As some of us have indicated elsewhere (Pollitt and Summa 1997b, 1998) there are institutional, cultural, and political inhibitions for SAIs actually developing into evaluation institutes. Of these, the basic institutional differences between SAIs and research institutes specializing in evaluation are probably the most important ones. Even if performance auditing may borrow methodological devices from evaluation (or from social science more generally), and may benefit from this kind of borrowing, the role of performance auditor is crucially different from that of evaluator. Public auditors are part of an authoritative system of controls in the set of public bodies that constitute a democratic government, and their work is based on statutory powers and a mandate which more or less defines the limits of their territory. By contrast, evaluators usually come from a range of different and differently placed organizations which are free to direct their work and choose their approach—as long as finance is provided. SAIs also have a wide freedom to choose their topics; but as far as their core function is concerned, they are not in the position of being 'bought in' to undertake a task at the behest of a commissioning authority. By contrast, evaluators are typically commissioned for purposes defined very much from the point of view of the commissioner, often to provide help in a specific phase of a programme management cycle. Even if SAIs, too, nowadays often describe helping the audited bodies to improve their performance as one of their objectives, they are very strict in defending their independence in defining their portfolio of topics and the choice of auditees.

There is thus a fundamental difference in the perspective from which performance auditors and evaluators work. As long as performance audit is carried out as a part of the work of an SAI, it is bound to be done from a perspective of guardianship and control, with a basic role of holding public bodies to account for the expenditure of public funds. SAIs may also give advice to departments and other public bodies to help them improve their management, but this secondary function, important though it may be, can never replace the primary function of guardianship.

Performance audit and monitoring of performance

In the most straightforward sense, performance audit could be understood as *audit of performance* so that the objective of the audit work would be to reach a judgement on the level of performance of the audited entity. A direct measurement or assessment of performance (with suitable indicators) would in this case be an essential part of the audit process, and judgements on the results of the measurements would be central to what would be presented in the audit report. As a matter of fact, this line of thought is close to what is implied by the widely accepted INTOSAI and GAO definitions of performance audit presented above.

These definitions are fairly unambiguous, and they seem to provide a clear role for performance audit, also giving it a legitimacy by distinguishing it clearly from traditional audit and attaching it to a focus (valid information on the performance of public organizations) about which no legislature can remain unconcerned. However, identifying performance audit with the study and review of actual performance of public organizations inevitably raises the question of the relationship between external performance audit and at least two other types of activity.

First, there is the internal monitoring of performance, which is conducted by the management and the steering bodies of the organizations themselves. The most usual distinction here is that monitoring of performance is carried out as a routine part of the management of the activity itself, whereas performance audit is external and independent of management. A common view is that it is the duty of management to develop and produce adequate performance information about the activities and results of the organization it is in charge of, and that the auditors' task is to see to it that this information actually is available and of adequate quality. This is the role that is offered to auditors by the professional code: one of the basic postulates in the INTOSAI standard is that SAIs should recommend to the audited entities that measurable and clearly stated objectives be established and that performance targets be set for them (INTOSAI 1992, pp. 15–16). The problem with this understanding of the task of performance audit is that it does not really distinguish it from financial or regularity audit: it appears to be limited to the same type of systemic control activity as any traditional form of audit. On the other hand, if performance audit were required actually to measure and evaluate performance in cases where no indicators or records of measured performance exist, it would turn auditing into a very broad and research-like activity (which in turn, in situations of limited resources, would mean reduced possibilities for a broad coverage of the audit field).

Second, there are also other forms of external control and audit functions, such as quality audits and accreditation of quality systems, or traditional forms of inspection. The relationship between such activities and performance audit is by no means always clear (Power 1995, 1997).

Our studies of the topics covered by performance audit work in the five SAIs show that strict audit of performance in the above sense is rare. Most of performance audit work is actually focused either on good management practices and standard processes in the audited bodies or on systems of monitoring and reporting on performance, rather than on substantive performance itself. This point will be developed later on the basis of an overview of the portfolio of topics and criteria exhibited by our samples of performance audit reports.

Public and private audit

Performance audit seems to be a concept and a practice that is discussed mostly in the context of public-sector organizations. The concept is well recognized by all state audit institutions, and international organizations of the SAIs have discussed and developed standards for good practice in performance audit. Power (1997, p. 52) relates the evolving agenda of value-for-money audits in the UK to the public-sector management changes known as the 'New Public Management' (NPM—see Pollitt 1993, pp. 186–7). It is true that related new variants of audit have emerged which are used mainly in the private sector, such as operative audits, management audits, quality audits, or environmental audits. The essential difference between these and performance audit as carried out by the SAIs is that these are characteristically internalized forms of corporate control, whereas performance or value-for-money audits are a part of the external control system operating on public organizations.

In the UK there has recently been a discussion on the nature of public audit, aiming to define a 'model' that distinguishes it from the 'normal' form of external audit that applies in the private sector (Evans and Thornton 1997; Evans 1998). The 'public audit model' was defined by the Chartered Institute of Public Finance and Accountancy (CIPFA) and adopted by the Nolan Committee (a committee set up to scrutinize standards of conduct in public life) in 1994. In this ideal model, public audit, as distinguished from private-sector audit, is characterized by:

1. greater independence of auditors from the organizations they audit;
2. a wider role of auditors and an extended scope of audits; and
3. extended reporting to stakeholders.

In this model, the wider role of auditors and the extended scope of audits refer particularly to responsibilities that public-sector auditors have for ensuring the arrangements made for securing economy, efficiency, and effectiveness and accuracy of performance. This, in turn, is seen to be connected to extended reporting requirements, in the sense that public audit reports are more informative than private-sector audit reports, and that separate reports are issued, also by the external auditor, on value for money.

Controversy has arisen on what the actual application of this ideal model of public audit would mean in practice, with some interpreting it as an attempt to widen the mandate of public audit bodies to cover all organizations using public finance, including all quangos (Evans 1998; Lovell 1998). Independently from what view is held on the implications or desirability of the widening of the actual application of the public audit model, it does squeeze out the essential relation of performance audit to concerns that are specific to the public sector. Performance audit, as practised by the SAIs, is intimately connected to a concept of public accountability. Even if 'technically' similar control practices are to some extent carried out in private companies, they are done on behalf of and in the interest of the owners or the management of the enterprise.

The differences in the financial and institutional frameworks in which public and private organizations operate suggest some reasons why performance audit is less salient in the private than in the public sector. As indicated above, external audit, in the sense it is conceived of in the private sector, is a function that is carried out primarily on behalf of the owners of the audited enterprise. The security and profitability of an investment can be judged on the basis of the enterprise's accounting information, its profit statements, and its balance sheets—provided they are correctly drawn. The *raison d'être* of independent audit for a company is to provide the owners with an assurance that the financial information on their investment can be trusted. Similarly, tax authorities have an interest in the credibility of an enterprise's financial information. Both from their and the owners' point of view, the correctness of 'numbers in the books' is an adequate source of accountability on the performance of an enterprise.

Furthermore, the performance of an organization that is financially independent and receives its income in the form of revenue from a market can be assumed to be more adequately reflected in its financial information than is the case for a public-sector organization which receives its income as an appropriation from the government budget. In theory, a competitive market provides a natural push towards good performance and efficient use of resources which makes institutionalized external control specifically targeted on the level of performance less necessary in the case of private-sector organizations. This is, of course, true only as long as we consider 'performance' narrowly in economic terms; including, say, environmental and consumer safety issues in the concept of a company's performance will bring it into the sphere of public accountability—and this is exactly the background for the emergence of audit-related practices such as statutory environmental impact assessments.

Even in narrowly economic terms, both knowing about performance and ensuring that the information provided on the level of performance is correct is more complex in the case of public organizations, the 'production' (or output) of which is often hard to quantify or to measure in money terms. More substantial forms of investigation are needed to measure or control the performance of public organizations, where notions of profit or return on investment do not apply. The development of performance audit is one attempt to ensure control and accountability in the specific conditions of public organizations.

However, certain recent trends point towards the need for audit information to become more similar in private and public sectors. It is exactly the above described condition of poor or vague accountability on performance that many governments have attempted to remedy through the reforms discussed in the previous chapter. Through the introduction of these measures, market conditions are 'simulated' within the public sphere so that performance can in theory be more easily assessed through the usual, financially based accounting information. In this situation, the correctness of accounting information becomes of crucial importance; this emphasizes the need for efficient financial audit but makes the 'added value' of performance audit less clear. At the same time, widespread corporatization and privatization of former government bodies have in several countries extended the 'territory' to which normal commercial accountancy can be applied (Pollitt and Summa 1997d), thus also widening the area for which financial audit has the same importance as in private organizations. For several reasons, therefore, financial audit has recently become a lively area for development within the public sectors in a number of European countries.

2.3 The Limits of the Territory: Mandates and Organizational Frameworks for Performance Audit

For all of the five SAIs we are studying, performance audit is included in their mandate and covers a considerable slice of their agendas, even if the concepts used for this activity, and the way the work is organized, differ. In some of them, considerable changes have been introduced into the objectives and modes of operating performance audits, whereas in others it has been a more or less permanent part of the work of the institution. In this section, the mandates of the five SAIs included in our sample will be briefly described, with the aim of giving a picture of the framework in which performance audit operates. (For other basic information on these SAIs, see Appendix 2.) Also, the resources used for performance audit and the main lines on how it has been organized in each of the SAIs will be described.

The mandates for performance audit

Supreme audit institutions are characteristically organizations with a clearly and explicitly defined legal basis for the purpose and scope of their activities. On the one hand, the statutory framework through which they are established usually ensures them autonomy in their work and access to the information they need; on the other hand it limits their mandate to certain types of enquiries and to specific categories of organization. Our five SAIs differ, for example, as to the scope of their mandates, as to how a mandate has been established and whether and when performance audit has been explicitly included in it. Table 2.1 summarizes some of the differences.

The generally strong legal status of SAIs is reflected in the fact that three of them (the Algemene Rekenkamer, the Cour, and the VTV) are established by a statute in the constitution, with a lower-level regulation specifying their audit remit. The UK, with its common law tradition, has established the mandate of the comptroller and auditor general by an Act of Parliament. Sweden is an exception—not only among our five SAIs but in Europe more generally (see NAO 1996a)—as the Riksrevisionsverket is established only through a government ordinance.

There are also differences as to how and on what basis performance audit is included in the remit of the SAI. In the Algemene Rekenkamer and the

Table 2.1 Performance audit in the mandates of SAIs

SAI	Mandate stipulated by	Scope of mandate	Establishment of performance audit in the mandate
Algemene Rekenkamer	Constitution; specified by Government Accounts Act	Ministries; other government bodies; 1989 extended to welfare benefits; state aided bodies, and corporations with 5% or more state-owned capital	Included in the mandate in 1976 by amendment of the Government Accounts Act; the 1989 extension covered also performance aspects
Cour des Comptes	Constitution; competencies specified in the Code on Financial Jurisdictions (*Code des juridictions financières*)	Government bodies (article L 111–3); public enterprises (article L 111–4); social security institutions (article L 111–5; bodies receiving public grants or aid from the state, from any other body submitted to the Cour's control, or from the EU (article L 111–7); use of funds levied through national charity campaigns (L 111–8); judgement of public accounts (L 131–1)	Implied by the Code on Financial Jurisdiction ('audit of proper use of public money' and . . . the management of public enterprises')
National Audit Office	National Audit Act, 1983	Departments and executive agencies; other public bodies specified by statute or agreement; bodies receiving public grants to provide public services	'Value-for-money' audits authorized by the National Audit Act 1983
Riksrevisions-verket	Government ordinance	State agencies (excl. ministries); public enterprises; some state-owned companies and foundations; state subsidy systems; income transfers	Since establishment in 1961; specified in a government directive which stipulates the organization and tasks of the RRV

TABLE 2.1 (*cont'd*)

SAI	Mandate stipulated by	Scope of mandate	Establishment of performance audit in the mandate
Valtiontalouden tarkastusvirasto	Constitution; state audit act	Ministries; state agencies; state enterprises; recipients of state subsidies; companies with >50% of voting rights controlled by the state	Implied by the basic regulation ('audit of the appropriateness of financial management'); specified by a government ordinance

National Audit Office, performance audit as a distinct form of audit work has been established through an extension to their mandates, even though in both of these performance audit-type audits were already carried out. For the other three SAIs, the mandate for performance audit is implied by their original audit remit rather than understood as a specific extension to this.

The Swedish RRV has the longest history of conducting performance audit as a distinct category of audit work. Performance-oriented audit has been a major part of its work since the establishment of the institution in 1961 by a merger of the State Accounting Centre and a former separate audit institution. For the period 1967–87 performance audit was RRV's main task, as during this time financial audit was decentralized to agencies and RRV had only a supervisory role in this area. In 1987 financial audit was 'recentralized' to the RRV, but performance audits have been continued since, as one item in the enhanced portfolio of tasks. The content of the performance-oriented audit work has, however, changed over time, and this is reflected in the terminology used by the RRV: what the 1961 Ordinance talks about would in direct translation into English be 'audit of administration' (*forvaltningsrevision*); later this was replaced by the concept of 'effectiveness audit'.

As for the Cour des Comptes or the Valtiontalouden tarkastusvirasto, no specific dates can be given for the establishment of performance audit in their audit remits, as in both cases the development of performance-oriented approaches was a choice of strategy under an interpretation of the basic law governing the institution (as distinct from a specific extension to their mandates). The French law (*Code des juridictions financières*) stipulates that the Cour is to 'ascertain the good use of public funds' (article L 111–3), and that it shall 'verify the accounts and management' of public enterprises' (article L 111–4). The audit of 'good use' and 'management' have provided a basis for an orientation towards both value-for-money aspects and regularity. For the VTV, the mandate given by the 1947 State Audit Act covers the audit of the legality and appropriateness of government financial management and compliance with national budget. The statutory right (or obligation) to audit 'the appropriateness of financial management' has provided the space for developing a type of audit which, in the English terminology, would be labelled as performance audit (a literal translation from the Finnish would be 'audit of activities').

In the Algemene Rekenkamer, the statutory basis for performance audit work was laid in 1976, and since then the Rekenkamer has been able to examine the efficiency and effectiveness of government programmes. The 1992 amendment to the Budget and Accounting Act explained the scope of these powers in more detail. The 1983 National Audit Act gave a statutory foundation for the new National Audit Office's value-for-money audits. Yet, this type of work had already been carried out without specific statutory authority, but with the encouragement and support of the Public Accounts Committee of the House of Commons.

The scope of the audit field

Our five SAIs also differ from each other as to what type of organization their audit remits cover. The scope of their respective audit fields has been summarized in Table 2.1. In our sample of countries there seems to be a tendency towards widening the coverage of the mandates of SAIs. On the other hand, changes in the structure of government, such as privatizations, may also limit the scope of the audit field of SAIs. These changes are, of course, related to the main theme of our investigation: the relationship between audit and public-sector reforms.

For example, the mandate of the AR was extended in 1989 to include inspection of welfare benefits and state-aided bodies, following considerable parliamentary concern that large volumes of public funding were passing through para-statal bodies which were less than fully accountable to the legislature. The Cour des Comptes' mandate has also been extended, even if with less prominent public debate. The Cour has been auditing the accounts and the management of the national public enterprises since 1976. In 1991 a decision by the Council of Ministers empowered the Cour to undertake and publish special studies. Since then, reports have been published on, for example, local collectivities' debt, the management of the national routes network, public housing support, anti-drug addiction policy, and social action by local collectivities. Since 1991 the Cour has also been allowed to audit the use of the funds that have been collected through national charity campaigns. Compared with the Cour's earlier activities, these can be seen as an extension to both the field and the mode of operation. In 1994 a new law (no. 94–637, 25 July) required the Cour to report annually to the parliament regarding the accounts of all social security organizations. In 1996 a new article was introduced to the Constitution (article 47–1) giving a basis for the Cour's annual report on the yearly social security finance act.

The audit mandate of the RRV covers state agencies, public enterprises, some state-owned companies, and foundations as well as state subsidy systems and income transfers. A difference from many other SAIs is that the RRV does not audit ministries or the Cabinet Office, which are audited by a separate, smaller parliamentary audit body. During the periods we have studied, the RRV's mandate was however exceptionally broad in another sense: unlike any other European SAI, the Swedish RRV had until 1998 a department that specialized in developing financial management systems and in giving advice to state agencies in management questions. The RRV also takes assignments from the government to this effect, and thus it has had an exceptionally direct role in the reforms of Swedish public management. At the time of writing, however, changes in these arrangements were in progress. Following an institutional review in 1996–7, a decision was taken to split the 'old' RRV into a 'pure' audit body (still to be known as the RRV, and still responsible for performance audit) and a new government advisory agency incorporating the previous RRV financial management department.

The Finnish VTV is formally in a position similar to that of the RRV (part of the executive), but it is not involved in direct consultancy to agencies, nor does it take assignments from the government. Its audit remit covers government ministries and agencies, non-budgetary funds, state subsidy systems and income transfers, and state enterprises and state owned companies as long as more than 50 per cent of the shares (counted by voting power) is owned by the state. This means that privatization by selling shares of fully or partly state-owned companies may exclude some of these from the audit field of the VTV. A recent extension to the audit field of the VTV has been the mandate in 1995 to audit the transfers of funds between Finland and the European Union.

Another aspect of the audit mandates of different SAIs is whether and how far their investigations can be extended to questions of the merits of *policies*, or whether they are expected to stay within the limits of efficiency and effectiveness in implementation and administration. This is particularly interesting from the point of view of performance audit, because it is in this type of audit work that the border line of questioning or not questioning policy objectives is most directly encountered. For some SAIs, particularly the NAO, questioning policy is a definite no-go area; for others the line is not so clear (Barzelay 1997).

In the UK legislation this is treated very explicitly. The comptroller and auditor general has full discretion over the nature of value-for-money audits conducted by the office. He decides whether, when, and how any VFM examination shall be carried out; and he decides whether, when, and in what terms the results of an examination are reported to the House of Commons. However, he is not entitled to question the merits of policy objectives. The

1983 Act explicitly restricted his powers to examinations focused on the means that departments have employed to achieve the policy objectives set by the government and approved by Parliament.

Like the NAO, the AR is not permitted to question the merits of the policy objectives themselves. On the other hand, its mandate in questioning policies is wider in the sense that it has the possibility for investigating effectiveness even at the stage of programme formulation, when the programmes have not yet proceeded beyond the stage of an initial decision to commit finance (NAO 1996a, pp. 148–50).

In the case of the RRV and the VTV, the watershed between policy objectives (as a no-go area) and the implementation or use of resources is not as salient an issue as with the NAO. Nevertheless, the RRV does announce in its self-explanatory material that performance audits are not designed to question policies, although they can analyse the effects of such policies when they are implemented (Riksrevisionsverket 1993, p. 5). In Finland as well, the policy/administration line has not been a central issue of debate when defining the scope for performance audits. The VTV regulations give no strict, official definition of the objectives of performance audit, and in practice its focus has changed over the years. (The same goes for the RRV.) It is generally described as aiming to ensure that public bodies and public activities are effective and appropriate; in practice this has led to audits (for example in the field of state grants and subsidies) which can be interpreted as questioning the merits of a policy.

In theory, the line between questioning policy objectives and only asking questions related to the 'three Es' in the implementation of policies may sound a clear-cut and unambiguous way of defining the mandate for performance audits. In practice, however, if a performance audit project is extended into analytical questions on *why* the observed effectiveness of an audited programme is unsatisfactory, it may not be easy to keep away from explanations that raise questions of relevance or realism in the specification of objectives. The NAO's interpretation of this precarious line indirectly introduces an important additional element into the audit mandate: even if the merits of policy objectives are not to be questioned, the accuracy and completeness of the information on which policy decisions are reached is a legitimate subject for a VFM audit—in addition to the means with which objectives are pursued and to the results achieved (NAO *c.* 1987, p. 4).

The resources of performance audit

Having established where performance audit fits within the mandates of our five SAIs, it makes sense also to look at the resources it consumes. Only the RRV and the VTV have organized performance audit into a separate department or departments (two in the case of VTV) within the office. In the RRV this has been the case since the creation of the office; in the VTV the separation of financial and performance audit was the result of a fairly recent reorganization (in 1991), the purpose of which was to make room for development of new practices and methodologies in both types of audit. In the other three SAIs, the main organizational principle is to divide work along the lines of administrative sectors. In the NAO and in the Rekenkamer, auditors tend to specialize in either performance audit or financial audit for their respective administrative sector, whereas in the Cour both aspects tend to be present in each audit project, and specialization of auditors into PA or financial audit is much less prominent.

Identifying the proportion of resources that each SAI uses for performance audit is not straightforward, particularly for those SAIs that do not separate financial and performance audit organizationally. It is particularly difficult to present exact figures on the development of the share of performance audit from the 1980s to the 1990s because of changes in the internal accounting systems of the SAIs. For instance, in the case of VTV, before the organizational separation of performance audit and financial audit there was no follow-up of the split of resources between these activities. As a consequence, we are not able to present fully comparable figures for the share of performance audit work in each of the SAIs, nor can we show exactly how this share has changed during the period our study covers. However, the overall picture of the weight of performance audit in the activities of each SAI in the 1990s is fairly clear.

A clear growth of resources devoted to performance audit has been visible at the Rekenkamer. Practically all the increase in the institution's capacity (about 40 person-years over 1985–95) has been allocated to performance audit. Exact figures (which are available only for the 1990s) show that the share of regularity audits has declined sharply and the share of performance audits has grown, the latter being more than two-thirds of all audit capacity in 1994 (see Table 2.2). The Rekenkamer's ability to rely on the work of ministerial audit departments for the purpose of certifying their accounts means that this kind of work represents only about one-third of its activities. The other two-thirds consists of 'audits to assess organizational and policy efficiency, the quality of decision-making, policy effectiveness and the monitoring of policy implementation' (Witteveen 1996, p. 27—but note that Chapters 5 and 6 below will provide a more critical analysis of the exact nature of this activity).

The share of the NAO's resources devoted to performance audit seems to have declined during recent years, having been over 40 per cent of direct staff costs in 1991/2 and only 34 per cent in 1995/6. However, interpreting this as an indication of reduced interest in value-for-money (VFM) work may be too simple, as other things have happened during this period. The number of value-for-money reports has increased during the 1990s, which means that more, but less costly, reports are being produced now than five years ago. Considerable time and effort has been invested in developing VFM work, as we will see in later chapters. Also, changes in the financial audit

Table 2.2 An indicative share of resources used for performance audit and financial audit in four SAIs, 1994[a]

Institution	Performance audit	Financial audit	Other activities
Rekenkamer[b]	69	31	
NAO	38	43	19
RRV	9	21	70[c]
VTV	48	35	17

[a] The percentages in the table are only indicative because the figures are not fully comparable. For the Rekenkamer, the split of total working time to financial and performance audit is presented. The figures for the NAO represent the percentages split of direct personnel costs between different activities. For the VTV the percentages are calculated on the total number of person-years and in the RRV on the total costs of the institution. As for the period of observation, in the NAO and in the RRV the period in question is the budget year 1994/5 and not 1994 as for the VTV and the Rekenkamer.

[b] The percentages concern only the share of audit resources in the two types of audit, not including other activities such as internal administration.

[c] In 1994/5, 46% of RRV's total costs were costs for the activities in consultation and development of financial management in state agencies. A corresponding activity does not exist in the other SAIs. The percentage of costs for internal administration was 24%.

side have influenced the share of resources devoted to each type of audit: the development of agencies and other independent public bodies has increased the number of financial accounts to be audited, and there has been an increased focus on work on the regularity, propriety, and risk areas, which are encompassed within the heading 'financial audit'. Central government's decision to adopt accruals accounting (resource accounting and budgeting) has also increased the NAO's workload on the financial audit side (National Audit Office 1997b, pp. 20–1).

The RRV differs considerably from the other four SAIs in the mix of activities it pursues. The share of performance audit in its operations is considerably smaller than the two other main parts of its activities. The so-called 'third leg' of the RRV (the development and consultancy-oriented financial management department) consumed in the 1990s close to half of the resources of the institution, whereas the shares of performance audit and financial audit were only about 10 and 20 per cent respectively of the total costs of the institution (see Appendices 2 and 3). This split will obviously prove to be different after mid-1998, when the financial management department was extracted from the 'core' RRV and set up as a separate agency. The RRV differs from all the other SAIs also in that it is to a large extent self financing. In 1994/5, 84 per cent of the costs of the economy and management department were covered by income from commissions. In the financial audit and performance audit departments the proportion of paid commissions has been considerably smaller, but it does exist there also.

In the Cour des Comptes, estimating the share of performance audit of its resources is more difficult because a single investigation by the Cour frequently combines a concern both with the proper legal use of public funds and with good performance (*la bonne gestion des fonds*). The Cour's internal organization follows sector-specific lines. The differentiation between the two types of audit is thus less distinct than in the other SAIs, and the use of resources is not measured on this dimension. Senior sources in the Cour estimate, however, that the bulk of the institution's efforts (about two-thirds in the mid-1990s) now go towards performance-related analysis (National Audit Office 1996a, p. 65). The estimated increase in performance-oriented audits can be attributed in particular to the extensions of mandate to the new areas of social security organizations and special studies.

With the Rekenkamer, the VTV is one of the SAIs in which the share of resources allocated to performance audit is considerable, and has clearly grown during the 1990s. About a half of the total number of person-years used by the institution in 1994 were devoted to performance audits. The share of performance audit, as measured both by total cost and by the number of staff (see Appendices 2 and 3), has grown since the reorganization.

Even though these figures are only indicative, they speak to the role and development of performance audit in the work of SAIs. Performance audit is firmly on the agenda of the SAIs we are studying, and there seems to have been some reallocation of resources towards this area of activity from more traditional forms of audit work. The growth of importance in performance audit does not, however, exhibit a uniform pattern across the SAIs. In the NAO performance audit had already reached a peak in its growth in the early 1990s, while particularly the Rekenkamer and the VTV were still strongly increasing the resources allocated to this branch of activity. On the whole, if we compare the 1980s and the 1990s, there has been some reallocation of SAIs' resources to performance audit, but the example of the NAO suggests that this is not necessarily a trend that will continue. As a preliminary conclusion, we may suggest that the increase of the share that performance audit represents within the total activities of the five SAIs has reached its peak, and, even if performance audit still is on the agenda of all the audit institutions we have studied, it is no longer necessarily the strongest growth area in their work.

3

The Changing Context

Christopher Pollitt

3.1 Purpose

The aim of this chapter is to summarize and compare the trajectories of public management reform in the five countries under study. This will provide the framework within which we can, in subsequent chapters, discuss the main trends in the development of performance audit. It is not possible in one chapter to give even a general history of all the changes that have taken place in Finland, France, the Netherlands, Sweden, and the UK. However, this is not our purpose. Our treatment is more focused and selective, concentrating on the 'big issues' that, prima facie, might be expected to affect and/or engage the attentions of the SAIs concerned.

We approach our subject matter in three stages. First, we need to take account of the 'starting points' for management reform, that is the different types of politico-administrative regimes that operated in each of the five countries at the beginning of the 1980s. The starting points were different in different countries. The regime within a given country provided the historical, political, and cultural foundations upon which that country's reforms were built. For example, decentralization was an important part of the reform rhetoric in many countries, but in France this theme played against the background of a famously centralized state apparatus, whereas in Sweden the same theme was applied to a situation which was already quite decentralized by western European standards. The prevailing politico-administrative regimes constitute the contexts within which our five SAIs conduct their work. In general, these contexts change only slowly—they are matters of constitution and culture and cannot be transformed overnight.

Second, we establish a broad classification of the main types of management reform that were 'in play' during the 1980s and 1990s. Some of these reforms may be seen principally as 'running repairs' within the particular politico-administrative regime of the country concerned. Others, however, exhibit larger aspirations. These more fundamental reforms sought, in effect, to shift the regimes in question in new directions. Our account concentrates on the key elements within these attempts at more fundamental change.

Third, we briefly describe the actual reforms within each country, relating them back to the classification established earlier. We also identify the possible implications of these reforms for SAIs, though only in general terms. A more detailed exploration of the links between management change and state audit follows in later chapters.

3.2 Types of Politico-Administrative Regime

Scholars have made a variety of attempts to classify types of political system and of administrative culture (Aberbach *et al.* 1981; Flynn and Strehl 1996; Hague and Harrop 1987; Lijphart 1984; Pierre 1995). One set of political scientists has concentrated on the nature of executive government and the patterns of party political activity that underpin it. Within this body of work an often-used and basic distinction is that drawn between majoritarian, intermediate, and consensualist types of government (Lijphart 1984). The majoritarian and consensualist models represent 'ideal types' at opposite ends of a spectrum of characteristics. In the real world, particular countries can be situated along this spectrum according to the mixture of characteristics they display. The essential characteristics of the two polar types may be summarized as follows:

1. *Majoritarian*: executive power is concentrated in a one-party or a bare-majority cabinet of ministers. It can usually count on getting its proposals through the legislature because it controls or heavily influences a majority of members. If there are two chambers to the legislature, one of them is much more powerful than the other ('asymmetric bicameralism'—Lijphart 1984, p. 7). Party competition tends to be between a small number of large parties, not a larger number of small parties, and tends to display an adversarial character. The electoral system is that of the plurality ('first past the post'). The UK is the classic case of this type of system.
2. *Consensual*: executive power is typically shared between a number of parties: 'the consensus principle is to let all the important parties share executive power in a broad coalition' (Lijphart 1984, p. 23). There is more of a give-and-take, balanced relationship between the executive (cabinet) and the legislature (instead of the executive dominance which characterizes the majoritarian model). If there are two legislative chambers there is likely to be a better balance between them also, often with special protection for the representation of minorities. The electoral system is one of proportional representation, usually giving rise to a legislature in which many parties are represented, with no one party achieving overall dominance. There are often special constitutional protections for subnational levels of government (counties, municipalities, communes, etc.). Belgium and Switzerland are cited by Lijphart as the classic cases of consensual democracies. Among our five countries, Finland and the Netherlands fall much nearer the consensualist than the majoritarian pole.

Between these two poles lie a number of other countries which possess a mixture of the two sets of characteristics identified above:

3. *Intermediate*: the USA, for example, has a majoritarian concentration of executive power and a plurality system for deciding elections, yet in other respects it is closer to the consensual model (balanced bicameralism and a good deal of give-and-take between the executive and a powerful legislature). Among the countries included in this study, France and Sweden are both classified by Lijphart as intermediate cases. France (under the Fifth Republic) has a multi-party system yet a strong central executive, dominated by a president who is identified with a single party; Sweden has proportional representation yet also tends to have single party or only minimal coalition cabinets.

Overall, the key characteristics of the five countries under analysis are as shown in Table 3.1.

So much for the dynamics of the political executive, and its relations with the legislature. We now turn to the administrative systems that serve both the political executive and the citizens. Here again, scholars have attempted to devise useful ways of classifying the different types of system that may prevail (e.g. Bekke *et al.* 1996; Farnham *et al.* 1996; Pierre 1995; Pollitt and Bouckaert 1999). From these various typologies we extract four features that seem to be of particular importance: the extent to which the careers of top officials are separate from those of executive politicians; the extent to which appointments to the upper ranks of the civil service are influenced by party political considerations, the extent to which the culture of the administration is primarily that of the classic law-bound, rule-following bureaucracy (often termed a *rechsstaat*); and the degree of decentralization of administrative authority within the system. The status of each country at the beginning of the 1980s in relation to these features is displayed in Table 3.2.

From the *rechtsstaat* perspective, the state is a central integrating force in society, and its focal concerns are the preparation, promulgation, and enforcement of laws. It usually follows from this that most senior civil servants are trained in law, and that a large body of distinctively administrative law—usually with its own courts—will have been created. The actions of both the individual public servant and the individual citizen will be viewed within this context of correctness and legal control. Both France and Germany, though different in many detailed respects, may be considered to possess administrative cultures of this type.

By contrast, a 'public interest' approach is characteristic of 'Westminster system' countries such as Australia, New Zealand, and the UK. Here, although law is still regarded as an essential component of governance, its particular perspectives are not so dominant as within a *rechsstaat* culture. Thus, in the UK law is not part of the training of most senior civil servants, and the system of administrative law is not so extensive and well developed as

TABLE 3.1 Executive government (as at 1980)

Country	Cabinet	Executive control over legislature	Bi-cameralism	Party competition	Electoral system
Finland (Consensual)	Multi-party coalition	Moderate	Uni-cameral	Multi-party	Proportional representation
France (Intermediate)	One party or minimal coalition	Strong (President)	Assymetric	Multi-party	Plurality
Netherlands (Consensual)	Multi-party coalition	Moderate	Assymetric	Multi-party	Proportional representation
Sweden (Intermediate)	One party or minimal coalition	Moderate	Uni-cameral (since 1976)	Multi-party but with long term dominance of one party	Proportional representation
UK (Majoritarian)	One party	Strong (Cabinet)	Assymetric	Two large parties dominate	Plurality

TABLE 3.2 Administrative characteristics (as at 1980)

Country	Minister/mandarin careers	Politicization of top ranks	Administrative culture	Degree of centralization
Finland	Separate	Moderate	Legalist	Low
France	Integrated	Extensive	Legal/Technocratic	High
Netherlands	Separate	Moderate	Generalist	Low
Sweden	Separate	Moderate	Generalist	Low
UK	Separate	Minimal	Generalist	High

in, say, France. The process of government (and note that 'government' is spoken of much more often than 'the state') is seen as one of seeking to obtain the public's consent for measures adopted in the public (general) interest. Government is supposed to play the part of a fair and trusted referee, with pragmatism and flexibility stressed as much as or more than legal or technical expertise.

The Netherlands and the two Nordic states probably stand somewhere between France and the UK in these respects. In all three, legal training for civil servants is probably more widespread than in the UK, but at the same time the state as a distinct legal presence in civil society is not quite so prominent or pervasive as in France.

One can see other patterns to the data. France and the UK stand out as the most centralized systems, but differ sharply from each other in terms of minister/mandarin careers and the degree of politicization of senior civil service posts. (France displays heavily intertwined political and administrative elites, whereas in the UK these two groups were and are much more separated.) The two Nordic countries and the Netherlands were all extensively decentralized, both in the sense of having constitutionally well protected subnational levels of elected authority and also in the sense of possessing a layer of powerful administrative agencies that enjoyed a significant degree of autonomy from the central ministries (e.g. Kickert and t'Veld 1995).

3.3. How Do SAIs Fit In?

The above constitutional, political, and administrative foundations also affect the work of SAIs. SAIs are obliged to operate in political environments and, despite their statutory independence, inevitably need to take account of political sensibilities. These sensibilities are structured differently in the different countries in our study. In the UK, for example, the comptroller and auditor general reports to Parliament and his reports are examined by the Public Accounts Committee of the House of Commons. The Committee has a long tradition of working on a bi-partisan basis, with differences of opinion on party grounds rare. However, in producing its reports the NAO needs to take account of the fiercely majoritarian and adversarial nature of the wider British political process, to maintain the tradition of independence and non-partisan assistance to the legislature, and to avoid being seen as a champion of particular policies (see e.g. Roberts and Pollitt 1994).

In France the Cour carefully guards its own direct relationships with the executive (and addresses its annual report direct to the President). In recent years it has also begun to develop a more active, direct relationship with the legislature (especially in relation to social protection issues). Its constitutional independence is strong and its status, as the 'home' of one of the 'Grands Corps' that dominate French administration, is high. Interestingly, however, the *procureur général* provides advice on legal matters as they affect the work of the Cour, and can act as an intermediary between the Cour and the judicial authorities. The *procureur général* may, for example, relay requests from the government for specific audits to be carried out, or he may report to the government on important matters arising from the Cour's investigations (NAO 1996a, p. 61).

In the other three countries the SAIs do not face such concentrated, single-headed forms of political power as in France and the UK. Of course, they must take some heed of 'government sensitivities', but the governments they work alongside are usually coalitions, displaying a complex array of cleavages and cross-interests. At the same time, however, the two Nordic SAIs report to their respective governments (since the Finnish and Swedish parliaments have separate, small parliamentary audit offices as well as the SAI). Until 1998, the Swedish RRV had one department specifically devoted to carrying out work for the government, helping the latter to improve its management processes; if one reads recent annual reports, it is clear that, although parliament is mentioned, the greater emphasis is on helping the government (Riksrevisionsverket 1997b). The Dutch Algemene Rekenkamer is different, in that, although it is not part of the formal machinery of the legislature (as is the comptroller and auditor general in the UK), an increasingly significant aspect of its activities has been the provision of advice to the Dutch States General (NAO 1996a, pp. 142–3; Witteveen 1996).

France is also an interesting case because of the extent to which the careers of the political and administrative elites are intertwined. Being a magistrate of the Cour makes one part of an elite that includes both ministers and mandarins. In none of the other SAIs would one expect to find ex-politicians taking part in the business of the day. Contrast this with the strict separation practised at the NAO, where, since the 1983 National Audit Act, staff are no longer even civil servants, instead being employees of the comptroller and auditor general. This change of status was deliberately intended to emphasize their independence of the executive.

In the Netherlands appointments to the governing body of the Algemene Rekenkamer are expected to reflect the kind of consensualist political balance that is so important for many Dutch institutions (NAO 1996a, p. 143). Influences of these kinds seem very likely to have *some* effect on the way that SAIs operate, but it is very hard to pin down precisely what these effects may be (especially since it is in the nature of these things that they are seldom openly discussed in print).

None of this is to deny the real independence that is enjoyed—in differing degrees and forms—by all the SAIs in our study. Rather, we are merely observing that no independence is absolute and that all organizations, however high the degree of autonomy granted by statute and custom, are bound to be subject to influences from their immediate environments, especially when those environments are partly composed of powerful politicians and elite public servants. Some commentators have gone further, and suggested that the nature of the relationships between SAIs and legislatures or ministries of finance/treasuries may directly affect the ability of the SAI to undertake the more sensitive types of performance audit:

> An audit body is probably less likely to face serious criticisms . . . if it serves a powerful legislative or executive client or if it has built up an effective cross-domain supporting coalition. As long as the clients or supporters are comfortable with the exercise of evaluative judgement in a relatively particularistic mode, the audit body may be insulated from serious challenge. (Barzelay 1997, p. 252)

For convenience, the main constitutional and structural features of our five SAIs are summarized in Appendix 2. A fuller treatment can be found in National Audit Office (1996a).

3.4 Dimensions of Management Reform

We now move forwards from 1980 and examine the modernization trends that have been visible in our five countries. Over the past two decades the process of changing the arrangements for public management has become virtually continuous. The specific types of 'modernization', 'streamlining', 'downsizing', or 're-invention' (to choose just some of the many terms that have come into use in the Anglophone world) have been numerous and varied. They include the restructuring of government departments, the building up of new budgetary systems, the introduction of service quality improvement techniques such as total quality management (TQM) or the European Foundation for Quality Management model (EFQM), the elaboration of sets of performance indicators, innovations in personnel management and payment systems, the launch of citizens' charters, 'outsourcing' and contractualization, and so on.

Building on other comparative work (Flynn and Strehl 1996; Hood 1996a; Jones 1993; Naschold 1995; OECD 1995, 1997b; Pollitt and Summa 1997a; Pollitt *et al.* 1997a, b; Trosa 1995b), we have here adopted a fairly conventional, multi-dimensional categorization of public management reform. For each country we have examined the significance of reform activity since 1980 along six dimensions:

1. privatization;
2. marketization;
3. decentralization;
4. output orientation;
5. quality systems;
6. intensity of implementation.

These six dimensions capture many, but not all, types of reform. They are abstractions: a form of shorthand for reducing great complexity to proportions that can be handled within a study of this scale. Some discussion of each dimension is necessary in order to illustrate their scope and limitations.

1. The first dimension is that of *privatization*. In some ways this is the most fundamental type of management reform since it involves a change of ownership which removes certain activities from the public sector altogether. The question here, therefore, is: to what extent has the ownership of state assets been transferred into private hands? For example, in the early 1980s the UK launched a major programme of privatization which continued through the 1990s and eventually embraced almost all the previously heavily nationalized utilities sector. France has also carried through extensive privatizations. By contrast, over the same period Finland and Sweden privatized only cautiously, selectively, and on a small scale.

Privatization may have implications for performance audit. Much depends upon the ability of an SAI to follow public money wherever it may flow, even if this is through a normal commercial contract into a private-sector company. Both law and practice on this point vary somewhat from country to country.

2. The second dimension of reform, *marketization*, concerns the extent to which use has been made of market-type mechanisms (MTMs). Where activities have been retained within the public sector (i.e. where they have not been privatized), they may nevertheless be subject to MTMs. The main MTMs are quasi-markets, contracting out, and the use of vouchers for entitlements to public services (OECD 1993). To some extent, net budgeting and user charging can also be thought of as MTMs, although of a weaker type since they do not necessarily involve any increase in *competition*, which is, analytically, the most important feature of markets. Here again, one can contrast the UK and Finland. In the UK the Conservative governments of Mrs Thatcher and Mr Major imposed MTMs throughout the National Health Service, community care, and much of local government; regular market testing of central government services was also put in place. Use of MTMs in Finland, however, has been limited and experimental.

Market-type competition can impact on the work of performance auditors in several ways. For example, it may lead to the adoption of more commercial-style (accruals) accounts. Also, it is likely to generate new types of performance information, which may well be of considerable interest to performance auditors. Furthermore, it is held by some commentators that competitive environments may encourage public officials to behave in less equitable or open ways, or to take unreasonable risks with public funds—all developments in which an SAI would have an interest.

3. Our third dimension is *decentralization*. This is defined in a general way as comprising the transfer of formal authority from a higher tier in a hierarchical organization to a lower one. More radically, decentralization may also take the form of a transfer of authority from a superior public body to a legally subordinate or separate public body (as when powers are *devolved* from central government to regional and/or local government). Either type of decentralization (within a single organization or from a superior to a subordinate or separate organization) can include elements of financial authority,

personnel authority, or other types of administrative power (e.g. the right to issue a licence or certificate). Analytically, this is rather a broad and heterogeneous dimension of change, and it is frequently helpful to subdivide decentralization into different types (Pollitt *et al.* 1998). For example, decentralization of *political* authority can be distinguished from decentralization of *managerial or administrative* authority. The great French decentralization programme of the early 1980s involved both political and administrative authority (Keating 1983; de Montricher 1996), but under the Conservative administrations of the 1980s and 1990s most decentralization in the UK was managerial, with central government most unwilling to increase the political authority of local governments (Pollitt *et al.* 1998). Another distinction is that between internal decentralization, which can often be fairly rapidly revoked, and a devolution of authority, which is more commonly enshrined in legislation.

In a number of countries decentralization of authority over certain activities has been taking place simultaneously with *increased* centralization of other aspects of public management (e.g. the central setting of output targets). A further issue is that different countries in our sample started from very different 'baselines' with respect to decentralization. Generally speaking, France and the UK had for a long time been more centralized than Finland, the Netherlands, or Sweden.

Decentralization certainly carries implications for performance audit. At its broadest, it means that auditors have to look 'further down' organizations in order to find the authoritative actors, especially in respect of the authorization of expenditure. Where decentralization is accompanied (as it frequently has been) by an increase in the number of operating units or agencies, it may also mean that auditors have more auditees to deal with. Furthermore, where an SAI's jurisdiction is (*de facto* or *de jure*) less active at the level of local government, devolution of activities to that local level may actually shrink the audit field for the national-level audit body. In the UK, for example, local authority accounts are audited by the Audit Commission rather than the NAO; in France, *chambres régionales des comptes* have been set up for subnational issues, and in Finland the VTV does not usually audit the accounts of municipalities.

4. The fourth dimension is that of *output orientation*. This denotes the extent to which control systems have moved away from their traditional bureaucratic emphasis on accounting closely for inputs and towards a more explicit emphasis on outputs (or even outcomes). Some of the management systems that have been introduced have a strong output orientation. Results budgeting in Sweden and Finland is one clear example; the performance indicators that are built into the framework agreements within which the UK's Next Steps executive agencies operate are another (Chancellor of the Duchy of Lancaster 1997b). Since 1996 these executive agency indicator systems have been developed further so as to enable the construction of an elaborate

benchmarking system for comparing performance across agencies, and with private-sector companies (Next Steps Team 1998).

Output orientation is strongly related to the previous dimension (decentralization). Frequently a new emphasis on output measures has been introduced as a counterpart to the decentralization of authority, in order to maintain or enhance accountability or control in the new situation. The example of the UK's executive agencies is again relevant here. Each of these is given extensive decentralized authority by its parent ministry, but is held accountable through a framework agreement which specifies a number of key output measures.

In theory, a growing output orientation ought to help performance auditors, since they, too, are interested in outputs, and should be able to make good use of improved output information. Nevertheless, this output focus represents something of a shift for many SAIs—not necessarily a sudden or dramatic one, but a shift none the less. The traditional attention given to the tight control of inputs, and to the correct following of procedures, is replaced (to some extent at least) by a concentration on what the organization has produced.

5. All five countries have introduced new *quality systems* into various parts of their public sectors, though in different degrees. Typically, these developments have been based on systems such as total quality management (TQM), the ISO9000 series, or the European Foundation for Quality Management (EFQM) model. For example, some Finnish municipalities have used ISO9000 as a basis for service quality initiatives, while TQM has been widely adopted (though not necessarily entirely successfully) in the UK and in France. More recently, some UK executive agencies have begun to use the TQM-derived EFQM model. (For a summary of the main models and a description of some applications, see Pollitt and Bouckaert 1996; for detailed case studies from the Netherlands, France, and the UK see Mol 1995; Trosa 1995a; and Next Steps Team 1998, respectively.) The introduction of quality systems is often connected to the adoption of a stronger output orientation (see previous dimension) because some of these systems (certainly TQM and the EFQM) encourage a focus on the extent to which outputs match customer requirements.

6. The sixth dimension is that of *intensity of implementation process*. This refers to the process rather than the substance of the reforms. The notion of intensity is intended to embrace the speed with which the reforms have been carried through, the vigour with which resistance to reforms has been addressed, and the extent to which the reforms have been forced through from the top rather than being negotiated with a range of interested groups. Thus, if a reform programme had been carefully negotiated with the institutions or groups concerned, had been cautiously implemented through pilot projects before being generalized, and had been targeted upon specific institutions rather than embracing whole sectors, then we would designate this

as 'low intensity'; if, however, a broad scope reform had been forced through at high speed, overriding widespread resistance and criticism, then we would designate such an implementation process as 'high intensity'. The 1989–91 restructuring of the UK NHS would be a good example of the latter. The French decentralization reforms of 1981–6 were also particularly bold and deep. The cautious, phased development of results-oriented budgeting in Finland from 1987 to the present day would be an example of a more gentle approach, as would the widespread use of pilot projects and piecemeal measures in Sweden.

Intensity of implementation is potentially relevant to performance auditors for several reasons. Very rapid change may produce disorientation or loss of expertise, which in turn can threaten the stability and continuity of public services. In the short term it may make auditing more difficult, as information systems are changed and organizational boundaries rapidly readjusted. Separating out the longer-term effects of change from the transitional impacts may be conceptually and practically awkward. Furthermore, the rapid adoption of novel approaches and techniques may require performance auditors themselves to undertake intensive retraining, if they are to be able to understand the new ways in which public bodies are now being managed. An alternative would be to recruit people with significantly different backgrounds from in the past—from merchant banking, for example, or other areas of private finance.

3.5 Comparing the Five Countries

If we now apply these dimensions to each of our five countries, we get the general picture shown in Table 3.3. This table is based on a series of studies of management change, but necessarily incorporates a considerable element of judgement (Hood 1996a; Pollitt and Summa 1997a; Pollitt *et al.* 1997a, b). The 'big picture' provided by the table can be related back to the two earlier tables, typologies of executive governments (Table 3.1) and administrative characteristics (Table 3.2). To generalize, one might say that intense, radical restructuring of the public sector was both more likely and more feasible in majoritarian systems and/or in systems where the 'weight' of the administrative law framework and of legalistic thinking was low rather than high. For example, probably the most sweeping management changes in the OECD world during the 1980s were accomplished in New Zealand, where a strongly majoritarian, centralized regime was only lightly encumbered with constitutional and legal constraints (Boston *et al.* 1996). On the other hand, a consensualist regime makes it more likely that management change will proceed on a cautious, incremental basis—which is mainly what we see in the cases of Finland, the Netherlands, and Sweden. A larger number of countries than five would make these linkages between regime types and the scope, speed, and content of management reform more obvious. (Pollitt and

Table 3.3 Dimensions of public management reform, 1980–95

Country	Privatization	Marketization	Decentralization	Output orientation	Quality systems	Implementation intensity
Finland	Low	Medium	Medium (mainly to local government)	High	Medium	Low/medium
France	Medium	Low	High (mainly to regions)	Medium	Medium	Medium (with high peaks)
Netherlands	High	Medium	Medium (to agencies and local government)	Medium	Low/Medium	Medium
Sweden	Medium	Medium	High (to agencies and local government)	High	Medium	Low/medium
UK	High	High	High (mainly to agencies)	High	High	High

Bouckaert, 1999, examine ten countries instead of the five that are the subject of the present volume.)

We will now turn to examine the process of public management reform in each of our five countries in slightly more detail.

3.6 An Abbreviated History of Recent Management Reforms

France

France is a country with a particularly strong administrative tradition, stretching back to at least the end of the eighteenth century. Though frequently portrayed as a highly centralized, even rigid, state, alongside this 'Jacobin' tendency there has always also existed a more decentralist 'Girondin' theme (Keating 1983). Furthermore, French political and administrative elites are closely mutually entwined (unlike, say, those of Finland or the UK), which means that administrative reform easily becomes the subject of intense political debate.

France is not usually classified as one of the countries 'leading' NPM-type reforms, but neither has it been as cautious in this respect as, say, Germany (Jones 1993, p. 4; OECD 1995). It could perhaps be said that reform activity in France, though continuous, has gone through three periods of particular intensity. The first of these was centred upon the socialist government's attempts to decentralize during the early 1980s. The second was a more managerialist wave of change in the late 1980s and early 1990s, the high point of which was probably Prime Minister Rocard's modernization circular of 29 February 1988 (Clark 1998). The third began in 1995 with the creation of *Commissariat à la réforme de l'Etat*, a body intended to develop in-depth structural reforms.

The decentralization initiatives of the early 1980s are closely associated with the name of Gaston Defferre, Socialist mayor of Marseille and subsequently Minister of the Interior and Decentralization. A law dated 2 March 1982 created the local collectivities as autonomous authorities. Article 72 of the Constitution states that 'the local collectivities manage themselves freely'. Further laws transferred to the communes, *départements*, and regions specific competences, financial and human resources, and shifted taxing and budget-making powers to local collectivities. Since then, all these local authorities have been directly elected and have raised their own taxes (within certain restrictions) and managed their own budgets. The departmental prefects, who lost their role of *tutelle* to the local authorities, and their budgetary powers, were given stronger coordination and control authority over the field services of central ministries. The reverberations of this fundamental reform echoed throughout the remainder of the 1980s and on into the 1990s.

During the same period, there was something of an oscillation with respect to privatization and state ownership. In the early 1980s the socialist government nationalized almost all the banks and main industrial firms. The succeeding, neo-liberal government headed by M. Chirac (1986–8) reversed this policy and launched an extensive privatization effort. A list of sixty-five companies that were to be sold off to the private sector was drawn up. In the relatively brief period before the socialists returned to power, almost half this programme was carried through. Nearly 300,000 industrial employees and 100,000 bank employees were transferred from the public to the private sector. Of this period, one commentator wrote:

> There was never any question, as was the case in the United Kingdom, of de-nationalising the public sector monopolies, gas, electricity, and coal. And industries which were perceived as 'strategic' (the state airline, steel, the aerospace industry) were left firmly under public control. It is also highly revealing that the state retained a variety of controls (potential and real) over the privatized firms and banks . . . (Wright 1989, p. 105)

However, the privatization process was far from over. In 1993 the conservative parties again gained the upper hand electorally and M. Balladur became prime minister. In 1995 M. Chirac succeeded M. Mitterrand as president. In the decade 1985–95 the public-sector share of total employment fell from 10.4 to 7.7 per cent. Furthermore, firms remaining within the public sector have had to face up to an increasingly demanding competitive context. Sharp internal reforms have taken place in companies such as SNCF (railways), Air France, and GIAT (military manufacture).

When the socialists returned to power in 1988, they embraced a theme of public-sector renewal that was incorporated in Prime Minister Rocard's circular of February 1989. This theme contained a number of separate elements, including the creation of 'responsibility centres' within ministries, a much more extensive use of evaluation, and a range of human resource management reforms. While these changes were significant, they did not amount to the kind of wholesale restructuring that was taking place in the UK at the same time. For example, the responsibility centres developed in a patchy way (some ministries effectively dragged their feet) and enjoyed only limited delegated authority (Trosa 1995a, pp. 64–5). Nevertheless, more than 200 such centres had been created by the beginning of 1994, and once units of this sort exist the potential for further delegations remains. There were also a number of attempts to introduce service quality improvement systems. After some early failures with quality circles and TQM, a number of less top-down and more user-oriented systems began to be developed (Trosa 1995b). As evidence mounted of a growing disenchantment with the state on the part of a significant section of French society, the rhetorical stress on the citizen and the service user became more pronounced. The Minister for the Civil Service declared that 1994 was 'l'année de l'accueil dans les services publics' (Ministère de la Fonction Publique 1994).

In the view of one knowledgeable commentator, what was being attempted was cultural change without the reinforcement of genuine structural change (Rouban 1995b). The pivotal position of the Grands Corps was preserved and their fundamental values of control and supervision remained relatively undisturbed (Clark 1998; Rouban 1995a, b). Other commentators offer slightly different interpretations, but there seems to be widespread agreement that:

> During the 1980s, decisive pressures arose mainly from decentralization, the making of the European Union and scarce resources. Consequently, administrative reform is a global concept in which various themes appear and disappear, with no coherent comprehensive strategy. Among those themes are globalization of budgets, deconcentration, productivity etc. (de Montricher 1996, p. 251)

The rapid institutionalization of evaluation after 1990 was an interesting feature of the French reforms, and one that survived the 1993 transition to M. Balladur's administration (Duran *et al.* 1995). Although a proposal for a National Evaluation Council was not implemented, a range of evaluation units and committees were set up at national and regional levels (de Montricher 1996, pp. 271–4). The Grands Corps, including the Cour des Comptes, were represented on the key national bodies. Eventually, in 1998, a National Evaluation Council was launched.

The overall picture of public management reforms in France is therefore mixed. According to the priorities of the particular government, the main focus has shifted from decentralization to privatization and from public-sector renewal to private-sector solutions. While the changes have been real and significant, it cannot be said that they have involved a fundamental restructuring of the central state's basic administrative architecture, as has been the case in New Zealand and the UK. The main thrust of the debate has been on how to streamline the state to deal with a changing environment. The Thatcherite and Majorite themes of minimizing the state and infusing it to the maximum extent possible with business methods and models have been considerably less popular in France. French governments have not abandoned the commitment to a strong administrative state, and a belief in the value of strategic planning, though diminished from that of the 1960s, remains a notable feature of the French approach. The experiments with organizational diversity and service user-led change, though significant, have been somewhat less prominent than in the UK and Australasia (de Montricher 1996; Pollitt *et al.* 1997b: Rouban 1995a).

Finland

The main Finnish public management reforms commenced in 1987, and there was a high degree of continuity in the implementation of these reforms, stretching through three different coalition governments (Holkeri, 1987–91; Ahonen 1991–5, Lipponen 1995–). The main components of the reforms were as follows:

1. *the introduction of results-oriented budgeting systems throughout the state sector*, leading to the development of systems of targets and indicators (Summa 1995). The piloting of these budgetary systems commenced in 1987 and they were steadily developed and extended over the ensuing decade. They have been credited with stimulating significant savings in running costs (Summa 1995);
2. *a State Enterprise Act (1987)*, which established the state enterprise as a new organizational form for state activities. Many public utilities and services were subsequently 'corporatized' into this format. Some (e.g. the railways and Finnish Post and Telecommunications) were then further converted into state-owned joint stock companies. By the end of 1995, twenty-four bodies had been turned into state enterprises or state-owned companies. Most of these achieved positive commercial results. They were also able to enter into take-overs and various kinds of commercial alliances with other companies. The level of detail of parliamentary control over their operations was reduced. Adoption of the state-owned company form may be regarded as an example of the use of market-type mechanisms (MTMs—see Table 2.3);
3. *a reduction in the authority and number of independent central agencies* (the traditional 'second level' of central government). Most of these agencies were abolished, merged, or converted into research and development centres; a few (e.g. the State Printing Company) were privatized. The slimming down of the agency tier marked a relinquishment by central government of detailed controls over the municipalities, linked to the adoption of 'frame budgeting' for central grants to local authorities (see (4) below). It attracted the attention of the VTV, which conducted a large study of the topic (Valtiontalouden tarkastusvirasto 1994);
4. *a reform of the grant system to municipalities (1993)*, which involved moving away from detailed, specific grants to a block grant. This transferred questions of detailed resource allocation between different services more firmly to the municipal level;
5. *reform of the provincial level of government*, merging and slimming down central state authorities at the provincial level but building up regional coalitions of municipalities. These changes were partly designed to provide Finland with a more effective way of dealing with the EU over regional policy issues and the European structural funds;
6. *a reform of civil servants' employment conditions*, to make them more similar to those of private-sector employees (Reform of the Civil Service Act, 1994). However, implementation was quite slow (Pollitt *et al.* 1997b, p. 78);
7. *the introduction of a version of accruals accounting.*

The general tempo of reform in Finland has been careful and moderate (Pollitt *et al.* 1997b). Sweeping privatizations and large-scale redundancies have been deliberately avoided, although, by one means or another, large numbers of staff have been removed from the central state 'books'. The approach has been one of modernizing the public sector rather than seeking to minimize it. A recent Finnish commentator described the style as 'technocratic/pragmatic' (Puoskari 1996, p. 4). A number of the initiatives have been launched by means of pilot projects, and extensive training programmes have been put in place to help civil servants adjust to new systems and circumstances. There has been a continuity in the main lines of reform, and most of the advice and guidance on reform have come from within the ranks of the civil service itself. The reforms have not been accompanied by widespread public or political controversy. On the whole, the habits of consensualism have prevailed. Another factor (in Finland as elsewhere) has been the relatively technical nature of most of the changes; as one civil servant said, 'there are only two or three ministers and 20–25 civil servants who understand the issues enough to conduct a public debate' (quoted in Pollitt *et al.* 1997b, p. 81). There is no parallel in Finland to the predilection that some Conservative UK (and, even more so, US) politicians have for attacking their own governments as being fundamentally inefficient, unresponsive, and generally inferior to the private-sector world of business and commerce. 'Finns are a people very loyal to the state, who see change as a governmental process rather than a grass root level reform of society' (Centre for Finnish Business and Policy Studies 1996, p. 2).

The Netherlands

Politically, the Netherlands, though formally a unitary state, is polycentric and corporatist (Kickert and t'Veld 1995). With a few brief exceptions, the process of management reform has been pragmatic and relatively fragmentary, although government rhetoric has occasionally made matters sound more programmatic and sweeping than they have actually turned out to be. The period 1982–9 was occupied by two centre–right coalitions ('Lubbers 1' and 'Lubbers 2'). In 1989 the Social Democratic party replaced the Conservative Liberal Party to form the 'Lubbers 3' government. In 1994 a left–right 'purple coalition' was formed and the centrist Christian parties were excluded from the governing coalition for the first time in eighty years. This new government declared itself in favour of restoring the 'primacy of politics' and criticized the undue autonomy which they considered had been given to some public bodies. Yet these changes of party mix between Lubbers 1, 2, and 3 did not generate any rapid or radical changes in the direction of management reform. Indeed, as the 1980s wore on, there were signs of some convergence between the parties with respect to issues such as privatization and the need to restrain expenditure growth (Roberts, in Pollitt *et al.* 1997b, pp. 91–130).

When the Lubbers 1 coalition came to power in 1982, considerable emphasis was laid on privatization. All four of the most prominent state companies were sold off (the Postbank, PTT Telecom, the Fishery Port

Authority, and the Royal Mint). Through this procedure, between 1986 and 1989 about 10,000 jobs were moved off the state's books. (A further 10,000 civil servants were also shed, mainly through wastage and other non-compulsory procedures.) As in the UK, privatization sales brought the government useful practical benefits in the form of one-off injections of cash to the state budget. However, the 'starting line' was different in the Netherlands, as a smaller proportion of the industrial sector than in the UK was in national ownership to begin with. While there was some controversy over the privatization policy, the predominant attitude seems to have been more accepting than in, say, Finland. One might contrast the relatively favourable media reception of the privatization of the Dutch Post Office with the critical publicity in Finland in 1993 when the Finnish Post Office (not privatized) closed a number of rural offices and transferred their services to private shop outlets.

Alongside privatization, the first two Lubbers administrations advocated decentralization of powers and discretion to lower levels of government (partly through a form of block grant), a simplification of legal procedures, and various measures of expenditure reduction. This was therefore political decentralization in our terms. However, administrative decentralization was also extensively implemented. A considerable number of ZBOs (quangos) were created, so that by the mid-1990s almost a fifth of the state budget was passing through this type of organization. Corporatizations (creations of joint stock companies in which the state holds all or a majority of the shares) were another type of decentralizing reform. A 1995 report from the Algemene Rekenkamer was sharply critical of the way in which many of the ZBOs lacked credible performance indicators, could not produce evidence of self-evaluation, and (in some cases) appeared to have an inadequate legal basis for some of their activities (Algemene Rekenkamer 1995). This was therefore an example of decentralization that sometimes lacked a corresponding strengthening of output measurement systems.

MTMs (e.g. contracting out) have been used in a modest way, but nothing has been attempted that would be equivalent in scale to the quasi-markets introduced in the UK health and community care sectors. Performance budgeting had previously been introduced by the Government Accounts Act 1976. This required ministries to provide annual performance data to support their budget bids. However, this was unevenly implemented, and a 1988 study by the Central Audit Department concluded that input indicators predominated over output indicators and that political and official interest in performance budgeting was limited. From 1991, however, a new wave of performance measurement was launched. Since then, progress on output measurement has continued, but still in a gradual and uneven way.

Also from 1991, a programme of agentification began. This was influenced by the UK 'Next Steps' programme and was also connected to the idea of restructuring central ministries as slimmed-down policy-making cores

(Committee Wiegel 1993). The availability of a sound framework of performance measures was one of the important preconditions for permitting a set of activities to assume agency status. The first four agencies were launched in June 1994, with three more in 1995 and six in 1996. These organizations use business accounting practices and enjoy the authority to vire expenditure between staff and other budget heads. Their creation has been a further step in the process of central ministries having to re-conceptualize their roles as 'steering' (hands-off) rather than 'doing' (Kickert 1997).

Service quality issues came to the fore at the end of the 1980s, especially at local government level. Experiments with 'one-stop-shops' and 'public service centres' were launched, and quality assessment and improvement techniques such as TQM were borrowed from the private sector.

In sum, there has been a great deal of reform activity within the Netherlands, but, true to the polycentric and consensualist character of its political system, this has tended to result in a series of ad hoc and sectoral or sub-sectoral initiatives rather than in grand national programmes. Doctrinaire solutions—or even the kind of ambitious 'systems thinking' that was much discussed in the Netherlands during the 1970s—have been largely absent in practice. The most accurate description of the overall process might be 'incremental pragmatism', with decentralization, privatization, and (more recently) agentification and corporatization as the main themes. Cost-cutting has always been on the agenda. Trade union resistance to some aspects of the reforms—and even more towards government wage policies—has at times been explicit. A major strike took place in 1983, and there was another serious dispute in 1990. The government came out as the main 'winner' on both occasions, and during the 1990s trade union leaders seem to have preferred negotiation to open conflict. The general intensity of the Dutch reforms could therefore be described as less 'hot' than that in Thatcherite Britain (the Dutch government did not launch specific attacks on trade unions in the way that the British Conservative government did) but 'warmer' than in Finland or Sweden.

Sweden

Throughout the period under study, Sweden maintained the largest (as a proportion of GDP) public sector in the western world. Since the early 1980s, the process of public management reform has been virtually continuous, under both Social Democrat (1982–91, 1994) and Conservative (1991–4) governments. Pierre (1995) divides this period into two phases: one of renewing the public sector and getting closer to the citizen (1982 to roughly 1988) and the second where the emphasis moved towards increasing organizational autonomy and making public expenditure savings (1988–96).

In 1976 the Social Democratic party fell from power for the first time in forty-four years. Post-election analyses suggested that the party had incurred the voters' displeasure for a variety of reasons, one of which was its association with the bureaucratic inertia of the state machine. When the

Social Democrats returned to government in 1982, they were determined to break this pejorative association by making the state machine more accessible to the ordinary citizen, thereby increasing its legitimacy. At the same time, they wanted to modernize the administrative apparatus through decentralization, simplification, and deregulation. The 1982 re-creation of a Ministry of Public Administration was symbolic of their intentions. Increasing use was made of 'frame legislation' which enhanced the discretion available to agencies and authorities; various powers were devolved from central government to the counties and municipalities, management by objectives was substituted for detailed *ex ante* and *ex post* controls by ministries over local authorities. The Government Modernization Programme of 1985 laid particular stress on decentralization from the central (state) sector to counties and municipalities. Between 1980 and 1994, fourteen different groups of activities were decentralized in this way, especially in the areas of welfare and civil defence. Increased user choice and user responsiveness was an important sub-theme. Quality was to be enhanced, not eroded. The state was to be 'renewed' (Gustafsson 1987).

Personnel powers were also decentralized, with agencies being permitted to set their own salary ranges, so long as increases were covered by productivity gains. In 1986 an individual pay system was introduced, and this is now fixed by individual employers. However, frame agreements are still centrally negotiated between the Swedish Agency for Government Employers (SAGE) and the three public-sector unions. By the mid-1990s Swedish public-sector pay arrangements could be said to be more decentralized than those of the Netherlands or France, but not as much as those of the most radical decentralizers in this respect—the UK and New Zealand (OECD 1997a).

Privatization was not (then) on the agenda. As one senior Swedish civil servant wrote, 'The Swedish government in principle rejects privatization as a method of solving the problems of the sector. The main objection is that this would lead to distributive injustices . . .' (Gustaffson 1987, p. 180).

This renewal programme did not proceed entirely smoothly. In some instances line ministries saw the efforts of the Ministry of Public Administration as depriving them of their controls over local authorities. The Prime Minister eventually had to resolve these 'turf wars', and did so in a way that made considerable concessions to the interests of the line ministries (Pierre 1995, p. 5).

A second phase of reform began in the late 1980s, and accelerated under the Conservative government that came to power in 1991. This period was dominated by a fiscal crisis and the acute need to make efficiency gains and savings. It included more extensive institutional reforms than during the earlier phase. Some agencies, their work-loads reduced by previous decentralizations, were abolished or merged. A total of 65 agencies disappeared between 1980 and 1994, but 45 new ones were created; 29 mergers took place, producing 13 merged entities.

Those agencies that survived were given greater autonomy within a more outputs-oriented regime. Results-based management was introduced on a broad scale from 1988, and from 1990–3 a series of financial management reforms were implemented, including accruals accounting and frame appropriations. Greater use of the voluntary sector became a theme as governments at various levels searched for alternative models of service delivery that would relieve financial pressures. Echoing UK developments (government as 'enabler' rather than 'provider'), some Swedish commentators have seen this as a shift from a model of a governing state to that of a bargaining state (Österberg 1995). The Government Administration Programme of 1991 stressed the notion of the 'refinement' of public administration, which included the separation of competitive from non-competitive activities. Between 1990 and 1996, thirteen agencies became public companies. Other agencies or public utilities had their financial bases altered so as to motivate them towards a more commercial approach (e.g. Statistics Sweden, the Swedish Meteorological and Hydrological Institute, the Civil Aviation Administration). However, the Conservative government's original plans for large-scale privatization were considerably reduced.

Overall, therefore, it can be said that Swedish public management reforms were characterized by a continuing concern to decentralize and make services more sensitive to citizens' needs. From the late 1980s, fiscal concerns also came to the fore. Privatization has not been a major agenda item except briefly, during the early days of the 1991 Conservative government. As in Finland, the broad objective has been to modernize and 're-legitimize' the state rather than minimize it. There are some signs, however, that this modernization programme has raised questions as to whether the control of elected politicians over the reformed apparatus has declined (Pierre 1995). There is also a question as to whether the term 'programme' is wholly appropriate in the Swedish context. While central government has from time to time made general pronouncements, it is in the nature of the (already) highly decentralized Swedish system that the actual implementation of reforms has varied greatly from one agency, county, or municipality to another. Sweden does not display examples of the kind of sweeping, uniform, compulsory, centrally imposed reform that took place in the UK with relation to (for example) health, education, or community care. It remains to be seen whether incremental change will provide a sufficient response to the fiscal crisis of the Swedish state (Lane 1995).

United Kingdom

Throughout the period surveyed by this study, the UK was ruled by a single-party Conservative government. This gave the executive an unusually extended opportunity to work out and implement their reform ideas (Hood 1996b). With some oversimplification, the Conservative period between the elections of 1979 and 1997 can be divided into three phases as far as public management reform is concerned. First, from 1979 to about 1982 there was a fierce but relatively crude drive for economies. Civil service numbers were cut by 25 per cent and civil service pay was brought under tighter ministerial control. The Civil Service Department, which had been seen by Mrs Thatcher as over-concerned to defend civil servants' interests, was abolished. Central government also embarked on a series of new legislative measures designed to tighten its grip on local authority expenditure.

However, the limitations of this economizing strategy were apparent from the beginning, and the government soon moved to emphasize efficiency rather than economy. This second phase lasted from the early to the late 1980s. Although the government constantly referred to the 'three Es' (economy, efficiency, and effectiveness—see Figure 1.2), most of the new procedures and performance indicators put in place throughout the public sector actually concerned the first two Es rather than the third. Huge efforts were put into improving the financial management skills of public officials. During this time new legislation redefined the role of the National Audit Office (1983) and set up an Audit Commission for local government (1982), both with mandates stressing the 'three Es'.

During this second phase, an increasingly ambitious sequence of public utility privatizations assumed a central position in the government's political programme. British Telecom was privatized in 1984, followed by British Gas (1986), the British Airports Authority (1987), water supply and sewerage (1989), electricity supply (1990/1), and British Rail (1994 onwards). The market capitalization of the privatized industries exceeded £100 billion. In ten years 800,000 employees were transferred into the private sector and the share of the gross domestic product accounted for by stated-owned industries fell from 11 per cent in 1979 to 5.5 per cent in 1990.

However, the third phase of reform was in many ways the most radical of all. After Mrs Thatcher's victory in the 1987 General Election, a confident and experienced government launched a series of public sector reforms which:

1. made much bolder and larger-scale use of MTMs (sometimes referred to as quasi- or internal markets) than ever before. The NHS, community care, and, to some extent, the education sector were all fundamentally restructured to promote more provider competition;
2. intensified organizational and spatial decentralization of the management and production of services (though not necessarily their financing or policy-making—see Pollitt *et al.* 1998). In a number of cases these changes involved shifting local units from local authority control to independent status, e.g. grant-maintained schools and colleges of further education;
3. laid constant rhetorical emphasis on the need to improve public service quality, and exemplified this by the launch of the Citizen's Charter programme (Prime Minister 1991, 1992; Pollitt 1994).

From the late 1980s, therefore, the public services were shaken out of their traditional bureaucratic forms. They were divided into, on the one hand, agencies set up to purchase services on behalf of communities and, on the other, a range of provider organizations (public, private, non-profit, and private for profit) which competed within MTMs to win contracts from the purchasers. This purchaser–provider split (in its various forms) was accompanied by a rapid extension of the use of contracts or quasi-contracts to govern relationships between public authorities.

Following the Next Steps report (Efficiency Unit 1988), the central government also drew a firmer line between the executive work of service provision and the policy work of the most senior civil servants. The traditional departments shed their executive work to more than 140 new executive agencies. These bodies were instructed to carry out their businesses within quasi-contracts termed *framework agreements*. Framework agreements specified performance targets, budgets, and personnel freedoms, and an annual report was published indicating how far these targets had been achieved (Chancellor of the Duchy of Lancaster 1997).

During Mrs Thatcher's premiership the public services were frequently chastised for inefficiency and self-interest while a series of business people and consultants were brought into central government in an attempt to transfer their allegedly superior management skills, techniques, and insights to the civil service. Under Mr Major in the 1990s, the anti-public service tone was reduced. For example, the Citizen's Charter programme was launched with a prime ministerial preface that praised public services and held out a vision of future improvement and excellence (Prime Minister 1991). At the same time, however, the drive to privatization continued and the government considerably extended its programme of compulsory competitive tendering and 'market testing' of public services (HM Treasury 1991). A Private Finance Initiative (PFI) was launched with the aim of promoting increased private-sector participation in public-sector capital projects (Terry 1996).

3.7 Public Management Reform and Performance Audit

In this chapter we have seen both diversity and similarity. Diversity is important in that different political systems work in different ways—what is possible or feasible in one may not be possible or feasible in another—and different SAIs occupy varying positions within their respective constitutional and legal frameworks. All this might be expected to produce significant variations in practice between the auditors in each country. On the other hand, although the variations in detail are endless, there do appear to have been some strongly similar themes in the management reforms that have affected all five countries since 1980.

Obviously, one of these themes has been the need to restrain expenditure. Everywhere, this has led to budgetary and financial management reforms, of a kind that could be expected to be of great interest to SAIs. A popular combination in all five countries (if to different degrees) has been a delegation of spending authority to lower hierarchical or governmental strata coupled with a strict application of budgetary 'frames', 'envelopes', or ceilings. This produces a situation where spending limits have been tightened at the same time as staff who would not previously have had much to do with financial management are now necessarily obliged to take some responsibility for it. The need for some auditing of such developments would appear unarguable.

A second theme has been that of increasing the productivity of public services—'getting more for less', or (in terms of Figure 1.2) raising efficiency. Again, such attempts are of salience for SAIs in general, and for performance auditors in particular, since efficiency is commonly acknowledged to be a crucial dimension of 'performance'. Adoption of the 'input–output model' (Figure 1.2), rhetorically and/or operationally, has been widespread. In effect, this creates a different set of criteria for expenditure control from that inherent within the *rechsstaat* model of public administration. Under the latter, the main aim is to ensure that expenditure is properly authorized—that it is lawful, that is being spent on the designated purposes, and that the correct procedures have been gone through (compliance). Under the input–output model, however, the main aim is to ensure the 'biggest bang per buck', i.e. maximum productivity through maximum efficiency of expenditure. There is thus a potential tension between the two models, both for managers themselves and for performance auditors. As we shall see, performance auditors may operate under mandates that stress the 'three Es' (economy, efficiency, and effectiveness), but that does not by any means imply that they have lost their interest in procedure and correctness.

A third theme—stronger in some countries than others but present in all—was that of responsiveness, of moulding public services more closely in accordance with the convenience and preferences of their users. The relevance of this trend for audit institutions is not quite so direct as was the case for the first two themes, but it has nevertheless been taken up by performance auditors in some countries. The grounds here are that it is hard to argue that a publicly funded service is providing good value for money if it is not satifying the requirements of its users. In approaching this topic, SAIs have found it necessary to move somewhat beyond their usual networks, in the sense that it is hard to assess responsiveness and user satisfaction without directly consulting users (i.e. citizens) themselves.

Finally, a fourth theme has been that of strengthening 'transparency', usually on the assumption that transparency is a feature of democratic governance and that more of it should strengthen public confidence in the workings of the state. Here again, the interest of SAIs (as institutions specifically devoted to the safeguarding of public accountability and assurance) is clear. It could be argued that the importance of SAIs as expert and independent sources of public testimony is enhanced during periods of time when public-sector organizations are undergoing multiple and sometimes rapid changes.

These four themes interact with each other, and may sometimes be in tension. (For example, decentralization and the fragmentation of the old, monolithic bureaucracies may conflict with the principle of transparency and accountability.) Both singly and collectively, they imply considerable changes to the ways in which public administration has been run in the past. Such changes are not likely to be straightforward, and success is by no means guaranteed. In these general terms, therefore, it would seem reasonable to expect SAIs to devote a good deal of attention to public management reforms. Public management reform has altered the contexts within which state audit operates. Furthermore, the character of many of the reforms resonated vigorously with the specific, professed concerns of performance audit, in that the reforms themselves were self-consciously to do with performance.

4

The Management–Audit Interface

Christopher Pollitt

4.1 The Implications of Public Management Reforms for Supreme Audit Institutions

In the Introduction we wrote of the 'multiple connections' between management reform and the development of performance audit. Now that the definitions of this type of audit have been explored (Chapter 2) and the context of management change has been described (Chapter 3), we can examine these connections more closely. Once they have been 'mapped' it should be easier to locate the more detailed material and examples which will be introduced in subsequent chapters.

At the outset it may be useful to distinguish a number of ways in which, in principle, public management reforms could affect, or be affected by, SAIs. In principle, such mutual influences could operate in either direction or both. That is to say, the widespread incidence of management change 'out there' (i.e. outside SAIs) could affect the way SAIs conceive of and organize performance audit 'in here', and/or performance audit reports and other products could have an impact upon the way public bodies pursued and implemented management reform. In practice, as we shall see, both types of connection exist. The broad picture is not a simple one of either management reform or performance audit coming (temporally) first, and the other development being 'caused' by it, but rather a series of intertwined mutual developments over time. Power puts the matter thus:

> auditing and the development of concepts of performance are mutually constitutive. (Power 1997, p. 119)

These mutual changes have proceeded at different speeds and with different emphases in different countries, but there has none the less been a shared general direction or vector. A recent OECD report gives the following (perhaps slightly *too* neat) overview:

> In general one could argue that, under performance management, input-oriented budgets are turned into performance budgets, cash-based accounting systems are changed into accrual based cost accounting systems . . . or performance reporting systems, and compliance and financial audits are complemented by performance audits and evaluations. (OECD 1997b, p. 21)

In at least one sense, we would go further than this. The interlinked developments of management reform and performance audit should not be thought of as being narrowly restricted to budgetary matters. The notion of 'performance' can be—and on occasion has been—construed very broadly indeed. Many performance audit studies (as we shall see) examine topics that are at several removes from questions of financial management—topics such as customer satisfaction with museum services, the management of health promotion programmes, or the accountability of non-departmental bodies.

Traffic across the management–performance audit interface could therefore be of many different kinds. Some of the more obvious possibilities are described below.

1. Public management reformers could aim directly at the reform of SAIs, e.g. by altering their mandates or powers, or by insisting on their adoption of particular organizational structures or techniques. This would clearly be an example of externally driven change affecting the very frameworks within which SAIs work.
2. Management reform might lead to changes in the public sector which altered the size of the audit field, e.g. where the public–private boundary is significantly shifted or where, as in the case of UK regulatory agencies, a new class or cohort of public bodies is set up which falls within the purview of the SAI. Again, this would be an external change, but one that was less direct in its effect than the above.
3. Management reform could complicate (or simplify) the pattern of organizations to be audited; e.g. a fragmentation of previously unified bureaucratic organizations into a larger number of agencies/units/public trusts/ corporations would increase the number of accounts within an SAI's purview. This is another species of external change, one that poses a problem for SAIs in terms of how they organize their work.
4. The adoption of new management techniques and approaches could affect the nature of the auditor's task; e.g., decentralized budgeting systems with many budget holders and greater virement than in the past might require a different audit approach from traditional systems that had been characterized by a high degree of centralization on a principal finance officer. This is, in effect, a more focused version of connection 3.
5. The adoption of new management techniques and approaches could directly affect performance audit by generating new data of considerable interest to the auditor, such as that derivable from contemporary systems of performance indicators.
6. The widespread use of new management techniques and approaches throughout the rest of the public sector could lead SAIs to reflect upon their own practices and decide to borrow some of these techniques and approaches for their own self-management. For example, an SAI might

decide to delegate greater authority to lower levels in the hierarchy of auditors, or to contract out a certain proportion of its audits, or to hire in management consultants to examine its internal procedures. This kind of connection is an example of an SAI being influenced by the external 'climate of thought' in such a way that it adapts its internal practices.

7. The increasing emphasis on performance measurement that has been part of many management reform programmes (see the discussion on output orientation above) could persuade SAIs to give more attention to performance audit relative to their other activities. This could make itself manifest in several ways, e.g. through an increase in the number of performance audits undertaken over time, or through internal reorganizations which separated out performance audit work from other SAI activities and gave the former heightened organizational status within the SAI.
8. The increasing emphasis on the specific criteria of efficiency, effectiveness, and service quality that has also been part of many management reform programmes could lead to SAIs applying these same criteria more explicitly and forcefully in performance audit—a sort of 'echo' effect.

All of the above are 'outside–in' influences, in the sense that they are ways in which reforms in the wider world of the public sector could influence the mandates, structures, standard operating procedures, internal resource allocation, and audit criteria of SAIs. However, the 'traffic' at the interface is potentially two-way, so we need to add descriptions of ways in which influence could work from the 'inside' of SAIs to the larger 'outside' world of public-sector institutions and programmes:

9. Individual performance audit reports (or sets of reports) could lead to changes in the nature of management reforms (e.g. the imposition of new safeguards in cases of privatization; improvements in the validity and reliability of data fed into performance indicator systems).
10. More generally, the cumulative weight of a series of SAI reports could influence the general atmosphere of debate around a management reform programme. For example, a series of reports indicating loss of financial control in newly decentralized agencies could encourage a wave of public and political scepticism concerning the advisability of this type of reform.

4.2 The Interface in Practice

Looking across our five countries, we have little difficulty in finding examples of *all* of the first eight types ('outside-in') of effects. Our research does not permit us to give quite such a confident answer in respect of the 'inside–out' possibilities, i.e. 9 and 10 (partly because our focus has been much more on the 'insides' of SAIs than the 'outsides'). Nevertheless, there is some material that allows at least tentative speculation about the impacts of SAIs, and this will be addressed more fully in Chapter 9.

1. One example of the first type of effect (point 1 above) occurred in the Netherlands during the 1980s, when the Dutch Parliament tried to exert greater influence over the SAI's choice of audit topics, partly in order to try to get it to look at certain issues connected with administrative reform (NAO 1996a, p. 146). Another is occurring in Finland at the time of writing, as reformers wish to transfer the VTV from its current location within the jurisdictional sphere of the Ministry of Finance to a position of serving Parliament, rather like the UK NAO. The Ministry has resisted this transfer. A third case is that of the transfer in 1998 of the financial management department of the RRV to the status of a separate government advisory agency. None of these examples is perfect, since the motives in each case were mixed—management changes were one issue among others, and were not necessarily the principal target of the reformers. Nevertheless, in a general way they illustrate how the modernization of the state machinery can lead to the role of the SAI itself being called into question. In the UK the extensive privatization of government services, the growing involvement of private-sector firms of accountants in public-sector work, and the market testing of much of the work carried out for the Audit Commission have led some to suggest that the private sector should take over more the work currently carried out by the NAO. Others have argued that a purchaser/provider regime similar to that used by the Audit Commission or for central government audit in New Zealand should be applied to the UK. Shortly before the 1997 election, a Conservative Government White Paper on *The Governance of Public Bodies: A Progress Report* stated that:

> The Government noted in Cm 3179 that there were benefits to be obtained from drawing on the experience of auditors from both the public and private sectors. The Government welcomes developments in the use of accountancy firms by the national audit agencies, though it believes that there is scope for subjecting more work to market testing. It has suggested that the Comptroller and Auditor General should consider allowing firms to compete with the National Audit Office staff to undertake certain audits, reporting to him. (Chancellor of the Duchy of Lancaster (1997a))

Despite this, however, there was little public pressure for major changes. The first year of the Labour Government headed by Mr Blair did not result in any proposal for fundamental constitutional change at the NAO, and the immediate pressure for privatizing audit receded. However, some medium-term restructuring of audit institutions remained in prospect, and prior to the election some leading Labour politicians had made no secret of their admiration for the Audit Commission, a body with a remit to audit local government and the National Health Service, and one that had made its name with a distinctive brand of quite popularly presented performance audit.

2. The second type of effect—changes in the scope of the audit field—is manifest in a number of countries. In France concern about the diversity of management of social security funds was a factor behind the promulgation of legislation which, from 25 July 1994, empowered the Cour to produce annual reports to Parliament on this topic. Meanwhile, in the UK the creation of a series of national regulatory bodies to oversee the newly privatized companies has provided a fresh target for performance audit (NAO 1996b). Also, the 'opting out' from local authority control of grant-maintained schools and the reform of colleges of further education has brought many additional organizations within the NAO's audit field.

3. The third effect—changes in the numbers and types of account to be audited—is equally unmistakable. In France the volume of funds collected through charity campaigns had been expanding rapidly, and questions arose concerning the control and management of these funds. A law dated 7 August 1991 empowered the Cour to audit these funds. Subsequently the Cour was able to uncover, for example, serious mismanagement within L'Association pour la Recherce Contre le Cancer (ARC). In the UK the introduction of MTMs to the NHS led to the creation of a large number of public trusts—corporate bodies that ran hospitals and community health services. Within a short period of time, this increased the number of NHS accounts to which the UK Audit Commission (the audit institution for local government and the NHS) had to attend from about 150 to over 3,000. In central government the NAO commented that, comparing 1993/4 with 1994/5,

> The number of accounts we audit rose by 45 in 1994/95 (to 542) and is expected to rise to over 600 over the next five years. This reflects the increase in the number of executive agencies which are preparing accounts for audit, and new bodies such as the Office of the National Lottery. (NAO 1995a, p. 8)

These increased numbers mainly affect traditional financial audit rather than performance audit, but they have implications for the latter in so far as performance audits are focused upon specific institutions (as they very often are in the UK).

It should be added that, *ceteris paribus*, a growth in the requirement for *financial* audits may demand additional resources within an SAI and thereby (within a static budget) limit the expenditure and staff effort available for performance audit. The clearest example of this happening is probably the introduction of the *Déclaration d'assurance* (DAS) procedure within the European Union following the 1992 Maastricht Treaty; providing this assurance to the European Parliament initially reduced the resources available for performance audit work. Another case would be the development of resource accounting in the UK. This has absorbed a good deal of attention from the NAO, which may, in turn, have placed an effective limit on any further net expansion of VFM work.

More generally, the numerous changes in both the shape of the UK public sector (effect 2 above) and the form of its constituent organizations (effect 3) have propelled questions about the scope and nature of public audit firmly on to the political agenda (HM Treasury 1996; Evans and Thornton 1997; Evans 1998; Lovell 1998). Indeed, in some ways the rapid development of new public management change has worked in the NAO's favour, and the comptroller and auditor general (C&AG) is regarded by politicians of all parties as a bulwark against the downside of rapid change (see. e.g. Sengupta 1998). Parliament's concerns have been that the traditional public-sector ethos (considered to be part of the reason for the perceived lack of corruption in British public life) is being eroded, and that the contracting out of public services is making it difficult for Parliament to follow how public funds are being spent. The multi-party Public Accounts Committee has regularly called for the C&AG to be able to follow public funds wherever they go, including to private-sector recipients. Before they formed a government in 1997, the Labour Party, keen to find ways of ensuring that its spending proposals had credibility, promised that, should it be elected, the C&AG would be given additional powers to follow public funds. This would enable the NAO better to play the role of 'sleazebuster', looking into irregularity and impropriety in the letting of contracts, etc. At the time of writing this idea has not been taken any further, but the general standing of the comptroller and auditor general remains high.

In the Netherlands the proliferation of quangos (ZBOs) has become a source of concern for the Court of Audit, which commented on the limited extent to which they were publicly accountable for their activities (Algemene Rekenkamer 1995). This influential report is also an example of an 'inside-out' effect (type 1) in that it was one of the factors leading to a shift of emphasis away from the ZBO organizational form and towards an agency model in which lines of accountability were more closely defined.

4. The fourth effect of management reform is to change the nature of the auditor's task. This is mainly a 'craft' issue and will be dealt with in Chapter 7. However, a few general indicators of the existence of this effect can be mentioned.

The RRV *Handbook on Performance Auditing* refers to the ways in which the renewal of government administration means that 'performance auditors will have to be prepared to follow these developments, review priorities and use new approaches and methods in their work' (Swedish National Audit Office 1996, p. 23).

In France, the *premier président* issues each year a notice in which he specifies the competences he considers necessary for individuals who seek to enter the Cour directly as *conseillers référendaires*. In 1995 he specifically required an in-depth experience in the social field and also, focusing on the increasing importance of the control of scientific and industrial bodies, stressed the need to recruit engineers.

The NAO also emphasizes that its work has changed and is changing as a result of the developments in public management. Its latest VFM handbook refers to: the expansion in the types of study that we do as a result of major changes in the way the government functions and accounts to Parliament. For example, the greater involvement of the private sector in the delivery of public services and more emphasis on performance measurement' (NAO 1997a, p. i). Or, again, the NAO's 1996 Annual Report stated that:

> Rapid changes throughout the public sector are leading to new demands upon our skills and resources. For instance, the Private Finance Initiative will be a key area for examination over the coming years. In focusing specifically on the issues of private finance, privatization and regulation, we are bringing together the specialist skills needed to examine these complex and demanding subjects. (NAO 1996c)

The report also pointed to the possibility of extending value-for-money work to commenting on comparative performance of non-departmental public bodies in response to comments arising from the recent examination of governance and audit issues. It further noted that the increased emphasis on the quality of public services had increased the need for the validation of performance indicators.

5. The fifth effect is the creation, as a result of management changes, of new data that is of salience and relevance for the performance auditor. This is perhaps most obviously seen in the introduction, in many countries, across many sectors, and at many levels, of systems of performance indicators (see e.g. Carter *et al.* 1992; OECD 1994, 1997b). In the UK there has been pressure from the Public Accounts Committee (PAC) and the House of Commons Public Services Committee (among others) for independent, external validation of agency performance indicator data. The NAO has supported this proposal (e.g. NAO 1997b, p. 1). Mr Major's government, however, resisted, proposing instead that this kind of work should be sought on an *ad hoc* basis, if agencies considered it worth while. At the time of writing the issue is still under discussion. In specific cases where validation has already been carried out significant inaccuracies have been unearthed (Hencke 1998; NAO 1995b). More generally, the wider availability of performance information has helped the NAO improve the quality of its analysis and develop an interest in benchmarking. Many performance audits now look at performance targets (e.g. NAO 1996d).

In both Finland and Sweden, validation of performance information has become an accepted part of the work of the SAI. In the VTV this work is undertaken by financial auditors rather than performance audit staff; in Sweden it is done jointly by financial auditors and performance auditors.

6. The sixth effect is essentially an imitation effect—SAIs feel the need to copy management techniques they see being increasingly employed 'out there' among the audited bodies. Thus, the adoption of performance-related pay (PRP), the use of contracting out, or the application of a systematic quality improvement scheme would be examples of an SAI 'going with the flow' by adopting techniques that are becoming increasingly popular elsewhere in the public sector. For example, as well as introducing and refining a PRP

system, the NAO has also made use of staff on short-term contracts and, on occasions, agency staff to augment core staff numbers, and has increasingly employed specialist consultants to provide outside expertise within VFM study teams. The training given to new entrants has changed from the traditional public-sector qualification—CIPFA—to a tailored version of the private-sector chartered accountancy qualification. The language employed by staff also mirrors changes outside the NAO, with audited departments and other bodies being referred to as 'clients', while concerns about the quality of service provided by the Office have been reflected in 'client relations' courses for staff. In practical terms, this has resulted, for example, in attempts to find ways of reducing the time taken to clear reports and in greater effort being made to keep audited departments informed of progress on studies and findings.

A further example is the arrangement currently under discussion within the Finnish VTV. The VTV is divided into four operational units, and a scheme is being negotiated under which there will be annual result agreements—effectively, internal quasi-contracts—through which units will commit themselves to certain levels of performance in return for given levels of resources (NAO 1996a; interviews at the VTV).

Several developments at the Cour illustrate this kind of effect. An internal committee has been created devoted to the improvement of methods and procedures. The practice of relating part of magistrates' annual remuneration to the quality of their work is growing. Training sessions have been organized for magistrates within the offices of leading commercial accounting companies.

For some time the NAO has contracted out a (growing) proportion of its certification (financial regularity) work, claiming that this enables it to 'benchmark our costs and methodologies against the private sector' (NAO 1995a, pp. 30–1). More recently, it has contracted out its first VFM study, and further examples of such 'outsourcing' continued under the Labour Government which came to power in 1997.

7. In some countries (but not all) the number of performance audits has increased, or the average size of a performance audit (person-days) has grown, and/or performance audit has been disentangled from traditional audit and given the status of a separate unit or division within the SAI. These trends are examined in greater detail elsewhere in Chapters 2, 5, and 7, and we may note them here as examples of effect 7.

8. The eighth effect should, in theory, be central to the whole development of performance audit. This type of audit is predicated upon a move away from the traditional audit criteria of legality, accuracy, and procedural compliance towards the application, through audit, of the performance-related criteria of efficiency and effectiveness. The National Audit Act 1983 required the comptroller and auditor general to examine: 'the economy, efficiency and effectiveness with which an organization has used its resources

in discharging its functions' (NAO *c.* 1987, p. 4). Similarly, Article 74 of the Dutch Budgeting and Accounting Act 1976 requires the Rekenkamer to 'give attention to the effectiveness of the management of the state and to the organization and functioning of the public service' (quoted in NAO 1996a, p. 148). In France article L 111–3 of the *Code des juridictions financières* requires the Cour to control the proper use of the credits, while article L 111–4 empowers it to verify the accounts and management of public firms.

The formal position is therefore fairly clear. All five SAIs included in this study proclaim that, in addition to applying the traditional criteria of financial audit, they also investigate effectiveness and efficiency (or, in the case of the RRV, 'effectivity'). What is more, they began to do so before public management reforms gathered international momentum in the late 1980s. It remains to be seen, however, how and how far these performance-related criteria are actually applied in practice. This is an issue that will be explored throughout the remainder of this book, but especially in Chapter 6.

9 and 10. The final two possibilities are of 'inside–out' effects that SAIs may have on public management reforms. An example of a study that led directly to specific improvements in the way the audited organization's performance measures were constructed was the NAO's VFM report on the UK Meteorological Office (NAO 1995b). Another example is the RRV performance audit of the Swedish Forestry Administration. The RRV came to the conclusion that the nursery business would best be spun off into an independent company. However, this was resisted by the Forestry Administration itself, which preferred the idea of a separate internal unit. A Commission on the Future of the Forestry Industry then referred favourably to the RRV's analysis, and eventually the government introduced a Bill that embodied the essence of the RRV's recommendations (Swedish National Audit Office 1995a, pp. 17–19). A third example is privatization in the UK, where in recent years the NAO has reported to Parliament on the risks to value for money where, in floating companies, government departments decide to sell all the shares at once rather than in stages. Having regard to the concerns expressed by NAO and Parliament over a series of privatizations, recent flotations have been conducted in stages.

Shifting the general terms of debate (effect 10) is an SAI impact of a larger order. One example of the cumulative weight of audits leading to this consequence could possibly be said to have occurred following the Public Accounts Committee report, *The Proper Conduct of Public Business* (Committee of Public Accounts 1994). The PAC, drawing on a series of NAO audits, focused public attention on the dangers that could accompany otherwise desirable moves towards more vigorous and decentralized styles of public management. This report attracted a good deal of media attention and increased the sensitivity of politicians to the importance of balancing the drive for efficiency with a continuing concern for public accountability and control. A similarly broad impact was achieved by the Rekenkamer's

1995 report of ZBOs (quangos), which concluded that there were serious weaknesses in the public accountability of many of these bodies (Algemene Rekenkamer 1995).

There are thus a considerable number of ways in which the processes of public management reform and the work of SAIs could interact. In this chapter these interconnections have been briefly identified (and illuminated by examples). The aim at this stage has been simply to establish the point that the management audit–interface has been a lively and important one, and that, conceptually, it can be characterized as including quite a number of specific types of mutual influence. In the remaining chapters we will explore these dynamics in greater detail.

5

The Subjects of Study

Hilkka Summa

5.1 Developing a Typology

Describing the practices of SAIs is one way of answering the question, what is performance audit? The main aim of this chapter is to give a first overview on what is actually being done in different SAIs in that part of their activities that they themselves classify as performance audit (or, more accurately, in the part that is translated into English as 'performance audit'). The overview will be constructed by comparing the types of subject chosen for performance audit projects in the five SAIs. For example, is it primarily an organization, such as an agency, a department, or a quango, or is it a public programme the implementation of which may involve several bodies, or is it possibly a function (such as the telephone system or procurement) that is present in most or all public bodies? Subjects can also differ in the characteristics of the phenomena studied: are they usually permanent, ongoing activities of the investigated bodies, or are they more often time-bound, exceptional operations or changes, such as privatization processes or investment projects? The portfolios of audit topics will also be compared between the two study periods we have chosen from the 1980s and 1990s, in order to get a picture of the trends and changes in the focus of performance audit across SAIs.

The type of subject is relevant in performance audit in a way that does not usually pertain in a financial audit. The natural subject of study in a financial audit is an annual account or a set of accounts that is included in the auditor's mandate. The financial auditor is expected to deliver regularly (usually annually) an assurance on the correctness of accounts produced by a set of well defined accountable bodies. Hence financial audit work has a cyclical character, whereas performance audits are individually planned and the portfolio of topics covered in a performance audit is the result of a (more or less conscious and explicit) strategy that each SAI has chosen. The strategies for organizing and designing performance audit projects are much more complex than those for financial audit. The dimensions along which an SAI can make choices when targeting its performance audits are multiple, and also, within each performance audit project the range of choices to be made regarding working methods, criteria, and outputs is wider than in a financial audit project.

The policy chosen by an SAI regarding the subjects chosen will be reflected in the types of *criteria* that will be characteristic of its performance audits: wide, policy-related subjects arouse interest for different types of questions and criteria than more narrowly focused studies (Keen 1998). For example, specific quantitative measurement of one or more components of the 'three Es' is more likely in an audit project focusing on the service activities of a single organization than in a project where the focus of study is a complex public programme involving several layers of administration. The type of subject chosen will also have consequences for the characteristic duration of projects and hence for the number and types of *outputs* it will deliver. The kind of *impact* a performance audit is likely to have also depends in part on the type of subject that is being studied. The questions of criteria, outputs, and impacts will be studied in the later chapters; here, the purpose is to clarify the basic choices that SAIs have made as to their subjects of study in performance audit.

In addition to the type of subject chosen for a performance audit, each SAI will need to make choices as to what administrative sectors, levels, and types of body will be covered by its audit programme. Unlike financial audit, in performance audit the SAIs do not have a legal obligation to audit all organizations in a certain category over a defined period of time: what is covered by performance audit is up to the SAI to decide in its work programme, within the limit of its mandate. However, the portfolios of performance audit projects of our five SAIs revealed that they all seem to end up with a fairly balanced coverage of all administrative sectors and the different levels of government included in their mandate—if not every single year, then at least over a limited planning period. This is not surprising, considering that all five SAIs have considerable independence in choosing such topics; to a large extent they are able to stand apart from the ephemeral tides of political interest in and/or neglect of that issue or sector. Furthermore, all possess internal organizational structures which, at least to some degree, divide work on the basis of administrative sectors. The resulting processes and criteria of selection are described in more detail in Chapter 7, Section 7.4. The key features in a topic that tend to attract the attention of performance auditors are:

- the volume of public resources used in an activity (large volumes attract attention);
- the likely risks to public funds;
- the desire of SAIs to achieve reasonably systematic coverage of their audit fields;
- evidence from previous audits that suggests that a follow-up may be necessary;
- current political salience.

These sorts of criteria were influential in all five SAIs; in other words, they were a reasonably common feature. Thus, the distribution of projects between administrative sectors or levels did not appear to be a variable that distinguished strongly between different SAIs. However, the *type* of subject chosen did exhibit some quite clear variations. Comparing the project portfolios of our five SAIs during the two study periods as to the type of subjects chosen revealed differences both between the SAIs and within them over the two periods. These variations may constitute evidence of somewhat divergent views among the SAIs as to 'what performance audit really *is*'. The observed differences can be summarized along three dimensions:

1. Is the performance audit project focused on a single organization, or is the study subject a programme, a function, or a set of activities that is either managed by or present in more than one organization (single *v.* multi-organization audits)?
2. Is the focus of the study the actual performance or core activities in the audited body, or does it concentrate on the systems for controlling and steering these activities (audits of substance *v.* systems)?
3. Does the audit concentrate on permanent, ongoing activities of the audited body or bodies, or is the subject of study a project, a change, or some time-bound, exceptional activity (audits of ongoing activities *v.* projects)?

In the first part of the empirical investigation of our five SAIs, their performance audit reports from the two periods were classified along these three dimensions to get an overview of the content of their portfolios of topics (see Appendix 1 for details). We assumed that the distribution of audit projects as to the type of subject chosen could be interpreted to reflect the SAIs' basic, often understated, views of the nature and purpose of performance audit.

First of all, there can be different views on whether performance audit is primarily about holding individual executives of public bodies accountable, or is mainly understood as investigating and producing information on the effectiveness of public programmes. If the ultimate objective of performance audit is seen to be the accountability of executives, audits will preferably be directed to single organizations rather than to sets of activities or programmes where it may be more difficult to single out the responsible individuals or authorities.

As for the second dimension—audit of systems or of actual substance of the audited body's activity—one may assume that the closer the identity of performance audit is seen to be to a financial audit, the greater will be the tendency to develop audit projects focusing on steering or control systems rather than on performance itself. Audit projects oriented towards steering or control systems can be more easily standardized and designed along the lines of financial audits, whereas investigations into actual performance will more probably develop into research-like complex projects which are very far from standard audit work. A systems-oriented audit is also more likely to be able to produce a conclusive statement on whether the audited target corresponds to some predefined standard or expectation than an audit that aims, for example, at investigating the effectiveness of a public programme.

The third dimension—subjects focusing on ongoing, 'normal' activities or on changes or project-type topics—can be expected to be related to the role that public management reforms have in the SAI's audit agenda. If an SAI takes an active role in auditing topics that arise from public management reforms, it will be likely to direct its audit projects towards project-type subjects. Audits of privatization processes or of the implementation or consequences of reforms fall into this category. Project-like topics can, of course, arise also from other interests, such as audits of investment projects.

5.2 Audits of Single Bodies or Programmes?

Table 5.1 indicates that the SAIs we studied did indeed make different choices concerning whether their performance audit projects are directed mainly to single public organizations or to functions or activities covered by several bodies. It also shows that the way this distribution has changed from the first period to the second differs between institutions.

Looking at the latter period, the 1990s, there is a clear difference between the NAO and the other three SAIs. The NAO's performance audit programme is directed mainly to single organizations, whereas more than a third of the audit projects of the other SAIs focused on topics covering several organizations. In the first period the pattern is different, the Rekenkamer and the VTV having done almost no multi-organization audits at all, and the NAO and the RRV having divided their capacity more evenly between

TABLE 5.1 The percentages of performance audit projects targeted on single organizations and on topics covering several organizations in the different SAIs in the 1980s and 1990s[a]

SAI	Period 1 (1980s)			Period 2 (1993–5)		
	Multiple organization	Single organization	(No. of reports)	Multiple organization	Single organization	(No. of reports)
NAO	31	69	(86)	21	79	(137)
Rekenkamer	6	94	(49)	40	60	(58)
RRV	44	56	(50)	35	65	(57)
VTV	10	90	(125)	35	65	(49)

[a] Figures are not available for the Cour, but our interview data and inspection of the published *rapports particuliers* enable us to offer qualitative comments: see text.

the two types. Hence the direction of change from the 1980s to the 1990s differs between the SAIs. In the NAO and the RRV, the proportion of single-organization audits increased considerably from period 1 to period 2, whereas in the Rekenkamer and in the VTV there was an increase in the share of multi-organization audits.

As for the Cour, it is clear that it can and does undertake multi-organization audits. Nevertheless, its basic role is to assess the accounts and management of single, specific organizations. This having been said, two recent trends have emerged. First, since 1990, some particular transverse analyses have been made (e.g. of national museums, local authority grants to firms, social policies to assist handicapped adults). Second, in a number of cases a single method has been employed to analyse a *set* of specific services or bodies. For example, such a method has been applied to the study of the costs and management of specific French embassies or groups of embassies, and a series of reports have been produced. Specific reports were produced on the embassies in Senegal, the Netherlands, and Spain (all in 1995), on pairs of embassies for the UK and Germany (in 1995) and for Gabon and Cameroun (in 1997), and on fiscal questions (1995), staffing matters (1995), and the representation credits of ambassadors (1997).

The observed differences between SAIs can be interpreted partly in the light of changes in the audit fields of the SAIs, and to some extent reflect the institutional setting in which they operate. For example, in the case of the NAO, the increase in the number of the newly established executive agencies and other public bodies in Britain has considerably changed the audit field: the number of individual organizations that are potential targets for performance audits has grown, and at the same time the elaboration of performance measurement systems and requirements for the agencies has made them more auditable in the sense of availability of information facilitating performance audit of these bodies.

To some extent, the distribution also reflects deliberate policy choices by the SAIs. As for the NAO, it expressed a preference to focus on audits of single organizations because these are easier to manage, particularly in the clearance phase. Also, the process of handling each performance audit report in the Public Accounts Committee favours projects where the findings can be attributed to one senior official—the accounting officer. Audits covering several organizations are more complicated to deal with in the delivery phase. Besides a reduction in numbers, there has also been in the NAO a change in the content of the multi-organization audits. In the earlier period, it was fairly usual for performance audit projects to deal with a certain theme or function by making comparisons between departments (e.g. *Department of the Environment, Scottish Office and Welsh Office: Enterprise Zones*, NAO 1986). In the 1990s the few multi-organization audits have usually dealt with a group of organizations operating in the same field (for example certain types of schools, museums, universities, etc.), and the point of the audit is to assess their performances through comparison. Clearly, the strategy chosen in the NAO has been to concentrate on performance audit projects focused on single public bodies.

In the Rekenkamer an opposite strategy has been chosen. In the 1990s, as part of a major reorganization of its activities, the Rekenkamer adopted a new concept of performance audits, called 'systems-oriented' audits. While performance audits focusing on single organizations were the dominant type in the 1980s (over 90 per cent of all projects), 40 per cent of projects now describe their subject of study as covering several public organizations. A special concept of 'government-wide audits' was developed in the Rekenkamer in the mid-1980s and carried on into the 1990s. According to Leeuw,

> A government-wide audit consists of analyses of the expenditures, activities and policy instruments common to most or all ministries and also includes co-operation. Often they focus on value-for-money aspects of the policies or policy instruments. Sometimes government-wide audits are labelled horizontal, this because other performance audits usually pay attention to separate ministries, and hence are called vertical. (Leeuw 1991, p. 25)

A related development is the fact that individual performance audit projects have also become wider in terms of the amount of working time allocated to them. It is not unusual for individual performance audit projects in the category of 'government-wide audits' to last for more than two years and take more than 500 work-days.

In the RRV the single-organization audits are the dominating type (65 per cent of all projects in the second period), and, unlike the Rekenkamer and the VTV, no dramatic change occurred in the distribution between single- and multi-organization studies from the 1980s to the 1990s. The proportion of projects focusing on single organizations increased somewhat between the two periods. The concept of 'systems-oriented' audits was used in the RRV in the 1980s, and the content that was given to this approach was clearly conducive to large, multi-organization studies. According to the view developed in the RRV in the 1980s, performance audits should study public activities within their systemic context, which covered the whole process from policy design and legislation to actual service delivery, instead of narrow, efficiency-focused investigations of single organizations. However, judging by the content of the RRV's performance audit project portfolio, this strategy never became the only approach: more than half of its projects in both periods were focused on single organizations. Characteristic topics in the 1990s have been audits of information systems or financial management systems in individual public organizations, or the functioning of steering systems in decentralized areas of activity.

Following the example of the RRV, the VTV adopted in the course of the decade, as the result of a large methodological development project (Toiminnantarkastuksen kehittamishanke) launched in 1992, an audit approach which it called audit of 'systems of activities'. This approach implied an orientation towards multi-organization performance audit projects, which were to cover the whole chain of political and administrative activities that produced certain outcomes, instead of investigating the performance of isolated public organizations. This approach was seen as a 'developed' form of performance audit, in contrast to 'less developed' earlier forms which had focused narrowly on the probity or efficiency of single organizations. One of the central ideas was that performance audits should be conducted like research projects, focusing on broad, cross-sectoral topics and producing in-depth knowledge of the mechanisms operating in systems of public activities. The new approach was chosen as a policy in the early 1990s, at the same time the decision was made to develop performance audits as a distinct 'product line'.

Like the RRV, the VTV has not fully put into practice its methodological 'declaration'. From period 1 to period 2 there was a clear shift towards a larger proportion of multi-organization studies, but two-thirds of all VTV's performance audit projects still have a single organization as their focus of study.

5.3 Audits of Substance or Systems?

Table 5.2 shows how the study objects of performance audit projects vary on the dimension of 'systemic' *v.* 'substantive' audits. *Systemic audit*, as a characteristic of how the subject of the audit project has been defined, gives a different sense to the concept of 'system' from the 'systems-oriented' methodological approaches defined by the Rekenkamer, the RRV, and the VTV which were discussed in the previous section. 'System' as an audit topic, as opposed to the 'substance' of the audited activity, refers to auditing the control or the steering systems through which the audited activity, and its level of performance, is governed, instead of directly investigating

Table 5.2 System-oriented and substantive audits: performance audit projects focusing on control systems and on actual performance in the different SAIs, 1980s–1990s(%)

SAI	Period 1 (1980s)			Period 2 (1993–5)		
	Substance	System	(No. of reports)	Substance	System	(No. of reports)
NAO	16	84	(86)	72	28	(137)
Rekenkamer	57	43	(49)	28	72	(58)
RRV	42	58	(50)	46	54	(57)
VTV	78	22	(125)	49	51	(49)

the activity itself. The distinction could, for example, refer to the choice between auditing the actual quality of service as experienced by the customers of a public organization, or investigating the procedures the organization has put in place for follow-up, control, and improvement of the quality of its service. The line is not, however, always clear-cut, and both aspects may be present in a single audit project.

On this dimension of comparison, the NAO has clearly moved in the opposite direction from the Rekenkamer and the two Nordic SAIs. Between periods 1 and 2, it practically reversed its strategy in the choice between systemic and substantive performance audits. In the 1980s more than 80 per cent of its value-for-money work focused on systems audits, covering topics like internal audit or management systems; in the 1990s such topics are hardly present at all in the NAO's audit programme, or are covered only as background factors influencing performance in the main activities of the audited bodies. Such a change might be seen to reflect a belief that attempting to assess the substantive performance of organizations, rather than only examine their systems, is more likely to provide a basis for improvement and lead to beneficial impacts.

The Rekenkamer and the VTV have chosen an opposite strategy. Between the two periods under study both of them considerably increased the share of audits in which the subject of study is a control or management system rather than an activity itself. For both bodies, this is a clearly expressed policy which goes together with the principle of favouring wide multi-organization studies over audits of single bodies. For the Rekenkamer, characteristic subjects of the approach adopted in the 1990s have been procurement and information systems, while in the 1980s corresponding topics would have been framed instead as, say, specific procurement processes or the functioning of a specific information system.

Approximately the same could be said of the VTV, where characteristic subjects of study for the performance audit projects in 1993–5 have been systems of state subsidies (for the municipalities, for hospitals, etc.), financial management, information, and internal control. This is not surprising, as the VTV declared in its activity plans in the early 1990s (Perkinen 1997) that steering systems would be its point of emphasis. Even if rhetorically close, the content of this emphasis is different from the methodological approach chosen as a result of the development programme in the course of the decade: audits of 'steering systems' were not expected to produce results concerning the fulfilment of society's needs, nor were they expected to cover 'wide systems of activities'. The interest in studying steering systems is closely related to the public management reforms carried out during and before the period; the central content of these reforms was to shift the financial and personnel management procedures to a more decentralized and managerialist model. (Indeed, in the Netherlands one of the most influential academic models of this shift is termed the 'New Steering Model'.)

Table 5.3 Changes in the proportions of different types of report by the Cour des Comptes on public firms (%)

	1980–3	1993–6
Compétence obligatoire	50	34
Reports on specific management aspects	10	18
Compétence facultative (subsidiaries)	40	48

Source: report by M. A. Delion, Conseiller Maitre, October 1997.

VTV's performance audits were largely directed to investigating how these reformed systems worked.

In the RRV there has not been any remarkable change in the share of systemic and substantive audits between the two periods. Our interview material indicates, however, that there was a change *before* the first period that was chosen for our in-depth investigation. Single-organization audits of the main function of the audited bodies had been the dominant approach in the 1970s, while audits focusing on steering and control systems increased throughout the 1980s. In the 1990s, again, there has been an increasing interest in investigating effectiveness and the achievement of objectives. However, the distinction between systemic and substantive subjects of study is less clear in the RRV's reports, as in many audit projects both aspects are investigated.

At the Cour there is no strict separation between substantive and systemic reports: each report tackles both dimensions. In the case of public firms, for example, the aim is to define the main areas of risk for management and the public authorities. However, a distinction can be made between reports that analyse the firms as a whole (where the Cour's scrutiny may be either mandatory—*compétence obligatoire*—or as a chosen study object) and those that focus on some specific aspect (e.g. training schemes), where the Cour is not legally obliged to report but chooses to do so (*compétence facultative*). This second category appears to have increased in salience since the early 1980s (see Table 5.3). It is apparent from this table that there has been a significant increase in the proportion of reports that are chosen by the Cour rather than being mandatory, and in those reports that concentrate on a specific feature of the organizations concerned.

5.4 Ongoing Activities or Time-Bound Topics?

Table 5.4 presents the distribution of the subjects of performance audit reports into those focusing on the 'normal', continuous activities of the audited

Table 5.4 Distribution of performance audits focusing on a project (or change, reform or other time-bound activity) and those focusing on ongoing activities in the audited body (%)

SAI	Period 1 (1980s)			Period 2 (1993–5)		
	Ongoing activity	Project	(No. of reports)	Ongoing activity	Project	(No. of reports)
NAO	83	17	(86)	74	26	(135)
Rekenkamer	82	17	(49)	90	10	(58)
RRV	84	16	(50)	79	21	(57)
VTV	80	20	(125)	67	33	(49)

bodies and those investigating time-bound, 'one-off', or exceptional phenomena. In all the SAIs, the majority of reports could be classified in the former category during both study periods. For the Cour, interviews confirmed that, there also, the subjects of audit projects would more often be the main activities of auditees than project type subjects.

Looking at the changes from period 1 to period 2, however, we can see that all SAIs except the Rekenkamer increased the share of audit projects focused on projects and reforms of other time-bound activities. Even if the trend is not very strong, it seems that audits focusing on the ongoing activities of audited bodies are in decline. This may be related to the SAIs' becoming interested in auditing the effects of changes related to public management reforms—which would, by definition, be time-bound. Yet, other motivations may direct performance auditors' attention away from the permanent processes in the organizations of their audit field, such as an interest in investments or in sales of government property.

In the NAO about a quarter of VFM reports deal with project-type subjects. Characteristic examples of topics in this category have been sales of government property, specific operations in defence administration (such as material and personnel transfers to and from the Gulf area), and the move of the Patent Office; audits of privatization processes have been another important category. In the RRV, in about a fifth of audits the subject is a project or other time-bound phenomenon, but the topics tend to be a different type from those of the NAO. Examples of RRV audit topics in the 1990s are investigations of development projects for information systems or the implementation of reforms of steering systems. The VTV is the SAI in which the increase in project-type subjects has been strongest, with about a third of their reports during the 1990s period addressing this type of subject. One explanation for this is that the VTV in the later period has chosen certain aspects of the Finnish public-sector reform policy as its priority area. Thus, many of its performance audit projects will have been framed as investigations of the effects of, or the implementation of changes in, the organizational structures and steering systems induced by the government's reform principles.

The Rekenkamer is the only SAI in which the share of project-type subjects has declined. This is another consequence of the audit concept adopted by it in the 1990s. Government-wide audits would characteristically frame their subjects not as time-bound changes or narrowly defined projects, but rather as investigations of certain functions across government organizations. In the 1980s the Rekenkamer performed audits focusing on project-type topics, such as investment projects or privatizations, whereas, according to the audit concept of the 1990s, the corresponding topics would instead have been investment *practices* or privatization *policy*.

As for the Cour's portfolio of topics, it is possible to get a limited picture on the basis of its public reports. For example, the list of public reports in 1995 contains a varied set of subjects, such as audits of the performance of single public organizations or functions (the National Centre for Regional Public Administration; public transport in the Ile de France), of subsidy systems for creating employment and for enterprises, of specific projects (France Telecom's mobile phone project), and of regional and local public entities. According to our interviews, in the unpublished audit projects the main activities of single organizations are the characteristic subject of study; other types of topic are not as frequent. One method of approach, which began during the 1980s, entails the thematic coordination of the audit topics of the Cour and those of the *chambres régionales des comptes*, so that certain themes will be covered at different levels of government. In some cases the targets for such audits will be single organizations, but in others more transverse topics will be chosen (e.g. a 1998 public report on drug addiction policy).

5.5 Alternative 'Identities' for Performance Audit?

Looking at all three of the dimensions on which we classified the subjects of performance audit projects, the big picture that emerges is that the SAIs can choose between two main orientations: performance audit as a scrutiny of the substance of the main, continuing activities of an individual public organization, or, alternatively, performance audit as an investigation of the functions, phenomena, or systems of activities that give a broader picture of the public sector at large. The former leads to choices of audit topics dealing with single organizations, with substantive rather than systemic approaches, and with continuous activities rather than projects; the latter, to multi-organization subjects, studied with a systemic approach, and often focusing on changes or other exceptional topics.

None of our SAIs is a 'pure' type on this simplifying dichotomy; yet it is clear that the NAO's portfolio of topics is closer to the 'single-organization strategy', and that, particularly in the Rekenkamer and the VTV, the identity of performance audit is closer to the 'systems of activities' focus. The RRV and the Cour are less easy to place on this typology, as their portfolios seem to represent mixtures of the two types.

One can of course ask what might be the background factors that could explain the choices that SAIs make in orienting their performance audit. Orientation towards single- or multi-organization audits may be interpreted to reflect the SAI's conception of its role. If keeping decision-makers and managers accountable is understood to be the main task of the SAI, an audit programme focusing on single organizations is a natural choice. One qualification to this would be the case where a minister was regarded as the responsible person, and a ministry was responsible for a range of similar organizations, such as embassies (the foreign ministry) or social security local offices (the social security ministry). From such a perspective, transverse or comparative studies could be combined with a focus on individual accountability. However, in so far as management reforms or statutory or cultural factors focus attention not on 'distant' ministers, but rather on the accounting officers or chief executives of individual organizations, the point would hold. By contrast, in the VTV type audits of 'systems of activities' or the Rekenkamer's government-wide audits, it is not fully clear who should be held responsible for the possible critical observations of the auditors. For VTV, accountability has never been a central theme in its motivations; it sees itself rather as a neutral 'producer of information' on the effectiveness of public programmes and policies.

Among other factors that influence the choice between types of subject is probably the pressures that the SAI faces in accounting for its own performance. One may assume, for example, that the NAO's strict practice in measuring its own performance with savings achieved through value-for-money audits is conducive to a choice of subjects in which quantifiable saving possibilities are most likely to be found. It could be argued that government-wide systems audits are less likely to result in findings that have direct savings implications than scrutinies of potentially wasteful procedures in specific organizations. Multi-organization audits are also expensive, and this orientation will probably result in a thinner flow of output from the SAI than the single-organization alternative. Against this line of reasoning, however, there are at least two counterpoints. First, as is much emphasized in the total quality management literature, the really big problems (and inefficiencies) are often to be found across departmental and institutional borders, i.e. in the *system* rather than within the individual organization. Second, comparisons (including benchmarking) can be powerful ways of exposing gross divergences in organizational performance, and therefore in value for money on a somewhat larger scale.

This chapter has emphasized the independence of choice that SAIs can exercise, and discussed the varying strategies that individual SAIs appear to have adopted in order to select their portfolios of study topics from the almost infinite range of topics that are available for scrutiny. However, perhaps not too much weight should be placed on the term 'strategy'. In the absence of much discussion of strategy formation in SAI documentation, it is far from certain that the actual range of topics investigated is, in any particular case, optimal, or even that it is the product of a coherent and systematic process of reasoning against clearly formulated criteria. The RRV has published a strategy for the auditing of social security and pensions into which particular audits can be fitted, and another for health and medical care, but these are relatively unusual. More generally, there seems, for most SAIs, to be only slim public justification for the chosen allocation of effort to one set of topics/objects rather than another. For example, is a 'balanced' programme across all sectors the only sensible approach, or is there something to be said for much more selective strategies? Are a few major studies likely to be more or less valuable than a larger number of smaller studies? What are the relative merits of substantive and systemic types of study, and how far can these be combined? The reports of SAIs offer a measure of *post hoc* justification for the studies they have actually chosen, but very little discussion of these larger strategic issues.

6

Criteria

CHRISTOPHER POLLITT AND ROBERT MUL

6.1 What are Criteria?

All judgements are based on *criteria*. Performance audits deliver a form of judgement (the organization/programme/project is functioning well/adequately/badly), and therefore performance auditors must (explicitly or implicitly) employ criteria. Logically, therefore, these criteria are central to the entire process of auditing. Evidence does not speak for itself; it acquires meaning only when gauged against a criterion. 'Speed of response to our clients has increased by more than 5 per cent per annum for the last three years' is a piece of evidence about a public service agency that is hard to interpret by itself. If we discover that the average increase in speed of response among similar agencies in the sector has been only 2 per cent per annum over the same period, we might judge the performance to be a good one. If, however, advances in information technology have permitted an average increase across the sector of 10 per cent per annum, then we might regard this particular agency's performance as quite weak. The relevant criterion, in this instance, is the average increase in the speed of response among similar agencies in a given sector.

We can already notice that a criterion can be referred to in at least two forms: a general one (the criterion of judgement is improvement in speed of response) and a specific and operational one (the relevant test is how the change in the speed of a particular agency compares with the measured average of change for agencies in that sector). We will need to return to this distinction when we come to look at the way in which performance auditors discuss and deploy the criteria they use in their work. However, the most fundamental point to be grasped is that performance auditing is not, and could not be, purely factual or 'evidence-based'. The facts have to be confronted with some criterion or criteria before a judgement or recommendation can be arrived at.

But what, definitionally, is a criterion? According to the dictionary, a criterion is 'a standard or principle on which to base a judgement' (*Chambers Encyclopaedic English Dictionary* 1994, p. 314). 'Standard' implies some measure —cardinal, ordinal, or nominal—that can be used as the baseline for purposes of comparison. Five minutes, 200 cm and $10,000 per annum are *cardinal* measures: they are points on regular, interval scales, so that the amount of difference between them and other values on the same scales can be precisely stated ($20,000 is twice as much as $10,000; one minute is a fifth of five minutes). 'More than the national average' and 'an improvement in the three-year running average' are *ordinal* criteria: they indicate a rank order (e.g., one can say whether something is 'more' or 'less') but not a precise interval (e.g. 'she is taller than him' tells you that she has more height, but not how much more). 'All patients in this category must be seen by a qualified medical practitioner' and 'the presence of an adequate accounting system' are *nominal* or *categoric* measures. Such measures classify phenomena in terms of whether or not they belong to a prescribed category or concept; they provide no information on either intervals or questions of rank order (one cannot say 'He is half a qualified medical practitioner' or 'She is more of a qualified medical practitioner than him'). At different times performance auditors can and do make use of criteria that embody all three main types of standard—cardinal, ordinal, and categoric/nominal.

The other key word in the above definition is 'principle'. That is, perhaps, a little less precise than 'measure'. The dictionary suggests 'a general truth or assumption from which to argue', 'a general rule of morality', and 'a norm of procedure' (*Chambers Encyclopaedic English Dictionary* 1994, p. 1010). Presumably rules and norms, such as that public officials must not take bribes or that records of public complaints must be maintained, would count as the kinds of principles in which auditors would be interested. However, the basic concept of a criterion has now been explored sufficiently for us to proceed to a more substantive examination of what specific criteria performance auditors are chiefly concerned with.

6.2 What Are the Criteria Applied in Performance Audits Supposed To Be?

Chapter 2 gave some important clues as to the nature of the criteria that performance auditors are supposed to apply. The INTOSAI standard quoted there mentioned three criteria:

- economy of administrative activities in accordance with sound administrative principles, practices and management policies
- efficiency
- effectiveness (INTOSAI 1992, p. 19)

In fact, this appears to us to constitute *four* criteria, since the first one contains two logically distinct proposals, namely, 'economy' and 'sound administrative principles'. (One could achieve economy without necessarily applying good administrative practices, and one could apply sound administrative principles without necessarily achieving maximum economies.)

Unfortunately, however, we cannot simply assume that the four INTOSAI criteria can be treated as an exhaustive and comprehensive list of the criteria actually used by SAIs. Such an assumption would be dangerous for a number of reasons. First, although the four carry the authority of a pronouncement by the senior international and professional body for state auditors, it is quite clear that, with respect to criteria, the mandates of the SAIs differ from each other in subtle but important ways. Second, there are sometimes difficulties in translating criterial terms from one language to another without losing some significant connotations. Third, in audit, as in other aspects of life, institutional rhetoric is not necessarily fully matched by actions. In short, we must proceed cautiously, noting the limitations as well as the strengths of our evidence as we go along. In this spirit the chapter will proceed as follows.

1. First, we will look at what each SAI says about the criteria it uses.
2. Then we will note some of the difficulties that face SAIs when they try to clarify or refine criteria for performance audit.
3. Third, we will briefly record some of the difficulties we encountered during the process of trying to classify the criteria that auditors used in the samples of reports we studied.
4. Next, we will set out what we found when we searched performance audit reports in the pursuit of criteria-in-use.
5. Finally, we will reflect on our findings and attempt to draw out an overview of performance audit criteria in theory and practice.

6.3 What SAIs (and their Mandates) Say about Criteria

In this section we will take each SAI in turn, and summarize three sources of information about the criteria that their performance auditors are supposed to apply. The first source is the mandate, or founding legislation, of the SAI concerned. The second is any significant references to criteria in guides or explanatory booklets that the SAIs may produce. The third is our own interview material, where some of our questions bear directly on the subject of criteria (see interview schedule at the end of Appendix 1).

Valtiontalouden tarkastusvirasto (VTV)

The founding law for the VTV established (in 1947) a mandate which included a requirement for audits to pay attention to what can best be translated as the 'appropriateness' of expenditure. It is upon this foundation that contemporary Finnish performance auditing is still based. However, while 'appropriateness' was originally interpreted to refer to *expenditure*, subsequent reinterpretation and debate effectively extended the term to cover *activities* as well as expenditures—a crucial step in enlarging the scope of performance audit. 'Appropriateness' is evidently a very general and therefore flexible criterion. In practice it has been used to cover, *inter alia*, adherence to laws and procedures, the achievement of savings, the enhancement of efficiency, and even effectiveness studies. The VTV's 1994 Annual Report elaborates on the criteria whose application it sees as the 'goal of performance audits' (State Audit Office of Finland 1994a, p. 7):

- the economy, efficiency, and effectiveness of the management of tasks
- the correctness and adequacy of external information regarding results
- the truthfulness of the grounds for setting objectives
- the efficiency of control, monitoring, and information systems
- the legality of the management of tasks
- compliance with the budget

This is obviously quite a wide range of criteria, and it should not be assumed that each and every element will be applied in every performance audit. It is interesting that the first element somewhat dilutes the normal meaning of effectiveness by adding 'of the management of tasks'. Effective management is not the same thing as an effective programme. Nevertheless, effectiveness has certainly been high on the VTV's own agenda since at least the early 1990s. An internal development project at that time articulated a methodological approach which favoured broad-scope audits of systems of public activities aimed at generating judgements of effectiveness (Valtiontalouden tarkastusvirasto 1992). However, this project does not seem to have been translated into any binding set of guidelines for auditors and, as we shall see (Section 6.6), VTV performance audits in the mid-1990s were by no means aimed mainly at effectiveness issues.

In our interviews at the VTV we were told that the most common 'management' criteria applied in practice were the existence of a clear division of authority, establishment of guidelines, and possession of a good system for following up actions and problems. These were described to us as general characteristics of good governance. However, another VTV auditor indicated that he thought that the criteria that were applied were frequently unclear, and that a good deal of latitude was accorded to individual auditors. He said that normally attention would be focused on the degrees of consistency obtaining between what a relevant law or auditee's set of standard operating procedures prescribed and what the auditor found was actually being done in practice. Finally, in a 1997 advice booklet, the VTV stresses that attention should be paid to efficiency and effectiveness, not simply to economy (Valtiontalouden tarkastusvirasto 1997, p. 3).

National Audit Office (NAO)

The legislative mandate for the NAO is significantly more detailed—and recent—than that of the VTV. The National Audit Act 1983 makes specific mention of three criteria: economy, efficiency, and effectiveness. In guidance produced in the late 1980s, the NAO comments:

> The Act does not confine the C&AG to examining only the *arrangements* for securing economy, efficiency and effectiveness. He may directly examine and report on the results achieved from individual projects, programmes or other activities. (NAO *c.* 1987, p. 4, original emphasis)

This same document explicitly defines each of the 'three Es'. It conceptualizes these in basically the same way as we have done in this book (see Section 1.4 above, especially Figure 1.2):

> *Economy* is concerned with minimising the cost of resources acquired or used, having regard to appropriate quality (*in short, spending less*).
>
> *Efficiency* is concerned with the relationship between the outputs of goods, services and other results and the resources used to produce them. How far is maximum output achieved for a given input, or minimum input used for a given output (*in short, spending well*).
>
> *Effectiveness* is concerned with the relationship between the intended results and the actual results of projects, programmes or other activities. How successfully do the outputs of goods, services or other results achieve policy objectives, operational goals and other intended effects? (*in short, spending wisely*). (NAO *c.* 1987, p. 5, original emphasis)

'Value for money' (VFM) is also a frequently mentioned criterion in NAO documentation; indeed, it is the informal title given to the series of 'green glossy' reports that form the mainstay of the NAO's performance audit output. However, VFM does not seem to have a separate meaning, distinct from the 'three Es'. Rather, VFM is a general term which embraces all three Es (NAO *c.* 1987, p. 5).

During interviews at the NAO it became clear that the formal emphasis on the 'three Es' needed to be supplemented by a recognition that other important criteria were also in play. One interviewee explained that the effectiveness of *management* was more often looked at than the impacts or outcomes of programmes. Examples offered of management effectiveness as a criterion were whether budgets were set and whether organizational systems actually worked. Another interviewee observed that criteria were often expressed in fairly general terms, and commented that this was partly because of the need to clear them with the audited bodies. A third interviewee expressed the view that he would like to see the NAO moving beyond procedural criteria to increase the number of genuine effectiveness studies it undertook. The view was also expressed that referring to 'good management practice' could be an easy way out for auditors, and that, if such a criterion were to be used, then additional effort would need to be made to assess how far an organization was from good practice, how much it would cost to bridge the gap, and what risks would be involved in not doing so.

Cour des Comptes

The Cour finds the legal foundation for the performance audit aspects of its investigations in its rights to examine the quality as well as regularity of management. There are a number of regulations that give legal basis to the Cour's authority and these have been gathered into the *Codes des Juridictions financières*. Two in particular refer to the Cour's duty to *s'assurer du bon emploi des crédits gérés par les services de l'Etat* (Article L 111–3) and to *assure la vérification des comptes et de la gestion des entreprises publiques* (Article L 111–4). However, rather like 'appropriateness' in the case of the VTV, *bon emploi des crédits* (good use of funds) and *gestion* (management) are very general concepts, which *de facto* have to be translated into more specific criteria for each specific context. For example, one senior member of the Cour explained to us that, for state services, notions of good management depended on the audited body adopting the means best calculated to achieve its objectives (and therefore also depended on its having formulated reasonably clear objectives), whereas for public enterprises *bonne gestion* tended to be translated by the Cour into questions of profitability and stability. Another magistrate made the same basic point in a slightly different way, by stating that it was not the job of the Cour to define what good management practice should be: rather, it was a matter of controlling the regularity of decisions and consistency of decisions, and investigating any specific problems that came to the magistrates' attention. Thus, considerable stress was laid on the *consistency* of management decisions (do they accord with the audited bodies' legal obligations and stated objectives?) and on their *instrumentality* in terms of being conducive to the achievement of the organization's declared goals.

Algemene Rekenkamer

The Algemene Rekenkamer was established as part of the Dutch Basic Law, but its specific powers to conduct given types of audit derive from periodically updated Government Accounts Acts. It was the 1976 Act that provided the first significant platform for performance audit. Article 74 of that Act required the Rekenkamer to give attention to the goal-orientedness of management of the state and of the organization and functioning of the public service. Goal-orientedness audit is a general term for performance audit at the Rekenkamer. Audits of the goal-orientedness of state management have focused on financial systems, contracts, and systems designed to ensure economy of expenditure. Audit of the *organization* of the public service (sometimes called 'small goal-orientedness audit') was meant to focus on economy and efficiency, and audit of the *functioning* of the public service (sometimes called 'large goal-orientedness audit') was intended to deal with policy effectiveness. Again, one can see that the legal text provides a fairly generalized formulation. It can, in practice, give rise to the application of a range of more specific criteria, but it can also afford ample opportunity for a flexible interpretation of what was intended by the legislature. The 1992 amendment to the Act was more specific, stating that the audit of effectiveness and efficiency included:

- auditing the effectiveness and efficiency of management, which includes all possible aspects of the internal management at (departments of) the public service
- auditing the effectiveness and efficiency of the organization; and
- auditing the effectiveness and efficiency of the policy (implemented). (Leeuw and Engwirda 1993/4, p. 17)

In the light of this, two former senior members of the Rekenkamer's staff concluded that: 'In view of its far-reaching audit possibilities, the Algemene Rekenkamer cannot be satisfied with describing, analysing and evaluating the implementation process, but it will have to extend the course of the process (or implementation) evaluation to actual effect evaluations in society' (Leeuw and Engwirda 1993/4, p. 17).

In interviews, Rekenkamer staff said that in the past many studies had concentrated on procedures and operational matters rather than results. It could be argued that having correct procedures and reliable systems were the stepping stones or prerequisites to efficiency, and that therefore the links between them and the 'three Es' were close. In recent years the emphasis on the importance of genuine efficiency and effectiveness studies had been increasing, and in 1995 the production of analyses of effectiveness became an office priority.

Riksrevisionsverket (RRV)

The RRV has practised performance audit since the 1960s, but over time the type of criteria applied and the balance between them is said to have changed. The 1996 *Performance Audit Handbook* straightforwardly identifies economy, efficiency, and effectiveness as the central criteria (Swedish National Audit Office 1996). An earlier review of the RRV's performance audit work placed particular emphasis on efficiency, stating that:

> the ambition of performance auditing is to point out central problems in efficiency; to serve as a driving force in a field that does not have private business's natural necessity to rationalise and improve efficiency in order to survive. For performance auditors, improving efficiency is not only a question of making savings or reducing costs. An audit focuses on the connection between operations and finances. In a wider perspective, the financial conditions are linked to judgements on quality and the resources used. In short, do the customers, the taxpayers, get their money's worth? (Swedish National Audit Office 1995a, p. 9)

> The Performance Audit Department is responsible for examining and promoting effectiveness and efficiency in central government activities. (Swedish National Audit Office undated, p. 13)

Elsewhere, however, it becomes clear that, although RRV performance audits do address issues of efficiency and effectiveness, they also apply other criteria. Examples of questions posed by RRV include 'Are there problems in planning? Are there shortcomings in the agencies' use of control instruments . . . are agencies able to adapt their activities and skills to meet new demands?' (Swedish National Audit Office undated, p. 12). This seems to indicate that the examination of management systems is an important feature of RRV performance audits, alongside or in the place of attempts directly to ascertain the efficiency and effectiveness of projects, programmes, and organizations.

Summary

Looking across the publications and interview data from the five SAIs, it is clear that, in most cases, formal mandates express the criteria that are to be applied only in very general terms. This is understandable, but it also leaves an extensive space for the SAI to develop more specific criteria in practice. This is perhaps slightly less the case for the NAO than for any of the others, because the 1983 Act actually specifies the 'three Es' in unusually precise language. From our interviews, it also seems clear that, in practice, many SAIs have found that a good part of their performance audit work has taken place on the basis of judgements not so much about effectiveness or efficiency, strictly defined, but about the presence or absence of good management practices (i.e., the criteria employed have been based upon categoric/nominative standards more than on ordinal or—still less—cardinal standards).

Yet, at the same time, during recent years all five SAIs have, in one way or another, expressed themselves as wanting to move more decisively into the area of effectiveness analysis. For example, as long ago as 1989 the Rekenkamer reported that, although its emphasis had generally rested on the criteria of economy and efficiency, 'nevertheless deeper insight is required to enable Parliament to assess the value-for-money aspect of government policy. This means that the Board should assign high priority to effectiveness audits . . .' (Algemene Rekenkamer 1989, p. 39). Since 1995 these sentiments have been translated into 'house policy'. Each directorate is expected to produce at least one effectiveness study each year.

NAO and RRV staff also suggested that further work on goals and outputs would be a key aspect of future work. In the NAO case this line of development may be given a further push by the new chairman of the Public Accounts Committee (from 1997), who made it known that he would welcome more examinations of the effectiveness of public service delivery. At the time of writing an NAO booklet has just appeared which argues that a greater variety of analytical approaches may be needed than in the past, especially in the areas of explanatory and interpretive studies (Keen 1998). And at the VTV a major review of the early 1990s laid the foundation for priority being given to broad-scope studies of the systems of governance and their implications for the effectiveness of government policies.

6.4 Difficulties Facing SAIs in the Development and Application of Criteria

Our SAIs may well be committed to clarifying criteria and moving more extensively into the analysis of efficiency and effectiveness, but there are, as usual, some obstacles that lurk between the rhetorical expression of aspirations and their realization in deeds. There are two broad points that can be made here. First, it is frequently very difficult for SAIs to identify, articulate, and apply clear and precise criteria to their performance audit work. Second, little research has yet been undertaken into the questions of how, in practice, auditors identify appropriate criteria and reach their judgements (Keen 1999). Our impression was that the selection of criteria (and the selection of methods—see Chapter 8) is usually made with a strong element of professional discretion and judgement. We have seen only limited material which directly addresses the criteria issue. Recent NAO advice states that:

> criteria should, where possible, be based on widely accepted standards, norms or targets, e.g. legislation; departmental regulations and guidance; professional standards; performance objectives and targets; management practices accepted by the departments; and contractual requirements. (NAO 1997a)

The same guide adds that staff should 'be sure to consult the department about your criteria and if possible agree them'. Yet, despite such helpful advice, clarity and precision may be difficult to achieve. The obstacles can be political (with a small 'p'), organizational, and/or conceptual.

A principal, and very common, obstacle is that the government itself has not defined a clear and well-ordered set of objectives and/or targets for the activity under scrutiny. It is widely recognized that such opacity sometimes occurs because of the political need to keep the objectives of a programme vague and general so as to secure the maximum coalition of support. As one magistrate at the Cour said to us, much depends upon clear objectives having been set by or for the auditee. 'Dans beaucoup des contrôles, les objectifs sont implicites', as one internal note put it, and then went on to recommend to magistrates that 'Il est cependant utile de s'interroger a leur sujet'. Interviewees at the RRV and the Rekenkamer expressed similar sentiments. In the UK a survey of auditors suggested that the lack of final outcome measures was a 'major constraint against the achievement of effectiveness auditing' (Pendlebury and Schreim 1990). In line with this survey, a number of the NAO studies from the 1980s which we examined referred to the absence of data within audited bodies preventing firm assessments of the success or otherwise of their activities. For example, a 1986 report on Enterprise Zones included the observation that:

the absence of essential information and analysis, and doubts about the reliability of some of the available data, make it impossible to draw firm conclusions about the merits of the Enterprise Zone concept, the true costs involved and the effectiveness of enterprise zones in securing the results achieved. (National Audit Office 1986, p. 10)

A less extensive, but still significant difficulty arises in the specific case of programmes with so-called 'eternal' objectives—to improve various underlying social conditions, reduce crime, improve the environment, etc. Here there may be endless scope for debate about the most appropriate time period to choose for assessment. In programmes of this kind final goals are, in practice, never or hardly ever achieved. Examinations of one or two years' worth of performance can be said to be too short-term, or to relate to an 'untypical' period during which contextual conditions were said to be in some way unusual. On the other hand, longer-term studies may face the problem that the programme delivery agencies have been restructured, or have adjusted their goals in some subtle ways—or may simply be criticized as 'too academic', and not suitable for audit. Against the background of these sorts of discussions, it can be extremely difficult to arrive at an agreed yet reasonably precise and challenging criterion of effectiveness or 'success'.

A third difficulty can occur during the process of discussing a performance audit with the audited body. Especially in SAIs where the clearance process involves securing the auditee's agreement to the final report text and/or the study design (as it does, most notably, at the NAO), attempts to include very clear and sharp criteria may run into opposition from the ministry or agency concerned. A report that discusses, in fairly general terms, weaknesses in management systems or in the degrees of conformity that have been achieved in respect of stated procedures may appear less potentially damaging to the reputation of the auditee than one that applies a precise (ordinal or cardinal) criterion and shows the audited body to have performed poorly against it. There is a sense in which the latter approach (sharp, numeric, or rank-ordered criteria) would 'raise the stakes' for both the auditor and the auditee. Any weakness in the auditor's calculations or reasoning would be plain for all to see, and the audit might become more vulnerable to the charge that it had presented a biased, one-dimensional picture of a complex issue. The performance of the auditee could be seen as being subject to a simple (possibly over-simple) 'pass or fail' test.

On the other hand, there can also be risks from keeping criteria fairly general. During 1996 and 1997, for example, several Dutch ministers criticized some of the Rekenkamer's reports for, *inter alia*, not applying sufficiently clear criteria. In the 1998 performance audit manual it is suggested that, if specific audit criteria are not derived from a law or departmental regulation, then they should be presented to the auditee at an early stage (Algemene Rekenkamer 1997, p. 14).

To return to the difficulties SAIs face in developing precise criteria, there may also be organizational and cultural factors which incline SAIs to apply broad tests of 'good management' or conformity to procedures rather than quantified measures of efficiency or direct tests of effectiveness. To examine the extent to which an operating system conforms to some model or rule of what is 'proper functioning' is, after all, close to the auditor's traditional task of verification (Chelimsky 1985; see also the later discussion of the craft of audit in Chapter 8). It interrogates the auditee on the firm basis of their own rules and operating procedures—criteria that are therefore hard for them to disown or reject. It does not demand the same level of skill in using analytic techniques as would, say, full-blooded economic efficiency analyses; nor is it entangled with the complexities of conceptualization and method that attend direct studies of programme or policy effectiveness. At the VTV, the NAO, and the Rekenkamer it was indicated to us that the availability of staff possessing requisite skills had at times been a factor influencing the types of study that were undertaken. Limited availability of certain skills may therefore reinforce existing cultural dispositions in favour of 'checking' rather than 'analysing' modes of audit, with an attendant emphasis on the application of fairly general, categoric criteria.

6.5 Criteria-in-Use: Towards a Classification

If SAIs sometimes have difficulties in establishing a firm basis for setting criteria, we as a research team certainly had difficulty in *classifying* the criteria that were actually used in the reports we read. Any notion we may have had at the outset that it would be possible simply to establish an agreed shortlist of performance audit criteria and then read quickly through audit reports in order to count how many times each criterion had been applied was soon dispelled.

To begin with, just at the conceptual level, establishing a list of operationally watertight and mutually exclusive categories ('economy', 'efficiency', etc.) was a complex and intensive undertaking. The key terms by no means necessarily translate into direct equivalents in each language. Neither are the meanings of the terms entirely stable within a single language—one finds significantly varying definitions of objectives, goals, effectiveness, efficiency, quality, etc., in the Anglophone literature, even among the documents issued by a single government. This variation is certainly not the exclusive preserve of the Anglophones; for example, it was clear to us that the Swedish equivalent of the term 'effectiveness' had, over the years, been used in a number of different senses within the RRV. Furthermore, it was apparent in a number of interviews, in several SAIs, that interviewees were using certain criterial concepts in loose or varying ways.

In the early stages of the research some of us examined a sample of performance audit reports and attempted, inductively, to draw out sensible and robust classifications of the criteria that had been used. The result, however, was a somewhat overlapping, but also significantly different, list of categories for each country. Subsequently, after further discussion the research team agreed upon a common categorization:

- Economy
- Efficiency
- Effectiveness
- Good management practice
- Good governance
- Quality of service
- Goal attainment
- Other

Some of these will bear a few words of further explanation. The 'three Es' have already been dealt with (Section 6.3 above). *Good management practice* is the fourth element in the INTOSAI definition of performance audit. It is a broad category in itself, comprising such tests as whether an auditee has sound accountancy systems or target-setting procedures in place, whether it reviewed complaints from users, whether it systematically deployed its human resources to the highest priority functions, and so on. The general idea is that in many areas there is a reasonable degree of agreement about what constitutes 'good management practice', and that the actual activities of auditees can therefore be compared with models or standards of good management.

Whereas good management practice refers mainly to the internal arrangements of specific public bodies, the concept of *good governance* is more holistic and externally oriented. Nowadays it is a commonplace that many public policies and programmes are delivered not through single organizations, but through networks or partnerships of various organizations, both public and, in some cases, private or mixed. Thus, it is the broad coordination and guidance of a whole squadron of organizations that will determine the ultimate effectiveness of the programme, rather than the individual productivity or efficiency of a single process or even a single component body. Assessment can be made of how well a parent ministry (say) 'steers' a programme within its jurisdiction. Are target-setting and results reporting properly organized? Are communications between the various organizations involved clearly structured and well understood? In this regard, the most relevant question for those who are interested in effectiveness is 'what are the outcomes from the operation of the *system*?' rather than 'what are the outcomes from individual organizations or functions within the system?' In a 1995 article the Swedish Auditor General put the point succinctly: 'A one-sided interest in productivity may result in the ever-better performance of the wrong tasks' (Ahlenius and Jonsson 1995, p. 7).

Quality of service was a criterion we included because we had already discovered a number of reports that focused specifically on this topic (e.g. NAO 1993c), but could not see that it fitted comfortably into any of our other categories. Here the criterion of success was the extent to which a public service met the reasonable expectations of its users.

Goal attainment involves establishing the extent to which the audited body has succeeded or failed in achieving its own, publicly proclaimed or legally prescribed goals. For example, if an audit focuses on the question of whether a public housing authority has met its legal obligation to provide accommodation for the homeless within its jurisdiction, then a goal attainment criterion is being applied. Using this criterion does not necessarily require the auditor to establish a firm *causal* link between the actions of the auditee and the level of attainment. For example, a school may have the goal of sending a certain percentage of its students on to university. The requisite percentage may be achieved, but whether that is because of good teaching in the school or because the school is lucky enough to draw on a wealthy and highly motivated catchment area may not be a question that is addressed.

Finally, we kept a residual category of '*Other*', in case any unusual or interesting studies were found to employ criteria that did not fall within our other categories.

Agreeing on this list made our task less difficult, but only slightly so. *Applying* these categories remained problematic. Of course, this may have been because our chosen categories were insufficiently clear and/or were overlapping with one another. However, while acknowledging some problems of this kind, we are convinced that, whatever categories we had chosen, there would have been difficulties in interpreting our 'raw materials'—the performance audit reports. This is so for several reasons. First, it is often the case that the criteria that have been used are not clearly stated on the surface of the text, but rather are assumed, or taken for granted, or referred to only in a brief and vague fashion. This comment holds true for at least some reports from all five SAIs—and for many reports in some cases. In consequence, criteria have to be inferred from the texts, a difficult and time-consuming task. Second, a single performance audit report may contain judgements that rest on a variety of criteria. (Again, this was the case for material from all five countries.) So there is the interpretive challenge of trying to decide which criterion or criteria are the most important within the context of the audit as a whole, or whether all should be given equal importance. Third, it is not necessarily always the case that the recommendations or judgements contained within an audit report are all based on the criteria that are announced in that report. Some recommendations may appear to be based on other, 'undeclared' criteria, which, once again, are left to the researcher to infer.

Many examples of these difficulties could be given, but perhaps one will suffice to illustrate the interpretative complexities involved. One of the reports we looked at was a 1993 VTV audit of the Finnish customs control function (Valtiontalouden tarkastusvirasto 1993). This particular audit set out to investigate customs controls with reference to the new challenges presented by, on the one hand, the opening of the Russian borders and, on the other, the closer relationship with the EU (which Finland joined in 1995). It concluded, *inter alia*, that there was overlapping work at different levels in customs organizations, that these overlaps should be eliminated, and that this could be done without endangering the level of control. On the surface, therefore, it might appear to be a straightforward exemplification of the good management criterion (eliminate internal duplications). However, a closer reading shows that a higher goal of making savings is heavily implicit in the report. (Minimizing the state budget was a very high political priority at that time in Finland, and one that the VTV's work reflected.) Reducing overlap will lead to savings. It looks, therefore, as though the best classification for the dominant criterion expressed in this report would be 'economy' (input minimization).

Despite these multiple hurdles, we did go ahead with the application of our set of categories to a sample of performance audit reports. We believe that the resulting findings (see next section) have some value, but need to be interpreted cautiously. For all the above reasons, therefore, we have refrained from making direct numerical comparisons between different SAIs. Our judgement is that the data are not quite firm and commensurable enough to support a 'league table' approach. Notwithstanding these hesitations, however, it *is* possible to discern some patterns in the data which are sufficiently large-scale to give confidence that they are not mere artefacts of the limitations of our methods.

6.6 Criteria-in-Use: Findings

In this section we will review the findings that are produced by applying our classification of criteria to samples of performance audit reports in each country.

Riksrevisionsverket (RRV)

One immediate difficulty with the RRV's material was that the terms 'effectiveness' and 'effectivization' (directly translated) were repeatedly used in a very broad way—going far beyond the conformity of final outcomes to policy or programme objectives—to include concepts that we would rather classify as economy, efficiency, or just good management. Much reinterpretation was therefore needed to 'convert' the language of RRV reports into the categories as defined by the research team.

TABLE 6.1 Use of the 'three Es' as criteria in RRV performance audits, 1993–1995[a]

Year	Economy	Efficiency	Effectiveness	Total reports studied
1993	2	2	0	20
1994	2	0	1	20
1995	3	1	0	17
Total	7	3	1	57

[a] Covers all performance audit reports in the period.

TABLE 6.2 Use of the goal attainment criteria in RRV performance audits, 1993–1995

	Conditions for GA	Goal attainment	Both	Total reports studied
1993	7	4	2	20
1994	10	1	2	20
1995	5	1	2	17
Total	22	6	6	57

If we begin with the 'three Es', and count the numbers of reports in which each 'E' figures as an obvious criterion (i.e. counting more than one criteria per report where several were applied), we arrive at Table 6.1. It can be seen that pure effectiveness reports were rare. More surprising, perhaps, true efficiency studies were not terribly common either. However, before rushing to any judgements about the RRV's lack of interest in performance, the picture must be balanced by examining the goal attainment category. Table 6.2 distinguishes between pure goal attainment studies (e.g. a 1994 study of how many disabled workers had gained jobs as a result of a system of payments to employers to support this kind of employment) and those that focus on the conditions necessary for goal attainment (e.g. a study of how far the radiation protection agency had the capacity to adapt to new circumstances).

Moving to the service quality criterion, this, too, proved to contain interpretive pitfalls. Reports that said they were focusing on quality issues could turn out to be about management system quality, process quality, or output quality, and might make no specific study of service users at all. For example, a 1994 study examined the quality of administration of a documentation and information system in Swedish universities (the LADOK system). Quite a

TABLE 6.3 Use of good management practice and good governance as criteria in RRV performance audit reports, 1993–1995

Year	Good management	Good governance	Both	Total reports studied
1993	9	3	5	20
1994	9	1	2	20
1995	4	2	2	17
Total	22	6	9	57

few studies addressed themselves to this type of management system quality (19 out of 57 reports studied during 1993–5), but these might be thought of as more appropriately filed under the 'good management practices' category. The number of reports that were specifically focused on output quality was quite small (4 of the 57 reports studied).

Studies of good management practices, or good governance, were fairly frequent, as Table 6.3 shows.

All the above tables refer to the second time period in our study—1993–5. We also carried out an analysis of the use of criteria during the 1983–5 period. This did not show any startling differences in the overall pattern compared with the later period. Good management practice, together with the appropriateness of actions and procedures for the achievement of declared goals, again formed the most frequent categories.

Of course, counting the number of times a criterion is used is a long way from determining its importance in terms of influence on the auditee and the wider world. If effectiveness, say, is measured only a few times, these particular audits may nevertheless become unusually influential. (The *impacts* made by audits can be hard to assess, and it is a subject reserved for detailed discussion in Chapter 10.) An example of a particularly important group of audits which attempted to apply the effectiveness criterion concerns those that the RRV carried out on the Swedish social security system during the mid-1990s. A set of three such audits compared the end results of the system—which at the time was dispensing benefits equivalent to 20 per cent of GNP—with its stated goals. These audits set out to:

- Determine the extent to which the primary economic goals of growth and balanced public finances have been achieved. The government's general policy of giving priority to the work first principle is an essential element in this context.
- Determine whether benefit payments to households achieve policy goals. (Ahlenius and Jonsson 1995, p. 8)

They represented a deliberate step beyond previous RRV work on social security, which 'had concentrated on administrative procedures and internal control' (Ahlenius and Jonsson 1995, p. 9). In the case of one of these studies, the RRV analysed the effectiveness of housing benefit as an instrument of housing and social policy, as well as the cost effectiveness of its delivery. During the last few years, studies such as these have come to be seen within the RRV as models for a new type of investigation which tries to look directly at effects.

Valtiontalouden tarkastusvirasto (VTV)

We now turn to the VTV. Here again goal attainment was a 'popular' criterion, but there were also many reports which used one or more of the 'three Es'. Table 6.4 shows the overall position. Goal attainment is clearly the most frequently-resorted-to kind of criterion. If we look 'inside' this category, we find that many of these studies reflect the legalistic culture of Finnish public administration, in so far as the audits are concerned to establish how far the activities of a body of function correspond to the goals or objectives laid down for it by the relevant legislation. This may sound a little like rule-following, but it goes beyond it in that the VTV wants to know how far *achievements* match up to goals.

A substantial portion of the 'three Es' category (the second most frequently used criterion) represents studies of achieved or potential *savings*. One might therefore say that, in practice, such reports tend to be concerned more about economy (and to some extent efficiency) than about effectiveness. In this, the work of the VTV would appear to parallel that of the RRV and other SAIs (see below). Nevertheless, some studies have directly addressed effectiveness issues, and have tried to do so by means of developing quantitative indicators of results. An interesting example here was a 1992–4 investigation of prisons. The VTV noted that the existing performance indicator sets for prisons included no measures of the actual effects of prison, either for the individual prisoner or from a wider social perspective. After an extensive study, the auditor proposed an indicator of recidivism as one way of operationalizing the effects of a prison sentence. This was vigorously rejected by the auditee, but the audit succeeded in stimulating a reconsideration of existing performance indicators and the development of new ones (Summa 1996; State Audit Office of Finland 1994b).

Table 6.4 The criteria used in VTV performance audits, 1993–1995

Year	'3Es'	Goal attainment	Service quality	Good management	Good governance	Total, reports studied
1993	15	14	0	11	9	20
1994	6	7	0	5	1	12
1995	8	12	0	3	6	17
Total	29	33	0	19	16	49

Good management practice is also a fairly frequently used criterion. In the VTV case this is closely connected to the management reforms launched by the Finnish government from 1987 onwards (see Chapter 3). These audits drew heavily on notions of good practice associated with the model of results-oriented management and budgeting which was being promulgated by the Ministry of Finance (Summa 1995).

Two final points of interest emerged from our examination of the VTV reports. A significant subgroup within the category of *Other* criteria (not shown in Table 6.4 but appearing in 15 of the 49 reports studied) was that of equality. Such reports could refer to equal treatment of municipalities within the system of state subsidies (studies in 1993 and 1995) or equality of farm tourist subsidies between regions (1995). The relative prominence of this concern reflects a longstanding preoccupation in the Finnish political system and culture.

Finally, it is noteworthy that the VTV certainly did not seem to catch the NAO's enthusiasm for service quality studies. Quality of service delivery simply was not mentioned in any of the reports we sampled. The VTV sees its task as studying audited bodies and functions from a specifically financial or economic point of view.

Algemene Rekenkamer

During our two periods the Rekenkamer produced a total of 252 performance audit reports, 151 in 1983–5 and 110 in 1993–5. Table 6.5 shows how many times each criterion was referred to in each period. These numbers are based on an 80 per cent sample of the total number of reports in each period (i.e. 130 reports in the first period and 84 in the second). It is quite clear that in both periods two criteria were used much more frequently than

Table 6.5 Frequency of references to particular criteria in Algemene Rekenkamer performance audits

Category	1983–5	1993–5
Economy	60	29
Efficiency	4	4
Effectiveness	2	3
Good management	101	76
Good governance	8	7
Service quality	0	1
Goal attainment	13	15
Other[a]	7	6

[a] The category 'other' here includes declared criteria such as giving information to Parliament and checking budget allocations.

any other. Good management practice was by far the most common, with economy in a distant second place; goal attainment was also quite frequently referred to. Thus, rather than examining the efficiency or effectiveness of programmes, many audits turned out to consider management procedures such as the availability of planning and control instruments. By contrast with this picture, we know that current policy within the Rekenkamer gives a certain priority to effectiveness studies (see Section 6.3 above—also mentioned during interviews). All we can say is that the effects of such a policy had not yet become very visible by the period 1993–5.

Brief reference to a major recent audit may help illuminate the Rekenkamer's approach. In 1996 the Rekenkamer published an extensive analysis of the government's financial relations with major Dutch companies. The auditors set themselves the following questions:

1. What are the long-term objectives of the Ministry of Economic Affairs with regard to the government's financial relationship with Fokker, DAF and NedCar?
2. In each case, were the decisions to alter the financial relationship taken with sufficient care?
3. In each case, were the decisions implemented with due care and was compliance with the conditions monitored?
4. How were the States General [the parliament] informed about the decision-making process and the implementation of the support operations?
5. To what degree have the instruments employed helped to achieve the long term objectives? (Netherlands Court of Audit 1996, p. 1)

It can immediately be seen that these questions strongly imply a mixture of good management, good governance, and goal attainment criteria. Question 3, for example, is a question about good management. Question 4 concerns good governance. Question 5 concerns goal attainment, and could conceivably result in a study going beyond goal attainment into a direct analysis of effectiveness (i.e. the outcomes of government financial support for these companies).

In its report, the Rekenkamer strongly criticized the government on a number of counts. It pointed out that various types of information of great potential relevance to governmental decision-making on these issues were not available. For example, the cost per job preserved was not known, and the audit report pointed to several issues where 'It was reasonable to expect the Ministry to have conducted the relevant studies' (Netherlands Court of Audit 1996, p. 2). The Ministry of Economic Affairs was also criticized for failing to involve the Ministry of Social Affairs and Employment in the decision-making process. Moreover, 'the Court of Audit is convinced that successive ministers have failed to comply with the norms for providing information to the States General . . .' (p. 4). Finally, the report recommended that a standard approach should be developed for operations involving financial support to companies.

Table 6.6 Criteria used in 35 NAO value-for-money studies, 1985–1987

Criterion	No. of times used
Economy	10
Efficiency	5
Effectiveness	7
Good management	28
Good governance	11
Service quality	0
Goal attainment	5

Table 6.7 Criteria used in 65 NAO value-for-money reports, 1993–1995

Criterion	No. of times used
Economy	23
Efficiency	18
Effectiveness	22
Good management	43
Good governance	5
Service quality	17
Goal attainment	18

In turn, this report was criticized by ministers, on grounds of both its methods and its judgements. The Rekenkamer gave consideration to these criticisms but decided that it was not necessary to make any fundamental changes to the report. The whole story is of interest in that it shows how far into policy-making the Rekenkamer is, on occasion, willing to go, and how it can tackle issues of broad scope in a single report. However, it also shows that, while the auditors were clearly aware of effectiveness as a criterion, they were in the end unable to apply it, because the government did not have the requisite data and the Rekenkamer evidently felt that it could not acquire them either. Thus, the report falls back on issues of good management and good governance as the mainstays of its analysis.

For the NAO we examined 100 randomly selected reports, 35 from the first period (1985–7) and 65 from the second period (1993–5). Identification of specific criteria was harder among the reports of the first period because the texts gave relatively limited information on this score. However, applying our categories as best we could, we arrived at the results shown in Tables 6.6 and 6.7.

Once again, therefore, good management practice registers as the most frequently resorted-to criterion. Good governance and economy are the next two most popular. However, many of the studies employing management practice as a criterion made little or no reference to where this came from. An exception was a 1986 report on work at MoD research establishments. This explained that 'the NAO examination took account of relevant practices adopted for the management of research by well-managed companies in the private sector' (NAO 1986). Examples of the use of a good governance criterion would be several studies which examined departmental arrangements for overseeing and controlling nationalized industries, and analyses of how new, coordinated approaches to industrial and commercial renewal were working out in practice.

Table 6.7 shows the same categories for the more recent period. Information about criteria used was more explicit in this period. Clearly, good management practice remained a very important criterion-in-use, but other criteria, including efficiency, effectiveness, service quality, and goal attainment, also became more significant.

Within the good management category, a study of clinical auditing in Scotland looked at how health boards had performed against government guidelines, while an examination of treasury management in NHS trusts used NHS Executive guidance and best professional practice as its benchmark criteria. Studies of the construction and sale of buildings drew on accepted private-sector practice in assessing the performance of public bodies performing similar functions.

One interesting contrast with the first period was the growth of studies applying a service quality criterion (usually defined as meeting the reasonable expectations of service users). Significant time and effort was invested in developing such studies (interviews), and this contrasts with the apparent absence of work of this kind in the VTV or Rekenkamer. It was a development that no doubt reflected the high political salience given to public service quality at a time when the Citizen's Charter and other quality initiatives were in full flood (Prime Minister 1991, 1992). This, therefore, constitutes a direct link between public management reform and the performance audit work of an SAI. The NAO studies of service quality included a study on NHS outpatient services, which focused on how long patients had to wait for an appointment, and how far Patient's Charter standards were being met. There were also examinations of the quality of service in both English and Scottish museums and galleries, and at the handling of small claims in county courts.

The apparent growth in the proportion of studies in which the effectiveness criterion was applied is interesting. These reports included one on the success of the council tax valuation exercise and another which sought to establish whether the telecommunications regulatory body had been successful in securing service improvements and lower prices. One might also mention an earlier study of job creation programmes in Wales, in which the auditors developed their own analysis of the net cost per job created or preserved, and included allowance for deadweight and substitution effects. This particular study was unusual in attempting an economic approach to the cost effectiveness of the programmes concerned (Roberts and Pollitt 1994).

Finally, the use of the goal attainment criterion comes through in many reports and well illustrates the NAO in its classic role of delivering public accountability. Several examples concerned privatization, where the auditors sought to assess whether the government's declared goals for the sales had actually been met (e.g. NAO 1993d).

Cour des Comptes

For reasons already alluded to, it is not feasible to tabulate all the Cour's performance audit reports. It is possible, however, to form an impression of the range of criteria in play by inspecting the *rapports particuliers* and other materials. These show that the magistrates of the Cour may apply criteria of economy, efficiency, effectiveness, goal attainment, good management practice, and good governance, depending on the context and purpose of the particular audit. For example, each year the Cour audits some of the more important chambers of commerce and industry (of which there are more than 180). These audits may address a variety of issues, including how efficient are their training courses and support activities for firms, how economical and effective are their investments in infrastructure such as ports, airports, exhibition centres. During the last decade there has also been a strong development—by the Cour and the Chambres Régionales des Comptes—of value-for-money audits. These have embraced such topics as military programmes (Brevel, in 1997) and infrastructure controls (Normandy Bridge, in 1994). The criterion of good management practice has been frequently applied—to central administration, administrative authorities, and public firms (e.g. Aérospatiale, in 1996; France Télécom, in 1997). During the mid and late 1990s the Cour has also applied the goal attainment criterion—for instance by assessing the extent to which industrial technical centres in steel (1995), textiles and clothing (1998), and clock and watch making (1997) have fulfilled their missions.

Unsurprisingly, in such a firmly law-based and law-imbued institution, conformance with the relevant laws and regulations is a frequently adopted criterion. Accountability and adequate financial control are therefore foci of concern in all the Cour's audits. However, this type of examination can go far beyond simple procedural correctness, to embrace goal attainment as well. For example, this occurs when the Cour investigates the extent to which an audited body has adopted those means and taken those actions that are best calculated to realize the objectives it has been set (or which it has set for itself). This is a frequent perspective for the Cour to adopt in its audits of state services.

Two cases may help to flesh out this summary of the Cour's approach. First, we may consider the 1997 report on national museums and national art collections (Cour des Comptes 1997a). The conclusions of this report make it clear that the Cour is here giving strong emphasis to the criteria of good governance and good management. Much of the report's criticism focuses on the lack of clarity of roles as between the various bodies involved in the museum sector, especially in terms of the respective boundaries of political direction, central coordination, and local operational management. There is also a comment to the effect that the Réunion des Musées Nationaux has difficulty in reconciling its new commercial and industrial responsibilities with its continuing public and cultural responsibilites. All this could be said to concern, in our terms, good governance. In addition, there are comments about somewhat narrower issues of good management practice, especially with regard to the storage and display of exhibits.

The second case is that of a study of social policies to assist handicapped adults (Lamarque, 1997). The Cour's study considered the implementation of two major pieces of legislation aimed at promoting the social integration of handicapped adults. Under these laws, financial assistance in various forms was provided (a) for such people to stay at home and (b) to help them secure external employment. The audit applied two main criteria: the *coherence* of the various measures of assistance, and the *efficiency* with which they were being put into effect. Coherence was defined as the existence of 'a systematic and logical set of relationships between the goals of the policy and the means of implementing it' (Lamarque 1997, p. 4). To assess this, data were collected on the numbers of handicapped adults present in different types of institution and the rate of employment of such persons in societies and public authorities, and on the extent of use of alternative solutions. Efficiency was considered in relation to the costs of training and the activities of the committees that existed to promote orientation and re-employment. The study went on to give direct consideration to certain questions of effectiveness. It looked at the rate of access of handicapped adults to jobs, and the rate of access to ordinary jobs by handicapped persons who had been trained in specialized institutions.

The report, which was presented to Parliament by the Cour and was the subject of a hearing, included stiff criticisms of the programme. It cited low effectiveness, pointing to the fact that most handicapped adults remained within specialized institutions instead of moving into the normal job market. It identified sub-optimal allocations of resources as between the various measures. It said that the committees for orientation and re-employment could not work efficiently because they lacked both human and material resources. Following these criticisms, the government did reform the regulations for grants to handicapped adults.

This was thus a multi-criteria study, which included within its scope issues of good management practice, efficiency, and effectiveness.

6.7 Reflections

The focus of the audit examination, and the criteria employed, are very likely to have a major influence on the direction of the study, the methods employed, and the outcome of the work. In general terms, the posing of more evaluatory or explanatory questions (such as are entailed by a focus on efficiency and effectiveness) will require the adoption of a greater variety of methods, including more complex ones such as modelling, theory-building, or experimental testing. (See Keen, 1998, for one closely argued exposition of this point.) The 'payoff' is that the impact of such analyses —where they have been successfully executed—may be greater than an examination of the same subject which restricts itself to questions about procedural compliance or the presence or absence of good management practices. The significance of this is understood by many auditors. Nevertheless, our overall impression, based on the reading of many performance audit reports across the five SAIs, is that the criteria that support the audit judgements have often been implicit rather than explicit, and are only occasionally discussed in any discursive or analytical way on the surface of the texts themselves.

Explicit reference to criteria, where these are made, tend to be of a general kind ('systems for handling complaints from the public are as yet unsatisfactory') rather than specific and operational ('average response times should not exceed 14 working days'). Where criteria can be confidently identified, the standards they embody are (in terms of the discussion in Section 6.1 above) most commonly nominal/categoric. Ordinal standards are reasonably common but cardinal standards are quite rare.

The clarity with which audit criteria are expressed (and, if necessary, discussed and justified) can be argued to be more than just a technical or professional issue of good audit practice. For such clarity is also an aspect of transparency, and therefore is important to the integrity of the democratic process more generally. At the same time, we have argued that it would be unreasonable to hold auditors entirely responsible for those occasions when audit criteria are unstated or vague. As Section 6.4 showed, auditors are frequently wrestling with policies and programmes that are themselves opaque or even contradictory, and their own capacities to force light into the fog have their limits. The power to call for persons and documents will not take auditors very far if the persons and documents are themselves studiously vague. Often, all the auditors can do is draw attention to inadequate specification of roles and responsibilities, or to a general lack of clarity—which is, indeed, what the performance audit reports we have examined very frequently do.

A very obvious pattern in our data is that the 'good management' category is heavily populated, in both time periods. For reasons explored in Sections 6.3 and 6.6, both direct measurement of input–output ratios (efficiency) and, even more, the explicit analysis of outcomes (effectiveness) are less frequent in performance audit than a focus on management practices or systems. This balance appears broadly to transcend differences of constitutional position and training across the five SAIs, and to have survived (thus far) declarations from some SAIs to the effect that they wish effectiveness work to feature more prominently in their portfolios. In this sense, therefore, the actual practice of SAIs has not in the past entirely lived up to the definition of performance audit given by the SAIs' own representative institution, INTOSAI. INTOSAI's text stressed the 'three Es' (as we saw in Chapter 2), but in performance audit practice at least two of these 'Es' (efficiency and effectiveness) have been much less frequently investigated than issues of management practice and procedure.

Now, however, a shift towards these second two 'Es' may be taking place. If it is, then, at least as far as 1993–5 is concerned, it would be fair to characterize this as an incremental change rather than a radical one. Equally, within this overall picture of a continuing predominance of good management and goal attainment criteria, it is also clear that some strong efficiency and effectiveness studies are already being carried out. Furthermore, there was certainly interview evidence of a strong desire (or perhaps a feeling of professional obligation) to increase the number of true effectiveness studies. This presumably strengthens the likelihood that the incremental changes we have registered will continue.

Finally, to take a slightly contrary line, there may be philosophical grounds for arguing that pursuit of precise criteria for the judgement of government policies, programmes, and organizations is in any case a conceptually mistaken quest, and that SAIs have therefore been perfectly sensible in avoiding any attempt to force a kind of clarity which is simply not to be had. This is not just a case of political motivation (the need to maintain broad coalitions of support, referred to in Section 6.4); rather, it is a question of the fact that policies, programmes, and complex organizations can never be reduced to single objectives, simple formulae, or sets of measurable standards. That is not their nature. On the contrary, 'policies' and even 'programmes' may be seen as agglomerations of aspirations and practices, intentions and resources, inherently multi-faceted and subject to constant shifts of emphasis between their component ideas. Their inherent complexity defies reductionism, and demands instead the kind of cautious, nuanced multi-criteria judgements that many performance audit reports could be said to embody. From this perspective, the audit report is not a 'final word' on an issue at all: rather, it is just a kind of scrupulous and independent summary of relevant authoritative statements and currently available evidence. Its role is to describe the status quo (in terms both of what has been said and what has been done) and to offer a judgement as to whether well established and widely recognized criteria have been met. This is a different role from that of generating new evidence by means of scientifically designed data collection and the application of analytic techniques. Such a perspective, stressing compliance with general criteria that have usually been laid down by government itself, is, if you like, the 'conservative' position. It stands in contrast to the 'progressive' arguments in favour of a future for performance audit which would lead to more technical sophistication, more causal analysis, and more empirically based recommendations.

7
The Auditor's Craft

JEREMY LONSDALE, ROBERT MUL, AND
CHRISTOPHER POLLITT

7.1 The Craft of Performance Audit

What *is* a performance auditor? What do they actually *do*? In this chapter we take a detour from our progression from study subjects (Chapter 5) to audit criteria (previous chapter) to methods (next chapter) to products, and finally to impacts. We pause in order to look more closely at auditors themselves, at the nature of their day-to-day work, and at how both their identities and the content of their work may be changing.

'You know what an auditor is?' ran a joke we were told at the NAO, 'an auditor is an accountant who couldn't quite stand the excitement.' While this might or might not be the beginnings of an answer to questions about the general identity of the community of auditors, it certainly does not fit the specific subgroup we are interested in—performance auditors. (Actually, even as a joke, it only makes sense in those countries, like the UK, where most auditors are indeed qualified accountants.) As we have already begun to see, performance auditors can have quite an exciting time. Far from applying some unvarying set of rules or standards, they are obliged to design each performance audit anew, as a unique product rather than a piece of assembly-line verification. They have to define their study objects, establish appropriate criteria, choose suitable tools for investigation, and exercise many other skills, including those of diplomacy and teamwork. Their work often receives considerable press and official attention (see Chapter 10).

We will be looking at these different aspects of the performance auditor's job in more detail below, but for the moment we wish to propose and explore the idea that performance auditing is a *craft* activity. That is, it entails the use of specialist skills to create a series of unique ('hand-crafted') products which are self-consciously intended to be made to high standards.

7.2 Magistrates, Accountants, Researchers, and Consultants

The relatively recent craft of performance audit does not exist in a vacuum. It draws upon a series of established professional and disciplinary sources for its practitioners and its ideas. These ideas include important aspects of

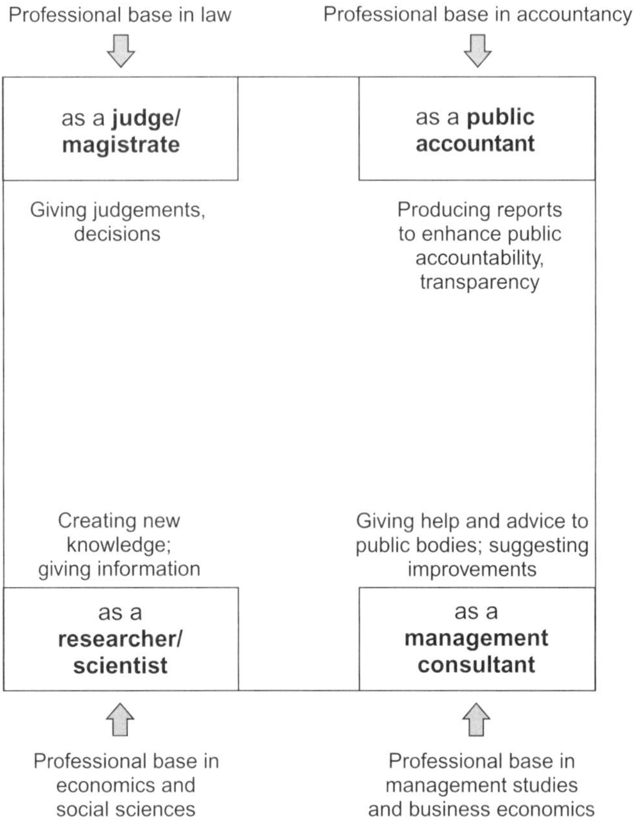

FIGURE 7.1 Possible roles for performance auditors

the self-image of performance auditors—the kind of mission they think they are engaged in. The particular mixture of these sources and influences varies from country to country. One way (but only one) of charting these different mixtures is shown in Figure 7.1.

In the literature and rhetoric generated by our five SAIs, at least four distinct 'images' or roles can be detected. In Figure 7.1 these four are shown as the corners of a kind of 'force field'. None of the SAIs is an absolutely 'pure' type—that is, all exist somewhere in the space *between* the corners. One might say, for example, that the RRV's statements usually place it in the lower half of the diagram and slightly to the right-hand side. This is because the RRV put considerable stress on giving help and advice to the government (a feature of its work that presumably is continuing after the splitting off of a part of it to form the National Financial Management Authority in July 1998), and also emphasized its role as an evaluator, providing research-based information that was relevant to better management of the public sector. It also mentioned its role as a public accountant, but this aspect was stressed less than by, say, the NAO. The fully fledged public accountant role, with its emphasis on accountability and transparency, is not as easily available to the RRV and the VTV as it is to the NAO, because in Finland and Sweden there are separate parliamentary audit bodies.

The NAO, closely tied to the parliamentary Public Accounts Committee as its main customer, is probably the closest of our five SAIs to the 'public accountant' role. Most of its annual reports, and most speeches by its senior staff, give first place to its duty to report to Parliament and the public on the wise use of public funds. Yet at the same time, as a secondary goal, it aspires to help departments, agencies, and other public bodies to achieve better value for money. Thus, one might place the NAO on the right-hand side of the figure, but further towards the top than the RRV.

Neither the work of the NAO nor that of the RRV involves a magisterial role of giving judgements and decisions. The Cour, by contrast, is closer to the top left-hand corner than any of the other four SAIs (Descheemaeker 1992, p. 25). However, it is not a 'pure type', either. With its annual public reports and its work for Parliament in connection with social security, and in a number of other ways, it is clear that the Cour of the 1990s is also active in the 'public accountant' role and even, to a lesser extent, in giving help to public bodies. Thus, one might think of it as being located somewhere in the top left-hand quarter of the diagram, but out towards the centre.

The work of the Algemene Rekenkamer is difficult to place. Many of its recent statements stress, in effect, the public accountant role (e.g. Witteveen 1996). Yet at the same time it has recruited a lot of economists and social scientists, thus creating, perhaps, some internal aspirations to be more 'scientific' and research-like in its investigations (bottom left-hand corner). Perhaps it should be placed somewhere slightly to the right of the diagonal line running from 'public accountant' to 'researcher/scientist', but in the top half of the figure to reflect the predominance of the public accountant role.

The VTV describes itself first and foremost as an information-giver (State Audit Office of Finland 1994a, p. 6). But it also mentions legality and, in practice, employs a good proportion of staff with legal backgrounds. Like the RRV, it is not a servant of Parliament, because of the existence of a distinct parliamentary audit unit. Nevertheless, it claims to be useful to Parliament in a general way. The VTV's emphasis on information-giving, combined with the adopted policy of broad-scope investigations (Chapter 5), might seem to indicate a role in the bottom left-hand quarter of Figure 7.1. On the other hand, it does not seem to have been at the forefront of the researcher-like developments of tools and methods (as we will see in Chapter 8). Its relations with other public-sector bodies are perhaps less clear-cut than in some other cases—in terms of Barzelay's analysis (Barzelay 1996), it lacks an obvious, powerful client for its products. This takes it further away from the consultancy and public accountant roles than either the NAO or the RRV.

This diagrammatic representation is intended mainly as a heuristic device —i.e. to encourage thought and debate—and should not be interpreted either mechanically or judgementally. Other 'personas' or roles could be considered as candidates; for example, there are some parallels between the craft of a performance auditor and that of an investigative journalist. Both journalists and auditors interview the key players involved in public issues, both gather large quantities of data, both have to assess the reliability of the information they have obtained, and both need to decide how to 'shrink' a mass of detail into a short, understandable report. In other ways, however, the comparison with a journalist is not an apt one. The journalist's circumstances encourage him/her to dramatize the findings, whereas most SAIs are quite cautious and conservative in the tone of their reports. The journalist tends to work alone, whereas auditors increasingly work in teams (to different extents in different countries, as we shall see). The performance auditor will have an extended professional training (as a lawyer, accountant, etc.) which many journalists lack. And, fundamentally, the performance auditor, however independent, is part of the overall apparatus of the state, whereas the journalist is not. SAIs cannot behave like newspapers, and newspapers cannot behave like SAIs, not least because they do not usually have the same privileged access to the official information as auditors.

To return to Figure 7.1, the most significant point is perhaps that in no case are performance auditors a 'pure' type. There is always some potential or actual tension in their roles—should they move more towards 'helping', 'judging', or 'reporting' roles? Our contention would be that they cannot do all at once—or, at least, they cannot do all of them well. For example, one cannot judge and pronounce upon an organization and simultaneously expect to act as a consultant and *confidant/e*. Or again, if one's prime concern is scientific rigour and the creation of new knowledge (bottom left-hand corner), it is unlikely that one will be at the forefront of offering timely, useful, practical suggestions to busy managers who need to know *now* (bottom right). To take a third example, the fearless public accountant, exposing failures and disappointments in public programmes to parliamentarians and the wider world (top right), is unlikely to be regarded with enthusiasm by auditees when they come to look for a helpful and supportive adviser (bottom right).

Of course, this is not in any case a free choice: each SAI is, as we saw in Chapters 2 and 3, constrained by law and history. Each therefore starts in a different place. Nevertheless, some cautious movement—or perhaps one should say change of emphasis—is possible. SAIs can choose and form strategies. Indeed, such shifts appear to have taken place, and to be continuing, as SAIs adapt to new demands. In this and succeeding chapters we will attempt to identify some recent and current trends—subtle changes in the character of the craft.

7.3 Practising the Craft: the Key Steps

Several descriptions of state audit have conceived of the auditor's task as a kind of journey, or exploration (Normanton 1966; Pollitt and Summa 1997c). We will borrow this analogy here as a way of structuring our consideration of the craft of performance audit into a sequence of key steps or operations. Several SAIs themselves describe the performance auditing process in a similar step-wise or cyclical fashion (Algemene Rekenkamer 1997; NAO 1997c; Swedish National Audit Office 1996). Following these precedents (see also Figure 1.1 above), the steps considered will be those taken in producing a report or judgement on a particular topic. In broad terms, at least, they are common to all five SAIs.

1. Selecting a topic to study
2. Planning how the topic can be approached
3. Carrying out the investigation itself (the 'fieldwork', or 'doing it')
4. Preparing the report or judgement (drafting and discussing the text)
5. Presenting the report or judgement to its intended audience(s)
6. Following through after the report has been presented

Sections 7.4–7.9 briefly discuss each of these steps in turn.

7.4 Selecting the Topic

Much financial audit is done on a mandatory, annual cycle. The accounts of the auditees in the statutorily determined audit field have to be considered each year. In that sense, there is no doubt about the choice of target, although there will still be a need to select and refine the most appropriate and cost-effective approach to the work. For none of the five countries covered by this research is the same true for performance audit. As was stated in Chapter 2, and elaborated in Chapter 5, performance audit topics are deliberately and consciously *chosen*, and all five SAIs have considerable freedom to choose, even if they are also prepared to listen to suggestions from 'outsiders'.

In approaching such selection decisions, a number of factors tend to be influential. The relative weighting of these can and does vary from time to time and SAI to SAI, but all seem to feature to some degree in all five countries. We can identify at least five such influential factors.

First, there is the *volume of public resources involved in an activity*, or its fiscal 'mass'. Although performance audits can be shown not to mirror exactly the size of government programmes, there is a looser connection, in the sense that an SAI which consistently ignored a very large area of spending would eventually be likely to attract criticism on that score. At the VTV, for example, economic importance is one of the four main criteria that are cited in internal literature and have been used to guide topic selection since the early 1990s. And at the RRV we find the auditor general arguing that the social security system should be a particular focus for performance audits because 'these benefits are such an important part of the economy' (Ahlenius and Jonsson 1995, p. 7). The Cour also pays attention to economic importance, especially in the case of cross-sectoral audits. For example, the programme set by the *premier président* for 1998 stresses the significance of the public service and its wages, partly because these represent such a substantial component of public expenditure.

Second, SAIs usually take account of the *likely risk to public funds* involved in a given activity. The programme concerned may not be the biggest in volume terms, but may have some feature or features that give rise to concern; for example, it may be a new, experimental programme, or it may fall within an area known to carry high risks of failure (advanced, high-tech weapon development: see e.g. NAO 1995c), error or fraud (certain types of benefit payments, e.g. the RRV's report on housing benefit, 1996, or the Cour's report on the Association pour la Recherche contre le Cancer).

Third, SAIs often strive to achieve something approaching *systematic coverage of the audit field*, over a period of years. While total coverage is an impossibility (given the resource constraints that all SAIs face, and the hugeness of their audit fields), there is a concern not to permit large tracts of public activity to 'lie in shadow' for long periods, and a desire, if possible, to gain additional benefits by allowing for 'between-report' conclusions to be drawn. The RRV, as mentioned earlier, has carried out not one but a cluster of performance audits on the social security system (Ahlenius and Jonsson 1995).

Fourth, increasingly, SAIs attempt to *follow up themes or topics where earlier audits demonstrated there were problems*. They return to the scene of former glories to see if the audited bodies have reformed their errant ways or, to put less dramatically, to assess how far previous audit recommendations were implemented. Such examinations are explicitly recommended in NAO guidance as one way of ensuring that the Office achieves a balanced programme of reports (NAO 1997c). The Cour's report on the troubled French finance corporation Credit Lyonnais could be seen as falling into this category, and all SAIs from time to time 'check back' to see if problems identifed at an earlier stage have been effectively addressed.

Finally, SAIs may decide to investigate *topics that are of strong political salience*, even if these are not big spending programmes or central policy issues. This may not be a particularly frequent occurrence, and it may be more characteristic of those SAIs that are close to legislatures (especially the NAO and the Rekenkamer), but it does happen. Although there can be sensitivity about discussing the rationale for selections in public, there is really no reason why at least a certain element within an SAI's portfolio should not be directed to topics of current interest to members of parliament or the government.

The UK comptroller and auditor general consults with the MPs on the PAC while planning the audit programme (NAO 1997b, p. 26), and the Rekenkamer, similarly, consults members of the States General (Witteveen 1996). The Cour, as we have seen, has developed links with the French parliament, especially in the social field. Such discussions may result in ideas for examinations that the SAIs may take forward.

Two points need to be stressed concerning these five criteria. First, they are not determinative, in the sense that application of all five main criteria still leaves plenty of room for debate within the SAI about exactly which topics should feature in the programme. Second, the SAIs are in the happy position of choosing a *portfolio*, not a single study. Thus, they can mix and balance different types of study chosen for different reasons. (For example, in a given year an SAI may decide to audit one quite politically salient and sensitive topic, but to devote the rest of its resources to 'safer' big-money programmes and to make follow-up assessments of the impact of earlier recommendations.)

If the above five are among the main criteria applied to the process of topic selection, we still need to ask: where, in practice, do the concrete proposals come from? Is the formulation of a programme of performance audits predominantly a 'top-down' or a 'bottom-up' process? The general answers to be drawn from our interviews were twofold: first, in every case many important ideas continue to rise up the SAI from the 'rank-and-file' performance auditors; but, second, in every case there was some evidence to indicate that the SAIs had recently moved to strengthen the degree of coherence or overall strategic thinking that informed topic selection. These two general answers must be qualified by the observation that the notions of 'top-down' and 'bottom-up' mean rather different things according to the internal structures, procedures, and cultures of the individual SAIs.

In all five SAIs, audit staff are relied upon to generate proposals for new performance audits; indeed, they are under an obligation to try to make suggestions without which the ongoing programme of work would dry up (Banefelt 1992). These are fed into what is usually an annual exercise and selections are eventually decided 'higher up'. In a monocratic and hierarchical organization such as the NAO, the final selections are made by the comptroller and auditor general himself, on advice from senior colleagues. In a collegiate organization such as the Cour, the *premier président* and the *présidents de chambre* will carry considerable influence, but the general process of discussion may be more collective, at least in spirit. Nevertheless, in both cases the most senior members of the SAI will perforce have to rely on ideas coming up from below; and, on the other side, rank-and-file auditors will know that their own reputations will rest partly on their abilities to review their particular field of interest and to come up with feasible and attractive proposals for audits. This relatively 'democratic' feature of the internal processes of SAIs seems to be of long standing (Normanton 1966, p. 165).

There are signs, however, that these 'bottom-up' suggestions are being increasingly guided and channelled to make more appropriate and cost-effective choices. At the RRV, the VTV, and the NAO, staff monitor particular areas (for example by reading official publications and press coverage, keeping in contact with officials, and consulting with outside experts), trying to select particular ideas that are coming up from below which will fit in with areas of interest indicated by senior staff. At the Rekenkamer the Board sets broad priorities—the EU and the environment are two recent examples—but nevertheless leaves considerable scope for staff to bring forward promising topics, while at the NAO strategic planning guidance is issued to staff, reflecting senior management interests. At the Cour, 1997 saw the introduction of a more explicit setting of 'strategic orientations' by the *premier président*, working in conjunction with the presidents of the sectoral chambers. This was intended to enhance the consistency of the overall work programme, and to reflect a growing interest in 'horizontal', intersectoral themes. The VTV introduced a new planning system in the early 1990s, which, while preserving the possibility for individual auditors to suggest interesting topics, established some broad criteria for selection among them, including the likely 'practical usefulness' of the audit and the risks to economy, efficiency, and effectiveness. The auditor general and the audit councillors (three second-tier audit managers) also made their own suggestions, and further ideas were sometimes sought from the ministries.

7.5 Planning the Way Forward

Once a topic has found its place within a strategic plan—and so is part of a programme of future work—more detailed planning has to begin. In the first place, auditors must develop a much more precise formulation of the chosen topic, in order to make it into an operational audit question. They must also establish the criteria they are to use for making their judgements. Second, auditors have to reassure themselves that the topic, however good an idea it may seem, is actually 'do-able' within the given time and resources constraints. All five SAIs meet this requirement by having some kind of preliminary or scoping study, designed to establish that relevant findings are likely to occur, and that sufficient evidence is likely to be available to make the commitment of resources to a full study worthwhile (and that resource costs of obtaining this evidence will not exceed the capacity of the SAI). Auditors may also be expected to forecast, with some degree of confidence, what they might expect to be able to report. Only when this has been completed satisfactorily will the senior staff give final approval for an investigation to go ahead. Some prospective studies fall at this hurdle—for example, in 1993 the VTV dropped about 16 per cent of its proposed topics on the basis of its pre-studies. At the NAO a small number of projects might be converted at this stage to reports to management, perhaps where the scope for a report worthy of parliamentary attention is not proven.

The selection and testing of appropriate tools and techniques for the investigation also usually takes place at this stage. Trends in tool use are described in greater detail in the following chapter. The NAO and the RRV have begun to make increasing use of expert panels to assist auditors in the technicalities of study design, and to comment on the focus and content of the proposed examination. The Cour has established an internal expertise 'hotline' through which auditors can check to see which other magistrates possess particular experience of a given topic, and contact them for advice. This is, in effect, a systematization of a process of informal, collegiate sharing of expertise which had already taken place and which appears to have been a key part of the development of the performance auditor's craft.

One rather fundamental aspect of preparation is the assembly of the relevant expertise (Pollitt and Summa 1997c, pp. 92–3). There is some variation between the five SAIs in the extent to which this part of the process is likely to include the use of specialists from outside the body of performance auditors themselves. While each of the five SAIs had made use of outsiders on some occasion, the frequency of this was much higher in the RRV and the NAO than in the other three. At the VTV we were told that 'We haven't really put the effort into that we should have', and that the budget line that had been established for hiring external experts had been underspent. It was also argued that including outsiders might blur the responsibility for the final recommendations—although this was not regarded as a problem, for example, at the NAO, where the consultants who are used are quite clearly contracted to work for the comptroller and auditor general. At the Cour it was explained that a few external experts had been hired over the past few years, but this remained unusual, and the budget for it was modest. The Rekenkamer uses advisory groups which contain externals, but seldom employs such persons as operational members of audit teams.

By contrast, the RRV has made increasing resort to outside experts, sometimes to test their conclusions but also to involve them in report-writing. At the NAO, too, use of outsiders of all kinds, including academics, management consultants, and specialists, has grown significantly since the end of the 1980s, to the extent that it is now unusual to find a study team that does not make use of outside skills, and the consultancy bill amounts to some 10 per cent of total operational costs. Our interviewees at the NAO believed that such assistance had had a profound and positive effect on performance audit work. Going one step further, the NAO has experimented with contracting out an entire performance audit (to an accountancy and consultancy company), but at the present time has yet to make this a regular practice.

It would be quite incorrect, however, to suppose that the planning phase is a purely technical business of checking data sources, refining the appropriate battery of techniques, and assembling a suitably skilled team. On the contrary, significant discussions—even negotiations—with the audited bodies may take place during this phase. None of the five SAIs launches performance audits 'blind', without talking matters over with the auditee(s). At the Rekenkamer,

> The first step is to hold introductory talks with the department concerned to determine the scope of the audit, the audit approach and the staff to be involved. Working arrangements are made and matters such as temporary accommodation and logistical facilities are settled. (Algemene Rekenkamer 1989, p. 32)

In earlier research, VTV staff similarly emphasized the importance of creating a good dialogue with the auditee right at the beginning (Pollitt and Summa 1997c, p. 94). This is also stressed in NAO guidance (e.g. NAO 1997c) and in the advice to *rapporteurs* in the *manuel de vérification* at the Cour. In short, the craft of performance audit demands not only a mastery of technical issues but also, from the very beginning of a project, the ability to discuss and negotiate with auditees who are not necessarily overjoyed to have been selected as a topic for investigation.

7.6 Doing it

Under this title we consider the 'fieldwork' stage of an audit, during which auditors collect, test, and analyse their evidence, make visits to the audited bodies (and sometimes to other 'stakeholders' in a policy or programme), and generally strive to realize the original aims that led to the topic's selection.

During fieldwork performance auditors will be called upon to practice forensic, analytical, and diplomatic skills. They must pursue the evidence they need and avoid being sidetracked into irrelevancies. They must continuously distil the wheat from the chaff—it is very common for performance audits quickly to amass vast quantities of documentary and interview evidence. They must keep relations with the auditees as smooth as possible, not least because a resentful and uncooperative auditee may have the capacity to slow down the investigation considerably, thereby putting timetables askew and probably increasing the cost of the audit. Yet they must retain the self-confidence to continue asking acute, analytical questions and not to be overawed by the powerful and senior staff they frequently find themselves dealing with in the audited body. And all the time, they must manage their own team, dealing with a range of circumstances including individuals sometimes being called away to work on other studies, sickness, skill shortages, and all the other 'normal' problems of personnel management.

Although hard to generalize, it is perhaps reasonable to characterize the fieldwork stage as the time during which rank-and-file auditors try to ensure they are in a position to fulfil all the promises they made to their senior management when they persuaded them that the subject was worth pursuing. It is the time when they search for the information that will justify their, often critical, assertions and enable them to make recommendations. After all the time invested in planning, auditors experience moments of truth for example, in the interviews, during file examination, and, as responses to questionnaires come in, in searching for the material they need. Increasingly, such work has not been left to chance. Before embarking on the work, the performance auditor will have planned how information will be gathered, and where and in what form it might be found. Questions will have been prepared, task lists drawn up, and in many cases provisional conclusions formulated tentatively, to be tested against the evidence gathered.

In general, performance audits at all our SAIs appear to be undertaken as a small-team activity, so that, to the extent that this is the norm, team management becomes another aspect of the auditor's craft. Some SAIs still carry out performance audits on the basis of an individual being sent out to 'bring back the bacon'; this 'solo' model of performance auditing seemed to be most prevalent at the Cour and the VTV, but even at those two establishments, teamwork was becoming increasingly common (e.g. Lamarque 1997; Valtiontalouden tarkastusvirasto 1994). Of course, these trends are connected to the choice of subject (Chapter 5). The more broad-scope, multi-organization or 'horizontal' topics are chosen, the less feasible it becomes for individual auditors to carry out the whole of the work. There is also the issue of mixing and matching skills and experience (the novice learning beside the 'master craftsman'), perhaps uniting the managerial and drafting skills of one person with the investigative abilities of another.

Another reason for pursuing a team approach is simply that two or three people are likely to be able to carry out the necessary fieldwork faster than one. Timeliness of reporting has become a key issue for our SAIs, and audit projects are time- and labour-intensive activities. At the RRV a typical performance audit may last about 12 months, and take up the time of two auditors. At the Rekenkamer it is not unusual for audits to take between 12 and 24 months, and for rather larger teams, of two to five persons, to be formed. At the NAO teams of three (including a director, who may have perhaps four or five such projects on the go at any one time) are normal, and the length of performance audits is typically around 12–18 months from scoping work to publication, of which 6–9 months is likely to be fieldwork. At the VTV the average performance audit in 1993 took up 193 employee-days (State Audit Office of Finland 1994a, p. 17). However, in all five SAIs, individual studies can depart widely from these averages, in terms of both the size of the team and the length of the study.

Fieldwork generates an enormous amount of information which performance auditors must sift and analyse. They must form judgements about what evidence is and is not relevant for the story they wish to tell, and decide what conclusions will stand up to detailed and critical scrutiny. How they go about this probably varies from individual to individual and, given the different clearance requirements in each country, between SAIs. Having examined the way in which NAO auditors carry out their fieldwork and analysis, one observer has concluded that 'VFM is predominantly a quasi-rational activity which embodies judgements based on the collections of large numbers of indicators—documents, interviews, expenditure data and so on—about events, and where the relevance and accuracy of the indicators are agreed by the auditee' (Keen 1999). Another view sees it as an iterative process, where 'Drafts are rewritten and expanded as a synopsis for the final audit report gradually takes shape . . . The analytical process usually takes place throughout the audit. Performance audit is an open, searching process in which new information or knowledge can significantly affect the auditor's perspective. Some hypotheses are confirmed while others must be modified, revised or rejected' (Swedish National Audit Office 1995a, pp. 12–13). During fieldwork auditors have (literally) to face up to the staff—often the senior staff—of the audited body. In a number of countries it is common for the auditors to work from offices sited in the buildings of the audited body. All this requires a measure of self-confidence and self-awareness, to keep relations with auditees as smooth as possible, yet not allow the audit enquiries to lose momentum or be deflected.

Finally, it should be mentioned that performance auditors at all five SAIs will seldom enjoy the luxury of being able to concentrate on only one audit at a time. As we noted earlier, SAIs have no more escaped resource pressures than have any other organizations in the public sector. Their productivity has, in general, increased. As a result, at several SAIs the number of days spent on any one project has tended to fall (at the RRV, for example, the average number of days for a main study fell from 299 in 1993–4 to 193 in 1995–6), and staff are commonly involved in several studies simultaneously, possibly (and perhaps ideally) at different stages of preparation. At the Cour and the NAO particularly, we were told of the increasing stress under which performance auditors operated, having to produce more, and to more exacting standards, within tighter timetables and budgets. Like other public service managers, performance auditors are experiencing an increasing *intensification* of their working lives which is encouraging them to identify ways of streamlining evidence-gathering and speed up other elements of their craft, such as the discussions with auditees about the draft report.

7.7 Drafting, Discussing, Re-drafting

The production of a draft report, as many performance auditors will recall with some misgivings, may be a long way from the end of the work on a particular study. Even when all the evidence is in and has been written up, there are still important aspects of the auditor's craft which remain to be exercised. The processes and discussions through which the draft is finalized serve several functions. One is simply to produce an *accurate* document, free from factual error. Another is to produce a *defensible* document, which the

SAI can stand behind, both in private debate with the auditee and, in most cases (except for the Cour), in the public arena as well. Defensibility includes, but can also go beyond, simple factual accuracy, encompassing for example the reasonableness of recommendations. A third function is to make the text *accessible*, that is to remove unnecessary technicalities, clarify concepts, and polish presentational aspects. One might think of all three as parts of the quality control of performance audit.

To help achieve quality in these three respects, auditors from all SAIs employ two sources of advice, and some have regular recourse to a third. The first source of advice and improvement, drawn on before the draft report is exposed to the auditee, is the SAI itself. All possess internal procedures by which draft reports are considered by other 'parts of the shop'. At the Cour there is a process of vigorous collective consideration within each sectoral chamber. At the NAO drafts are given detailed critical scrutiny, not only by the relevant assistant auditors general (the third tier from the top of the Office), but by internal reference panels of colleagues from elsewhere in the Office. At the VTV the counsellors (second-tier) consider reports at the draft stage. These processes are important not only for the fate of the individual report, but also because they are occasions on which the work of a particular auditor (or team of auditors) is exposed to the searching gaze of its peer group and senior colleagues. Reputations can therefore be made or lost. It is also a time when the performance auditor, steeped in perhaps more than twelve months of 'eating, drinking, and sleeping' a particular subject, can seek the assistance of fresh, less jaundiced eyes.

The second source is the audited body. All five SAIs show the draft to the auditee and discuss it with them, in some cases having given prior warning or preliminary presentations of key findings. There is then an attempt to reach agreement on all factual points, but often also on questions of emphasis and interpretation. In the case of the NAO, a convention has been established, with the firm backing of the Public Accounts Committee, that the final texts of the NAO's reports as presented to Parliament will have been agreed with the auditee. The purpose is to avoid arguments during committee hearings on reports about facts, and so allow attention to be focused on conclusions and recommendations. On occasion this can lead to prolonged argument over drafts, line by line (Roberts and Pollitt 1994, p. 534).

In other countries the consultation requirement takes a different form. For example, in France audited bodies may add their comments as annexes to the Cour's public reports; in the case of the *rapport particulier* on museums and art collections, the commentaries were almost half as long as the text produced by the Cour itself (Cour des Comptes 1997a, pp. 161–234). But in the Cour, the Rekenkamer, and the RRV it is nevertheless regarded as good practice to seek to obtain the maximum possible agreement with the auditee before finalizing a report (Algemene Rekenkamer 1989, and interviews). The VTV describes the process of clearing the draft with the auditee as one of thesis–antithesis–synthesis. Finnish auditors also regard it as important to give auditees a clear opportunity to correct any factual errors that may have crept in.

Both these forms of advice are common to all our SAIs. An additional source of help is external opinion. As we noted earlier, outside expertise is quite widely used by the NAO ('reference panels'), the RRV, and the Rekenkamer (advisory groups), but is unusual for either the VTV or the Cour. Where SAIs report to parliaments, there may even be processes for offering MPs a 'preview' of what is going to be in a report, and an opportunity to comment. In recent years the Rekenkamer has been discussing the 'main messages' of its studies with members of the States General before the final reports emerged (Witteveen 1996, p. 28).

7.8 Presenting and Publicizing

Once a report is finalized, there remains a good deal of work to ensure that the final product is professionally prepared and presented, and that it reaches the right audience(s) at the right time. Much of the detail of this process is discussed in Chapter 9 ('products'), but suffice to say here that there is considerable evidence to demonstrate that all SAIs have given greater attention to presentational aspects over the last decade or so (drawing on lessons learnt from professions such as public relations), and that performance auditors themselves have been heavily involved in these developments. SAIs appear to have drawn a line in different places in terms of where their performance auditors must release their grip on their product. While NAO audit teams, for example, remain solely responsible for all aspects of editing and proofreading the report prior to despatch for printing (in recent times, even selecting and ensuring that the audited department is happy with the photograph on the front cover of the final report), performance auditors at the Rekenkamer pass their report on to a separate editorial section, where it is refined and readied for publication.

Even if auditors themselves may not present their findings, they will have to work alongside increasingly professional SAI press and media offices to ensure that press releases present the main messages and that journalists are clear about the SAI's conclusions. Increasingly, however, auditors—and not always the more senior ones—find themselves in the front line. The more experienced members of NAO audit teams are now receiving media skills training to prepare them to give radio and television interviews. A number of magistrates from the Cour are now involved in regular meetings with parliamentary committees concerned with the social security area. Contacts between the Rekenkamer and the States General have multiplied (Witteveen 1996), and the RRV has expanded its presentations to parliamentary standing committees. The VTV, perhaps, is of the five the least involved with this kind of public and political interface.

The particular procedures in place in the UK, whereby performance audit reports are routinely examined by a committee of members of parliament, means that, even after publication, audit teams responsible for particular reports provide briefings—written and, on occasions, oral—to the Public Accounts Committee (NAO 1997c, p. 50). Most, perhaps all, of the team will be present at the Committee hearing, and will then assist the chairman in drafting the committee's report, containing their recommendations, which will then be agreed by the members of the Committee and published. To those who do not escape to pastures new within or outside the NAO once the study has been completed, it may feel that a particular report will never quite lie down and die.

7.9 Following Up and Following Through

As every performance audit is a unique investigation, there is always something that participants can learn from the experience. As a result, a number of SAIs have developed systems of *following up*—in the sense of internal procedures which assess the quality of their work after the event. At the lowest level, there are simply checks that studies have been completed to time and budget and, if not, some sort of enquiry as to what got 'off track'. Beyond that, however, some SAIs have introduced more thorough forms of *post hoc* 'quality control', to examine what went well and what didn't, as well as to establish what lessons have been learnt for the future. At the Rekenkamer post-audit evaluations are carried out by teams within three months of the publication of a report, and at the NAO such enquiries form part of a broader quality assurance process that also involves seeking the views of the audited body (see Chapter 10) on what it feels it has gained from the examination and how fairly it considers the work to have been conducted. At the time of writing, the VTV was just beginning a process of review of its reports by an external expert, using a predefined assessment scheme (Valtiontalouden tarkastusvirasto 1998).

Every SAI also *follows through* to some extent; that is, it goes back to the auditees after a period to find out whether, and to what extent, recommendations have actually been implemented. Some SAIs expect their staff to attempt to measure the proportion of recommendations that have been acted upon, or even the extent of savings that may have been achieved. Perhaps more importantly, there is then the *expectation* that auditors will monitor progress within audited bodies over the coming years. At the Rekenkamer follow-up audits take place two to three years after the original audit. The prospect that the auditor may return is, of course, designed to provide further encouragement to auditees to take promised action, but, as we saw earlier in the chapter, there is always the possibility that a new examination will arise from the reconsideration of the subject. The audit process will have gone full cycle.

7.10 Who Are They? The Performance Auditors' 'Guild'

Auditors tend not to have a very colourful public image. 'Men in grey suits' is probably the most widely shared popular view. In the past this was probably tolerably accurate (see Normanton, 1966, for discussion of the background of 'national auditors' in several countries in the post-Second World War period), but there is evidence of change—and not only in the carefully selected photos of women and shirt-sleeved men in the NAO's annual report (NAO 1997c)! There are perhaps several salient features of recent trends in membership of the performance auditors' 'guild':

1. the development of a distinct and prominent subgroup of performance auditors within four of our five SAIs (the Cour des Comptes being the exception);
2. an increase in the educational level of recruits;
3. the development of more sophisticated in-house training and guidance provided;
4. some broadening of the skills base, but within a framework very different from one SAI to the next (i.e., the most common disciplinary and professional background at one SAI is not the same as the others); and
5. growing demands on performance auditors in terms of their performance and development.

We noted earlier that in all but the Cour des Comptes performance audit was now undertaken by a separate group of staff, giving performance audit a distinct presence within the SAIs. At the RRV the existence of a separate Performance Audit Division for some years has meant that performance auditors have been an identifiable grouping. In the past, auditors at the NAO undertook both financial audit and value-for-money work, but since 1991 qualified staff have opted to specialize in one or the other discipline, the belief being that both were becoming too complex for a generalist approach. A similar, if slightly less clearly drawn, division occurred at the Rekenkamer, where some overlap has continued and financial and performance audit specialists come together for financial management work. In all these cases performance auditors are a sizeable proportion of staff within the five SAIs —some 50 per cent at the VTV, for example, around 20 per cent at the RRV (a far larger body in 1996), and some 30 per cent at the NAO. A significant proportion have many years' experience of the work, providing a continuity of approach and an understanding of relations with government and parliament that many see as essential to the SAI's authority.

Another trend has been the general increase in the educational standing of staff. In the 1960s Normanton noted with some concern that auditors in the UK from the 1920s were in the anomalous and sometimes uncomfortable position of being lower in rank than the directing grades in the departments whose financial activities they are supposed to examine and criticize—the exact opposite of the position in France (Normanton 1966, pp. 272–3). The more recent trend of almost entirely graduate entry at the NAO for many years would no doubt be to his liking. At the RRV 73 per cent of all staff have a university education or similar level of education, and at the Rekenkamer, where the figure was 78 per cent, those interviewed emphasized that this growth reflected the increased demands on the office and the increasing complexity of the work. At the VTV staff all have university degrees, in particular in accounting and business (NAO 1996a, p. 44), while most of the Cour's magistrates are postgraduates of the prestigious Ecole Nationale d'Administration, with qualifications in public law, economics, or finance.

The higher educational qualifications on entry have been added to by the development of increasingly sophisticated in-house training and guidance. At NAO training has changed and increased in recent years. Previously based around a core of mandatory courses, staff are increasingly expected to develop their own programme to suit needs identified with their line manager and others. Thus, training will include internal courses, but will be augmented, for example, by outside courses, work experience, work shadowing, secondments, and one-to-one tuition. At the Cour there is now a Magistrates Committee dedicated to improvement of professional skills, and it has set up a training programme within which magistrates can choose what to learn. Similarly, although a wide range of internal courses are in place at RRV teaching basic skills such as the audit process, statistical methods, and the organizational setup of European Union, staff are also encouraged to develop themselves. Accordingly, they attend relevant seminars and lectures on specialist subjects. At the VTV in 1994, training for performance auditors took up an average of 11 days per auditor per annum (16 in 1993) (State Audit Office of Finland 1994a, p. 12).

A further feature has been the broadening of the skills base inside the performance auditor's guild, but within a framework very different from one SAI to the next. At the NAO, for example, the tradition has been to train staff, usually fresh from university and with a wide variety of unrelated academic backgrounds, as financial accountants, enabling those who choose to do so to take up value-for-money work after qualification. At the Rekenkamer, social science and public administration backgrounds have traditionally predominated in performance audit, with accountants carrying out the financial audit work. More recently, though, several of our SAIs—in particular the RRV, the NAO, and the Rekankamer—have begun to question whether the balance of skills they have is the right one to undertake more difficult or innovative studies, and in particular to carry out the more elusive effectiveness studies (Chapter 6). To this end, for example, the NAO has increased the number of staff it has recruited mid-career with a range of backgrounds in operational research, statistics, and economics, or with specialist knowledge of defence, health, or privatization issues. In recent years, the RRV too has followed a deliberate policy of recruiting staff with previous professional experience to replace members of staff who are leaving. Our interviews at the Rekenkamer also indicated a desire for greater awareness of econometric techniques, cost allocation methods, and cost-effectiveness analysis among auditors, while at the RRV more staff with an economics bent (albeit preferably still generalists in outlook) was seen as a necessity.

A common theme of our interviews was that SAIs expected a great deal of their performance auditors and that the demands were growing all the time (although this was matched by their requirements of financial auditors). At the RRV one interviewee suggested that staff needed to be 'intellectual doers', with analytical capacity and courage, while another said that he was looking for 'specialists in generalism', able to respond to the changing demands of the work. At the VTV staff were expected to be able to ask penetrating questions, to classify things, and to sustain concentration on one thing for several months. They had to know 'what was right and wrong'. At the Cour, as we saw in Chapter 4, the *premier président* indicated in 1995 that there was a particular requirement for recruits with experience in the social field, and for engineers. Faced with increased complexity in their environment, all our SAIs seem to have been pushing their staff hard.

Taking these trends together, it makes sense to talk of a process of increasing professionalization within performance audit, characterized by improved technical competence among a group of people better qualified now than their predecessors, and undertaking higher levels of continuing professional education. That being said, there may be a danger that performance auditors will be asked to become jacks of all trades while failing to be masters of any. If performance auditors are to be adequately trained in accountancy and financial management, is it realistic to expect them also to become proficient at economic analysis *and* at the use of social science techniques, including quantitative methods such as multiple regression analysis and surveys? And if they are to develop their investigative skills to enable their SAI to break new ground, how far can the performance auditor's craft be stretched to encompass the handling of the media, the designing of reports, or following up of the impact of studies? On the other hand, it could be argued that what is really required is not necessarily the 'hands-on' expertise that would enable auditors to use sophisticated accounting, economic, statistical, and social science techniques *themselves*, but rather the inculcation of a level of understanding that permits them to select appropriate experts and intelligently assess and integrate their contributions to the overall performance audit project in question. Either way, to varying degrees all five SAIs have recognized that performance audit requires a growing range of skills, and have taken steps to bring in a wider range of staff, draw on outside consultancy assistance, and promote training. It will be interesting to see whether this richer mix, however it is formulated in each case, responds to the demands made on it.

7.11 The Identity of the Performance Auditor: Secure or Insecure?

We have made some progress in answering the questions 'what do performance auditors do?' and 'who are they?' The picture that has been built up contains contrasting elements. One way to represent these contrasts might be to enquire about the 'identity' of performance auditors in the late 1990s. Are they secure in their craft, clear and settled in their vision of themselves? On the basis of the evidence we have reviewed, the answer to such questions appears to be 'yes and no'. Yes, they are secure, in so far as they are now well established members of longstanding, well respected, and sometimes powerful organs of democratic governance, which have the capacity to command parliamentary and/or governmental attention. And they have become a distinct sub-species within all but one of our SAIs, their skills sustained and developed through distinctive training, and their thinking influenced by disciplines somewhat removed from those relevant to their financial audit colleagues. They are also developing an increasingly sophisticated technical literature, making links with other types of researcher and developing international contacts that are helping to disseminate good practice and ideas.

The identity of performance audit is fairly clear also in more specific and practical ways. Actually doing such audits entails going through a series of recognizably similar steps in each country (Section 7.3); the work generally requires similar attributes. In every country, performance auditors need to be self-confident enough to deal with senior people in the audited bodies; they need to have good drafting skills, to be able to manage their time well (especially where they are juggling between several projects simultaneously), to be acutely conscious of their SAI's reputation for independence, while also remaining sensitive to the legitimate concerns of auditees.

However, in other respects, the specific identity of performance audit within each SAI is less certain. The boundaries between performance audit and other activities are not always clear, as was shown in Chapter 2. The labels affixed to performance audit have been multiple ('VFM' in the UK, a multiplicity of tags within the RRV, an even longer list of special labels at the Algemene Rekenkamer, no separate designation at all within the Cour). More substantially, perhaps, the scope of performance audit has exhibited wide variations —from broad analyses of systems to in-depth substantive investigations of particular contracts, and from a focus on a single function within a single organization to thematic treatments of whole squadrons of organizations (ZBOs in the Netherlands, public utility regulators in the UK, museums in France—see Chapters 5 and 6).

Furthermore, behind these different kinds of study lie quite profound differences in disciplinary background and professional training. The British performance auditor is (currently) likely to be a trained accountant and to have a university degree of little direct relevance to audit, the French auditor to be a graduate of ENA, the Swedish auditor to be an accountant/economist or social scientist, and so on. They may usually work alone (VTV) or more commonly in a team (NAO). They may make extensive use of outside expert advice (NAO) or very little indeed (Cour, VTV). Interestingly, as far as our specific interest in the relationship between performance audit and public management reform is concerned, it would also appear that rather few performance auditors have either training or experience in public management *per se*. This remark has to be qualified in the case of the Cour to the extent that magistrates spend periods of their careers outside the Cour and may return bringing with them experience of having been on the board of a public enterprise or even a private-sector corporation. In other SAIs also, entrants may occasionally come from backgrounds that have afforded them management experience. On the whole, however, performance auditors, though they frequently *comment* on the quality of management (Chapter 6) tend themselves not to possess much management experience beyond that of managing their own small audit teams.

In sum, one might say that the craft of performance audit shares some broad procedural features across all five of the countries in our study, but that both the characteristic scope of the work and the standard requirements for membership of the guild vary extensively from one to the other. Whether this marks a healthy dynamism and inevitable diversity, or an uncertainty about the nature of the core tasks and about the best ways to approach them, is a matter for further debate. There is some evidence—we would not want to exaggerate it—of incremental convergence, in that training requirements have now come under closer scrutiny in all five SAIs, and exchanges of personnel and ideas between European SAIs have grown in recent years. Equally, though, there are plenty of signs of the continuing strength of diverse national traditions and attitudes, and we see little sign, in the near term, of a single, uniformly executed, performance audit 'craft'.

8

Methods

Jeremy Lonsdale

8.1 Approaching Performance Audit Methods

Chapter 7 examined the 'craft' of performance audit, highlighting what we described as the growing technical competence of the work in each of the countries examined. It also drew attention to the changing demands on practitioners, many of whose work has extended beyond simply undertaking audits, and now requires that they draw on skills of negotiation, are conversant with a range of computer software, or, on occasion, know how to handle the mass media and outside consultants.

Despite this expansion of their role, performance auditors are employed primarily to plan and carry out audit examinations, and to do this use a range of methods to collect and analyse information. This chapter focuses on the methods they use, which have a vital bearing on the success of their work. In particular,

1. it considers what SAIs say about the methods their staff use;
2. it summarizes the findings from our examination of SAI reports to identify what methods have actually been employed;
3. it looks at the factors that may have determined the choice of methods made by SAIs;
4. it examines the extent to which SAIs explain their methodologies in their reports; and
5. it concludes by asking what our findings suggest about the nature of performance audit.

The methods employed by performance auditors—defined here as the tools or instruments employed to gather and analyse empirical evidence—cannot be considered in isolation. For example, the type of question posed by auditors will influence the methods drawn upon. As we noted in Chapter 6, examinations of effectiveness usually require significantly different approaches to studies of a more descriptive nature. The methods employed are also likely to influence the nature and extent of the impact of the work. For example, where methods generate original data and provide new insights, they are likely in many cases to be more penetrating than when reliance has been mainly on an analysis of published material. In addition, performance auditors do not conduct their work in a vacuum. Their backgrounds and experiences are likely to have a major influence on the choice of ways to tackle a particular problem. Individually and as a group, they may have developed their own 'baggage'—established means of tackling problems —which they may be unwise, unwilling, and unable to shake off. Yet they are also subject to outside influences. In addition, there are others, including consultants or academics, examining the activities of public bodies from a number of different perspectives, whose approaches may attract the attention of performance auditors.

Performance audit is provided for in legislation of some kind in each of the countries we have studied. Perhaps not surprisingly, however, this gives little or no guidance as to how SAIs should actually undertake their work. The UK's National Audit Act 1983, for example, provides for access to documents and to those people holding such documents, as does the Ordinance containing directives for the RRV in Sweden. However, neither prescribes any particular approach once the SAI has exercised these rights. In the Netherlands, the provision on effectiveness auditing in the Budget and Accounting Act (Article 57) has been described as an 'experimental article' (Leeuw and Engwirda 1993/4, p. 18), allowing the Rekenkamer room to develop the auditing tradition considered most desirable and, presumably within this, making use of the methods considered most appropriate. In addition, although careful thought has been given by representatives of many SAIs to international standards for performance audit (see Contact Committee 1998), and guidance has been developed that includes reference to methods commonly employed, there are no detailed prescriptions governing how performance audit should be undertaken. Thus, when the RRV states (Swedish National Audit Office, undated) that it undertakes performance audit in accordance with 'generally accepted auditing standards for performance audits', such standards are neither mandatory nor particularly technical.

The lack of external direction is not surprising. Although SAIs may take account of auditees in deciding how to carry out an audit, discretion as to how their work is conducted is considered by all of them to be a fundamental aspect of their independence. The Rekenkamer, for example, considers it is 'free to decide on the way in which it conducts an audit and to determine what it publishes', including this among the 'foundations' and 'building blocks' for 'optimal auditing that is at once objective and independent' (Algemene Rekenkamer 1991, p. 5). Similarly, the RRV has stated clearly that 'No-one from outside the Division is entitled to dictate the way in which the audit is carried out' (Segergren 1992, p. 35). Instead, decisions on how to undertake individual studies, along with what methods to employ, are for teams within SAIs to propose, and for their senior management to approve. Thus, in the Cour des Comptes, a magistrate undertaking an audit (the *rapporteur*) has real scope to choose the most appropriate methods among those described in the *manuel de vérification*. If necessary, he or she can seek advice from a more senior member of staff (the *contre-rapporteur*). At the VTV the head of unit decides on the design of the study, and in the NAO the tools employed are outlined in detail within the overall framework for the design and execution of each study and come as part of a package presented to the comptroller and auditor general, which also addresses resources, the risks that make the study worth pursuing, and the anticipated level of interest in the proposal.

8.2 What SAIs Say About the Methods They Use for Performance Audit

Published material produced by SAIs provides some insight into how they view their use of methods of collecting and analysing information of performance audit. From our reading of these documents, a number of characteristics appear to be emphasized by the institutions. In particular,

1. the range of methods they use for performance audit is constantly evolving;
2. they are becoming more sophisticated in their choice of methods;
3. they are outward looking and fairly eclectic in their choice of methods; and
4. they take a pragmatic and practical approach to the application of particular methods.

Several of the SAIs have stated that their approach to the methods used is constantly evolving. The RRV has commented that the approaches applied in performance audit have been changing continuously (Swedish National Audit Office 1996, p. 19), while, significantly, the NAO's 1997 conference for performance auditors was entitled 'Innovations in Value for Money', the purpose being to draw attention to methods developed recently by certain audit teams within the office. Change has come quickly at the VTV, where staff referred to the loss of their 'familiar tool kit' and the need to replace it with new ways of working, following a period of rapid administrative change in the 1990s. Such developments were ongoing at the time we undertook our work, and one senior auditor considered it likely that the VTV would borrow more from evaluation research methods in the future (interviews, 1996 and 1997).

Such evolution is seen by SAIs very much in terms of growing sophistication of their approach to selecting and using methods. Our discussions with a number of senior auditors in several SAIs provided support for the view, expressed in published documents, that, compared with ten years ago, considerably more thought was given to designing studies and choosing appropriate ways of obtaining information. At the Rekenkamer, staff told us that attention to methods and methodology had become more systematic, while at the NAO auditors contrasted the detailed way in which they designed their studies now with more haphazard approaches of the 1980s. At the Cour and the VTV also, internal committees or training courses or manuals of advice had appeared addressing methodological issues. A number of our interviewees spoke of anticipating problems in evidence collection and analysis, and of thinking through how to reduce or eradicate them at the earliest possible stage.

The same SAIs consider that their approach to performance audit has become more outward-looking and eclectic, with their staff keen to look beyond the confines of the more traditional audit methods of documentary examination and interviews. An examination of the work of the VTV carried out between 1989 and 1992 concluded that performance audit in Finland should move to adopt a 'broad, research type approach'. An RRV consideration of methods (Swedish National Audit Bureau 1992a, p. 44) acknowledged that 'Performance auditing combines by tradition different methods and sources in audit work', and elsewhere the RRV has drawn parallels between the methods employed in its work and the evaluations and investigations carried out by research workers or government commissions, studies of the rationalization and restructuring of government carried out by special government bodies, and the assignments carried out for public bodies by consultants.

Similarly, the NAO has referred to its value-for-money work as drawing on techniques that 'have their origin in a number of different disciplines—audit, social science, management or the professions, for example' (NAO 1995d, p. 10). In addition, in recent years the NAO has shown interest in the work of different types of evaluation. Some of the internal VFM guidance issued in the early 1990s drew attention to the evaluation work of the GAO in the United States (although this did not spark off a rash of GAO-style evaluations), while more recently the Office has employed a research fellow with an evaluation background to try to identify ways in which evaluation methods might be drawn on more fully for audit work.

Despite this, SAIs have drawn clear distinctions between the way they and others examining public-sector activities undertake their work, emphasizing, in particular, what they consider to be the very practical nature of their role. In discussions, auditors at several SAIs made the point that they were not research institutes, but rather were concerned primarily to produce information that was 'useful' to their audiences, rather than to offer definitive insights into problems. Emphasizing the point, senior RRV officials suggested that auditors had to use professional, adequate, and cost-effective methods to get valid and reliable results, but would not necessarily look to innovate in methodological terms or make use of what they described as 'elaborate methodologies'.

8.3 Methods Used for Performance Audit

Against this background, we now consider what methods SAIs have actually used, and examine whether there has been any change over time. We are not aware of any systematic analysis of the methods used by SAIs, and so we reviewed performance audit reports published over a period of six years— an appropriate period of three years chosen from the 1980s contrasted with 1993–5. Table 8.1 summarizes our findings.

TABLE 8.1 Methods used by SAIs during the 1980s and 1990s

Method	VTV[a]		AR		RRV		NAO	
	1980s	1990s	1980s	1990s	1980s	1990s	1980s	1990s
Document examination	42	49	27	48	47	52	86	137
Interviews	23	41	27	46	39	50	86	137
Review of secondary data	11+ 7[b]	14+ 22	21	40	31	27	25	19
Questionnaires/surveys	4	16	1	14	15	15	6	44
Observation of activities (site visits)	24	—	2	5	10	12	27	47
Correspondence with auditee	—	—	8	1	—	—	—	—
Benchmarking/internal comparisons	12	18	—	—	1 (incl. international)	4 (incl. international)	—	5
International comparisons	—	7	—	—			7	14
Case examples	—	2	—	5	5	6	13	34
Statistical techniques	—	—	—	—	3	3	1	14
Consultation with third parties/expert groups	—	—	1	5	9	16	15	78
Modelling	—	—	—	—	—	2	—	2
In-depth interviews	—	—	—	1	—	—	—	6
Sample examination	—	—	9	14	—	—	20	27
Expert interviews	—	—	—	4	—	—	—	—
Focus groups	—	—	—	—	—	—	—	4
No. of reports examined	42	49	60[c]	60	65	79	86	137

[a] For the 1980s the most suitable period for each SAI was chosen for examination. For VTV this was 1985–7, for the Rekenkamer 1983–5, for the RRV 1983–5, and for NAO 1986–8.

[b] The first figure indicates the number of cases where results from earlier VTV audits were used as a source of information, while the second figure indicates the number of reports that refer to studies by research institutions or scientific research as sources of information.

[c] A sample of 60 reports for each period were chosen for examination. For the first period this amounted to around a third of all performance audits, and for the second period, around a half.

There are a number of caveats to the data.

1. We were able to count only those methods actually referred to in reports. However, as we discuss later, it is clear that SAIs have not always included such details in their publications. Thus, there may be an element of under-reporting.
2. We have assumed that auditors have accurately recorded the methods used.
3. Even where methods are recorded, some descriptions were sufficiently vague for there to be some doubt as to classification.
4. Our treatment of the Cour had to be different as it does not describe methods used in its reports: instead, only a record of the methods used—the *dossier liasses rapport*—is maintained with the documentary evidence supporting each report, making the information inaccessible within our resources. As a result, the discussion of methods used by the Cour in this chapter is based on interview evidence alone.

Valtiontalouden tarkastusvirasto (VTV)

Our analysis of the methods used by the VTV was limited by the fact that it has not been customary to explain the methods for data collection or analysis within reports. This was particularly true in the 1980s, and more information was available in the more recent period, along with some attempts to assess the validity of the results. Despite this, it would seem clear that in the first period performance auditors mainly employed what we might refer to as 'traditional' audit methods, such as document examination and interviews. Similar methods also predominated in the period 1993–5, when most reports stated that audits consisted of 'getting acquainted with the relevant documents' and 'having discussions' with those involved.

In addition, the data suggest a slight shift in the 1990s towards greater use of non-traditional methods, although this should not be exaggerated. There appears to have been greater use of questionnaires, although we have included all references to sending out questionnaires as a means of collecting data, even where, in many cases, what was done may have been closer to corresponding with representatives of audited bodies, rather than carrying out a systematic survey. There has been a tendency to use more comparisons with other bodies, although in many reports these findings are presented in an illustrative or anecdotal way, rather than as the basis for the conclusions and judgements of the report. Finally, some comment must be made about the apparent ending of site visits. This does not seem to have been the case; rather, it seems likely that the VTV auditors ceased considering such work as a special technique worth mentioning in their reports, particularly since the 1947 Act states specifically that audits should, as far as possible, take place on the premises of the audited body.

Cour des Comptes

Our discussions with staff at the Cour des Comptes also indicated a slight widening of the range of methods used by auditors. However, the examination of documentary evidence appears to have been the bedrock of audit work here as well, with the most commonly examined documents being internal reports and instruction manuals, as well as reports from other external auditors. Interviews and questionnaires also predominated in both periods, along with the review of existing statistical and accounting information.

During the 1990s, other methods have been employed on occasions. Meta-evaluation, drawing on work undertaken by ministries, has been used, while case studies have been used more frequently in recent years. In the 1990s programme evaluation techniques have been developed as a way of analysing the full effect, both direct and indirect, of government programmes (NAO 1996a, p. 66). The Cour is developing its evaluation methodology and has included text on evaluation in its *manuel de vérification*, the magistrates audit guide. Although there has not been widespread use of economic modelling and statistical techniques, some magistrates do employ them, and specific training courses have been set up. Benchmarking and other means of comparison have been used on many occasions.

Algemene Rekenkamer

The range of methods used primarily by the Rekenkamer appears to have been fairly stable between the two periods, with the picture obtained from the analysis of reports confirmed in interviews with staff. The most prevalent reported methods used by performance auditors in the sixty reports examined in the first period (1983–5) were the examination of documents and interviews. Analysing existing data was also a common activity, and a number of reports drew on information provided in correspondence with the auditee. Questionnaires and the direct observation of administrative processes were rarely used. In the second period (1993–5) the use of interviews and document examination again predominated, along with an examination and analysis of existing data. The most significant increase was in the use of questionnaires, while a number of other methods were used for the first time in the second period. These included case studies, in-depth interviews, and expert interviews.

Riksrevisionsverket (RRV)

A majority of the RRV's performance audits in both periods appear to have made use of the analysis of documents and interviews, and many involved examinations or analysis of existing data. Table 8.1 also indicates the use of a small number of other methods. In both periods an identical number of reports made use of questionnaires, although this represented a decreasing proportion. The second period saw a growth in the number of reports using explicit consultation with others, such as seminars or expert groups, as a way of gathering information. There was also an increase, from a low base, in the occurrence of benchmarking or international comparisons. In contrast, limited use appears to have been made of statistical and modelling techniques. Case studies have been used occasionally, the term here being used where auditors had visited the audited body to gather new information. In general, there appears to have been a broadening of the range of methods employed between the two periods, although the tendency has not been particularly strong, as even in the early 1980s some studies employed non-traditional audit research methods.

National Audit Office (NAO)

Perhaps the most noticeable change can be seen at the NAO. Here again, we note the importance of document examination and interviews. Indeed, in the 1986–8 period these appear to have been the major, if not the only, methods employed for most of the studies examined. In addition, the NAO's other main means of obtaining information were site visits, and the examination and analysis of existing data, perhaps from the department or bodies involved. Questionnaires and international comparisons were rarely used.

The second period saw a continuation of the use of interviews and document examination in all studies, as well as site visits in a large proportion of cases. In addition, however, a number of developments appear to have taken place. The figures suggest a noticeable growth in the use of questionnaires and surveys, which have become an important feature of NAO work in the 1990s. In 1994, for example, twenty studies published in that year made use of this method. Another feature has been the growth in consultation with third parties, with more than half of reports examined from the later period making extensive use of consultation with interested parties.

Finally, a feature of the second period has been what we might call a small-scale, but nevertheless noticeable, increase in experimentation and thus the use, on one or two occasions, of new methods such as focus groups, decision analysis, and modelling, not seen before. Discussions with NAO staff indicate that further experimentation has taken place since our analysis occurred. These findings accord with other research which has suggested that the NAO's reports of the early to mid-1990s appeared 'methodologically considerably more adventurous than those of the previous period' (Pollitt and Summa 1996, pp. 40–1).

8.4 Implications of the Data

The findings from our analysis of SAI reports are not out of line with lists of methods commonly employed by performance auditors that have appeared elsewhere. The RRV identified what it described as the 'most common techniques' (Swedish National Audit Bureau 1993, pp. 87–94). These were: interviews, seminars, and 'hearings', experts and reference groups, direct observations, studies of documentation, case studies, questionnaires, processing statistics, and making estimates. A more recent INTOSAI working group, which acknowledged that 'performance audits can draw upon a large variety of methods and techniques' (Contact Committee 1998, p. 164), added audit sampling, focus groups, benchmarking, before–after studies, quasi-experimental methods, meta-evaluation, cost–benefit analysis, and cost-effectiveness analysis.

In view of this, we believe that Table 8.1 allows us to draw several conclusions about the methods used by our SAIs over the past two decades (considered in more detail below):

1. There has been a tendency in each SAI to employ a slightly wider range of methods in the most recent period, compared with the 1980s, although more so at the NAO, for example, than the VTV.
2. Despite these developments, SAIs continue to rely heavily on document examination and interview evidence in their work, as well as to make widespread use of existing secondary material.
3. There are signs of increased consultation with users and providers of public services, evidenced by the growth in the use of questionnaires, as well as consultation with other interested parties in various ways.
4. In general, where they have branched out beyond more traditional audit methods, SAIs appear to have drawn primarily from the social sciences, rather than other fields such as statistics.
5. Although there has been growing interest in forms of benchmarking, there has been only limited use of international comparisons.

8.5 A Widening in the Range of Methods Used

The data summarized in Table 8.1 do not suggest that a revolution has taken place within our SAIs between the two periods examined, in terms of the methods employed in performance audit work. If anything, it suggests that SAI rhetoric in this aspect of its work, examined earlier in the chapter, is slightly in advance of practice, with the range of methods employed not yet fully reflecting the degree of interest shown in finding new ways of undertaking the work. However, in our view there is evidence of a slight widening of the range of methods used, and stronger signs of growing interest in new ways of carrying out examinations. Thus, we see the appearance, for example, of focus groups (NAO), the more routine use of questionnaires (several SAIs), greater use of international comparisons (VTV), and some first attempts at modelling (RRV and NAO) and meta-evaluation (Rekenkamer and Cour des Comptes).

8.6 Continued Reliance on Documentary and Interview Evidence

More significantly, Table 8.1 suggests overwhelmingly that documentary and interview evidence are the two most important methods employed in performance audit, a finding in line with our expectations, with statements made by SAIs, and with the work of other researchers. The RRV has described the study of official and unofficial documents as of 'central importance' to an audit (Swedish National Audit Office 1996, p. 85), while the *manuel de vérification* used by the Cour des Comptes stresses the importance of magistrates starting their work by checking that they have the proper documents regarding the legal environment in which the organization being audited exists, as well as the activity itself.

The reasons behind the central importance of documents do not seem hard to identify, and appear closely linked to the unique role played by SAIs. The strength of their rights of access to documents—a feature of their work in contrast to many other types of researchers—is crucial. The Algemene Rekenkamer, for example, has stated that, 'Although [their powers of access to documents and officials] have been debated in parliament during the post-war years, problems rarely occur in practice' (Algemene Rekenkamer 1989, p. 31), and this is also true for the NAO. In extreme circumstances, some SAIs can enforce these rights of access. In France, those who try to prevent the Cour from doing its duty may be liable to a fine of up to 100,000F (article L 140–1 of the *Code des juridictions financières*). Similarly, in Finland the VTV's powers under the 1947 State Audit Act allow for fines against anyone failing to provide documents on request within a set time limit, a provision they have apparently yet to use (NAO 1996a, p. 45). There is also provision in legislation for the VTV to request the preparation of explanatory papers by auditees to aid their work.

SAIs see other strengths in document examination. At the Cour des Comptes great store is placed on being able to produce rigorous evidence to substantiate findings and recommendations, and documents provide this. The NAO regards it as 'a very efficient way of collecting evidence', while the RRV has emphasized the 'richness' of the written documentation available in most cases as a result of the activities of government agencies (Swedish National Audit Bureau 1992a, p. 44). Documents also assist in the more confrontational aspects of audit work. Where there is a need to convince audited bodies about audit findings (and, in the case of the NAO, to reach agreement on the text of a draft report), documents, particularly from within the audited body, are generally considered by all to be authoritative evidence; and they give a contemporary view of events, rather than the rationalizations that might emerge from interviews conducted months or years after the events in question.

The second most common means of gathering evidence employed by SAIs is the interview. As with access to documents, an SAI's ability to require officials to answers questions, in some countries (e.g. France) at the risk of being fined should they refuse, is a powerful weapon. From an auditor's point of view, interviews help impart an overview of an activity or allow for clarification of areas of uncertainty, and provide the opportunity to seek quick access to, and guidance about, key documents and other material. Additionally, in most cases auditees expect to have such discussions in order that they can explain their work. In France, for instance, interviews usually begin with the head of the organization under examination and later involve those at a more technical level with the detailed knowledge. Interviews are organized not only with staff members, but also with those working outside the organization who have contact with it. Thus, civil servants responsible for the field in which the audited body operates, external auditors, or other interested parties will be interviewed to obtain a comprehensive view.

Our discussions with staff at SAIs suggest that greater attention has been given to interview technique in recent years, and all now provide training of some kind on how to conduct interviews and minimize obstacles to their success. There are also indications that greater thought has been given by auditors to conducting interviews. A greater variety of interview approaches can be seen in the work of some SAIs. Although many remain of the 'informal conversation' type, designed to establish basic facts, others make use of interview guides containing a list of topics to be explored in a structured manner, or are based on written questionnaires sent to interviewees in advance. A minor development in the second period at the NAO and Rekenkamer has been the use of in-depth interviews, seeking qualitative data to augment quantitative material. Despite this, some (see e.g. Pollitt and Summa 1996, p. 41) have suggested that the transparency of approaches used by SAIs tends to fall short of those employed by academic evaluators, with interview schedules seldom included in published reports, and the number and types of interview, as well as the conditions, seldom published.

8.7 The Use of Secondary Material

Another common means of obtaining audit evidence has been the review and analysis of secondary material. At its most basic, SAIs use the work of others—perhaps the reports of internal auditors within a body or consultants employed by them—as part of evidence gathered for a study. They may draw on data available at the audited body or elsewhere (see Goldsworthy 1996 for an example from the NAO), perhaps examining it from new perspectives or using computer software to provide significantly more data than had been available within the audited body.

Associated with this has been the development of interest in meta-evaluation by the Algemene Rekenkamer and Cour des Comptes. The Rekenkamer has examined the use of the large number of evaluations undertaken by government ministries and agencies in the Netherlands (Kraan and

Rozendal 1997). Meta-evaluations have also been used occasionally by the Cour in the 1990s; for example, a study of highways policy in 1992 took two evaluations undertaken by government ministries and studied the quality of the work, comparing their methods and seeking to explain the differences they noticed in their results.

In addition, the appearance of bibliographies in some audit reports (for example in those of the NAO) suggests that some auditors are starting to undertake more systematic literature searches for relevant published material. In general, and in contrast to the work of other researchers, audit reports have tended not to highlight this aspect of their work by including footnotes or bibliographies. As has been noted elsewhere, 'A typical academic evaluation will be festooned with references to other studies and may well include some kind of formal literature review. Such papers convey a sense of the evaluators adding to some cumulative and collective body of knowledge and insight. SAI reports read more as stand-alone products' (Pollitt and Summa 1996, p. 41).

8.8 The Development of Consultation with Users and Suppliers of Public Services

A theme discussed elsewhere in the book (particularly in Chapters 7 and 9) has been the way in which SAIs have engaged much more with other parties in recent years, be they auditees, the recipients of the services under examination, the audiences for their work such as parliamentarians, or the media. To some extent, this is also reflected in some of the developments identified in our examination of methods and in the increased consultation with interested parties of all sorts during audits.

The most popular method aimed at eliciting the opinions of others has been the questionnaire or survey. All SAIs in this study have used them, although they appear to vary considerably in format and style, and in terms of whom they address. At the NAO questionnaires, organized in-house or conducted for the NAO by outside market research firms, and conducted either face-to-face, by telephone, or by post, have sought the views of, among others, users of museums, galleries, and overseas embassies, or companies making use of particular government services. The RRV has also used questionnaires on many occasions, seeing them as valuable for obtaining information from a 'large and often geographically widespread population' and establishing 'facts that are not available in any other way' (Swedish National Audit Bureau 1993, p. 92).

A development at the NAO in the mid-1990s, although apparently not elsewhere, has been the use of focus groups. An effective example can be seen in a study of the handling of calls from the members of the public by the police in London (NAO 1994b), where focus groups explored the ways in which officers dealt with calls. One outcome of this was a list of twelve key rules for dealing with callers which were included in the report as recommendations in the study, while the discussions also helped identify problems in the working of the communications room, and provided quotes to illustrate the views of officers. As an indication of its faith in the method, the NAO has since produced a guide for staff on making use of focus groups (NAO, 1997e).

Another development, perhaps most pronounced at the RRV and the NAO, has been the growth in the extent of consultation with third parties in the course of designing and executing audits. In part, this appears to reflect a desire to ensure that reports are authoritative and accurate, by allowing as many interested parties as possible to provide evidence. It also increases the likelihood that errors will be identified prior to publication. Consultation takes a number of forms, from simply interviewing third parties, to perhaps involving them in identifying future audit projects. The RRV obtains outside views (Swedish National Audit Office 1993, pp. 88–9) through seminars, where experts, researchers, and government representatives are invited to help identify new ideas or, during a study, to discuss and test the observations and conclusions of the audit team. Hearings, similar to seminars, are also used at the start of audits to enable the team quickly to obtain relevant information about the field to be studied.

8.9 The Predominance of Social Science over Other Methods

The appearance of questionnaires and focus groups within the methods employed by SAIs indicates that, where they have expanded beyond traditional audit methods, SAIs have tended to look towards the social sciences for inspiration. Another example of this trend is the use, on occasion, of longer case studies or, more usually, shorter case examples to help highlight particular points or explore certain topics. Case examples have been used to inject life into their reports, a point that staff at the Rekenkamer and the NAO considered was of particular importance in helping non-specialists, particularly parliamentarians, to understand their reports. Some NAO reports have used a small number of case studies to form the basis of a whole report (such as in a study of the management of overseas programme aid—NAO 1994c—which examined aid to four countries). More usually, a large number of small case examples have been used throughout many reports to illustrate particular points, provide supplementary information, or add colour and insight. The RRV has also shown itself an advocate of this method, recognizing its value to provide in-depth cause and effect analysis, often in combination with other methods (Swedish National Audit Bureau 1993, p. 91).

Many examinations by SAIs involve an element of evidence-gathering by observation, although most stop short of what researchers might consider ethnographic methods. Much tends to be fairly passive observation, intended mainly for familiarization purposes. More participative evidence collection has been much rarer, with perhaps the most adventurous NAO example being where an auditor visited an Antarctic research station to gain first-hand experience of their work. In general, SAIs appear to have been cautious about this kind of technique for collecting primary evidence, considering that, short of photographic records, it can be difficult to substantiate findings obtained in this way if they are disputed. Auditee aversion to such a method may also be a factor; the NAO's approach of visiting a sample of heritage sites anonymously in 1993 to assess the quality of service provided does not appear to have been repeated, even though the audited body agreed the methodology.

In contrast to the use of qualitative social science research tools, SAIs appear to have made much less use of economic models and concepts. At the VTV, staff advised us that economic techniques were used less now than in the past, and staff at the Rekenkamer observed that there had been a lack of economists within the office over the years. While some NAO reports indicate an awareness of concepts such as deadweight and displacement effect, and have commented on whether auditees have made use of such approaches, they have very rarely been employed by auditors themselves (see Roberts and Pollitt 1994). At the Cour, staff reported that there had been some interest in cost–benefit analysis, for example in a recent examination of family allowances, while at the NAO some use has been made of modelling, in particular in a defence report (NAO 1993f), where, in order to look at the financial impact of departures from departmental guidelines, the NAO constructed a model of the 'average' high-value fixed-price contract and estimated the scale of premium payments under the Ministry's scheme. SAIs appear also to have made fairly limited use of statistical analysis. Time-series analysis does appear, but multiple regression analysis and correlation have been infrequently employed. Sensitivity analysis or its absence in departmental reviews has often been referred to in NAO reports, but the technique itself has been used less frequently.

8.10 Drawing Comparisons

For many researchers, drawing comparisons between organizations is an obvious way of forming a view about performance, but our analysis suggests that this is far less so for the performance audit work of SAIs. Table 8.1 shows that high-level comparisons between audited bodies and others were used by the VTV in the period 1993–5. A number of NAO reports have also made use of different kinds of benchmarking and comparisons in recent years (NAO 1997b). Again, however, these have tended to be 'high-level' comparisons between bodies, although courses covering performance and process benchmarking have been delivered recently at the NAO, and there are some examples of this kind of work in reports produced since the mid-1990s.

Despite this, there is evidence to support the view that 'SAIs appear to be slightly more cautious than evaluators about entering into comparative analysis that goes beyond the organizations immediately under investigation' (Pollitt and Summa 1996, p. 41). As the article suggests, this may well reflect difficulties with agreeing on conclusions drawn on this basis, which is, in itself, a reflection of problems in establishing suitable comparisons. Such problems appear to be magnified when international comparisons are considered. Although such work has been carried out—for example, reports by the RRV compared the performance of the Riksgaldskontoret (the National Debt Office) and the decentralized rail authorities with corresponding bodies abroad (Swedish National Audit Office 1995a, p. 15)—in both cases exact comparisons could not be drawn, and the purpose was more to widen the perspectives of the discussions. Similar work has been carried out by the NAO, with studies undertaken in the 1990s proving more substantial in terms of analysis and research than those of the 1980s, but some of the auditors involved have acknowledged the time and resource constraints on such work, and the need for it to begin before the main fieldwork is under way so that it can be ready in time (Goldsworthy 1996, p. 9).

8.11 Factors Influencing the Methods Used by SAIs

We now turn to look in more detail at the factors—both internal and external—that appear to have influenced the choices made by SAIs, as well as those that may have constrained the use of a wider range of methods. In their repertoire of methods, change (to date) has been incremental rather than revolutionary.

Factors encouraging interest in a wider range of methods

The changing and increasingly complex environment in which SAIs have operated has, perhaps, had the most significant effect on the amount of attention given to developing sounder study methodologies and, within this, thinking more about the methods employed. Several SAIs have drawn a clear link between the growing complexity of public administration in their country and the need for clearer approaches and sharper tools to assess the performance of auditees. The NAO has stated that 'We are continually striving to improve the quality of our reports and respond to the demands of the environment in which we operate' (NAO 1995a, p. 16). One aspect of this has been to apply 'rigorous methodologies that provide robust, defensible findings and conclusions'. Similarly, the RRV has stated that, as 'new demands replace old demands, and conditions constantly change, performance auditors will have to be prepared to follow these developments, review priorities and use new approaches and methods in their work' (Swedish

National Audit Office 1995a). In Finland, too, the reform of the state administration in the early 1990s led the VTV to think of new ways of carrying out its work. Meanwhile, in France, general demands for greater transparency in public administration have led the Cour to adapt its procedures in various ways.

As we discussed in Chapter 4, these public management reforms appear to have impacted on SAIs' choice of methods in a number of ways. In the first place, improvements in the quality and quantity of performance information characteristics of public management reforms have also opened up new possibilities for making use of certain methods not considered possible before. We noted earlier how the NAO has begun to look towards benchmarking, and there has also been growing interest in the examination of performance measures. Both initiatives become more feasible with the availability of improved information. In the Netherlands, the expansion of programme evaluations within ministries and agencies has encouraged the Rekenkamer to develop the use of meta-evaluations.

The changing approaches to public service provision have also led to increased interest in different methods. In the UK, the importance attached by successive governments to the quality of public services—most notably under the 'Citizen's Charter', but also more generally in a range of other initiatives—appears to have led directly to the growth of effort by the NAO to gauge public satisfaction levels or public opinion, in particular through the use of questionnaires, which had hardly been used at all in the C&AG's reports before the late 1980s, but also through focus groups. Similarly, the fragmentation of government in the UK has opened up the possibility, as yet not fully exploited, of a variety of benchmarking studies, drawing comparisons between these bodies.

The growing professionalism and the greater flexibility of the public sector in recent years—for example the greater recruitment of specialists, the wider exposure of public bodies to outside influences and the increased number of senior figures appointed from the private sector—have also led to different attitudes within public bodies to the criticism traditionally associated with audit. Unused to such public criticism, more auditees have responded by questioning the basis of this censure, and SAIs have thus found it more important to have watertight methodologies.

Within SAIs, a number of factors have encouraged wider thinking about methods, including the attitude of the heads of SAIs, the example set by colleagues who use innovative methods, and the introduction of staff with new skills and experience. Staff at the NAO told us that Sir John Bourn, the head of the office since 1988, had encouraged interest in more innovative methods, and there had also been senior management backing for workshops designed to raise awareness of new methods that might be appropriate for VFM studies. At the RRV, the encouragement of the current auditor general has had a similar effect in stimulating interest in broadening performance audit approaches, while at the Cour the *premier président* recently created a committee, chaired by a former *président de chambre*, to consider new methods.

Discussions with auditors in several SAIs revealed how important the example of their peers had been in encouraging interest in new methods among performance auditors. As a result, another key factor in widening the range of methods has been the presence of staff within SAIs with particular skills. Staff in the Algemene Rekenkamer considered that the relatively common use of statistical sampling techniques in their work in the 1990s reflected the presence, for some years, of a specialist statistician in the office who provided advice. Conversely, they linked the very limited use of quantitative techniques to the lack of economists and others with such skills. We noted in Chapter 7 that the Cour had begun to encourage the recruitment of individuals with specific disciplinary skills, such as engineering. The recruitment of staff with a wider range of disciplines, and the use of consultants on most studies, also appear to have enabled the NAO to draw on new methods; whereas in the 1980s professional staff were almost all trained or experienced accountants, the NAO has subsequently recruited a significant number of people with expertise in economics, operational research, programme evaluation, performance measurement, and statistics, to work on studies or be part of the VFM guidance team.

Finally, there are two other significant influences on the development of the methods used by the NAO, if not the other SAIs. First, the role played by a number of public administration academics in encouraging greater interest in new ways of undertaking performance audits has been important. Since 1993 all VFM reports have been reviewed against a number of criteria by a team of academics, and their comments and recommendations have helped to formulate NAO guidance and create a climate where performance auditors are expected to, at least, consider the scope for innovation. Observations on methods used have been wide-ranging, and comments have fed directly into internal NAO guidance. Second, the desire to identify potential financial savings, a key published measure of the NAO's success discussed in Chapter 10, has encouraged greater attention to the ways in which examinations are conducted and the methods used.

Factors working against a widening of the range of methods

If these factors have had some influence on encouraging an interest in using a wider range of methods, or a more sophisticated use of existing ones, perhaps the most important factor working the other way has been SAIs' perception of the strength of their existing tools, primarily the ability to demand documents and require answers from staff within government bodies. That SAIs make extensive use of, and have great faith in, interview and documentary evidence is not surprising, given the statutory powers provided to them. Staff at the Rekenkamer suggested that the relatively limited range of methods used in recent years reflected the fact that they could obtain the answers needed from a small range of tried and tested methods. Thus, the extensive powers of SAIs may have had a dampening effect on the need for SAIs to look at other ways of obtaining information.

In each country, the choices of methods are guided also by the SAI's own self-imposed standards (influenced in part by internationally agreed guidelines), by its view of what performance audit entails, and by judgements about what can be achieved within the time scale and budget set for a study. The choice of method will also reflect what auditors and the senior management of SAIs consider are appropriate ways of collecting the amount and type of evidence they consider adequate. To this end, the nature of SAIs and audit may well have encouraged a degree of conservatism about appropriate methods which worked against innovation. Given their constitutional positions, SAIs are keen to maintain their reputations as providers of reliable reports, and it is perhaps not surprising that they have not rushed to embrace new ideas without some evidence that they are sound and reliable.

The backgrounds and knowledge of SAI staff are also likely to have contributed to a concentration on more traditional audit methods. Largely trained in accounting, audit, law, public administration, and social sciences, performance auditors have, not surprisingly, looked to these disciplines to inform their thinking. At the VTV, staff interviewed suggested that many auditors did not have a very wide knowledge of different methods that could be used, and some staff at the Rekenkamer noted the difficulties the office had had over the years in recruiting economists and bankers to complement the social science and public administration emphasis among their staff. In the past, some observers (see Anand 1988) have drawn a link between the NAO's limited attempts to undertake effectiveness studies and the type of training provided to staff, which involved a minimal mandatory level of training in economic techniques. Staff at the NAO indicated that things had moved on a long way since then, although some still felt that their office was uneasy about innovative methods, unless they could be guaranteed to work.

Another constraint has perhaps been concern about the authority of evidence gained from methods previously untried by SAIs. Technical guidance states that 'The requirement to obtain competent, relevant and reliable audit evidence (INTOSAI Auditing Standards, paragraph 152) will normally influence the decisions taken by the auditor regarding appropriate methodologies. For performance audits in particular, the auditor will be concerned about the validity and reliability of the methods used to collect and analyse data' (Contact Committee 1998, p. 160). Reports must also be based on evidence capable of standing up to scrutiny in the review or clearance processes and in the eyes of specialist opinion. According to one former Rekenkamer auditor, in general 'Empirical evidence from mail, telephone or face-to-face surveys is not enough foundation for auditors' judgements so the analysis and conclusions rely heavily on documentary evidence' (Leeuw 1996, p. 52).

Despite the number of interviews often undertaken during fieldwork for a study, NAO staff emphasized that these were rarely regarded as authoritative enough on their own to include in a report unless opinions or perceptions were considered the most valid measure for assessing success or failure (see also Keen 1999). Such considerations restrict the ability of the SAI to experiment, and are a factor encouraging the conservatism referred to above.

Given the efforts, described elsewhere, that SAIs make to satisfy their main audiences, including parliamentarians and the government, the absence of much pressure from this direction in the past may well have acted as a discouragement to innovate. In the UK, there is little evidence of interest in Parliament in the methods used in studies; rather, attention has been focused on the main messages and the conclusions and recommendations. Where concerns have been expressed about study methodologies, for example poor response rates to NAO questionnaires, disquiet has been more a concern that the work of a parliamentary officer had been ignored than about any methodological shortcomings of the results. The same seems to hold for the Rekenkamer, although the use of case studies and more qualitative evidence was seen by some at the Rekenkamer as a reflection of the interest shown by parliament in real-life examples, rather than detailed statistical analysis.

In contrast, the interest shown by auditees in the way SAIs seek to obtain and analyse their evidence may have also acted as a constraint, especially given the efforts made by some SAIs to elicit the views of auditees on methods to be used. Recent NAO guidance emphasizes the need to 'test innovative methodologies or established methodologies being applied in new areas, and gain the audited body's agreement to the use of these methodologies, especially sampling and survey strategies, in order to avoid misunderstandings at a later stage about the acceptability of findings or extrapolations' (NAO 1997c). It is impossible to say to what extent an auditee's views result in SAIs dropping particular methods, although the relatively small number of comparisons between bodies in NAO reports (Pollitt and Summa 1996, p. 42) can perhaps be linked to this since, in general, bodies regard their work as unique, and comparisons with others, even in the same field, as impossible because of different circumstances and environments.

Time considerations inevitably impact on the range of methods that can be employed within the fieldwork period of a study, which might only last between three and six months. The fact that in the 1980s it was unusual for any audit examination at the VTV to take more than 50 days' work inevitably restricted the scope for more time-consuming methods. More recently, the amount of time taken over studies has grown significantly, so that by 1995 the average was 223 days to carry out work leading to a final report (NAO 1996a, p. 49), making it more realistic to try innovative approaches. Time constraints also mean that SAIs have tended, for example, not to conduct examinations tracking the progress of groups of individuals over time. Such studies would be possible, but currently do not fit in with the ways in which SAIs tend to plan their work. In part, this reflects the need to fit into the broader political processes, where there is an expectation among recipients of SAI reports of a regular stream of deliveries. In the UK, this has led some to suggest that the link between the NAO and Parliament constrains the use of methods 'because the need to satisfy political time-scales may exclude the possibility of more ambitious, elaborate and lengthy studies' (Roberts and Pollitt 1994, p. 547).

Inevitably, cost considerations are also important, and some SAI staff commented that there was a clear conflict between trying to introduce more sophisticated methods at a time when resources were tightly controlled. Staff in several SAIs commented on the need to ensure that methods were cost-effective, given the requirement on them, as on any other public institution, to keep down costs and increase efficiency. The NAO has stated on a number of occasions that it seeks to reduce the cost of its studies (NAO 1996c), and staff suggested that this has impacted on the ability of auditors to utilize more expensive methods, or on its ability to confirm findings from various sources. Such consideration may have encouraged SAIs towards more 'traditional' audit methods, considered by some to be cheap (Anand 1988).

8.12 Coverage of Methodology in the Reports of SAIs

Given their role in ensuring the accountability of others for their performance, SAIs might be expected to explain the methods employed in their work as a key part of their own accountability. In addition, given the political sensitivities associated with many of the subjects examined by SAIs, it might be thought that auditees and those at whom the reports are aimed would expect methods to be fully explained to give credibility to findings that can often have significant impacts on government policies and personal reputations, and which gain widespread media attention. Finally, it might be assumed that, given the similarities between performance audit and research of a more academic nature, SAI reports would bear great similarities to research reports, which provide detailed methodologies and sources.

Overall, these assumptions appear to be only partly true, with significant variations between countries. Consideration has been given elsewhere (Pollitt and Summa 1997b) to the amount of information that SAIs publish about their activities. This review found a wide variety of approaches. From our research, a similarly varied picture appears in the amount of information provided about methods in SAI reports, with the ones publishing the most information about themselves (NAO and RRV) also revealing the most in their reports about their methods.

Reports from the RRV vary considerably in the extent to which they describe the methods used. Some, from both periods, mention them only in passing, while others contain a more explicit methodological discussion.

Some include appendices showing the methods used, and on occasion coverage of methodology has been even more comprehensive. A report on human resource management (Swedish National Audit Bureau 1992a), for example, included an appendix on the experience gained from the methods used in the project, which discussed a range of issues including 'in-depth interviews and software as methods and sources'. However, there appears no clear connection between the nature of the audit project, its methodological complexity, and the appearance of a methodological discussion in the report. Rather, the logic appears to have been that, when new or inventive methods are employed, they are covered in some detail in the published report. More recently, methods have been described on a more regular and relatively standardized basis in the RRV's reports.

Something of a shift appears to have taken place over time in the reports of the NAO. In the 1980s few gave more than scanty details of methods employed. Where methods were mentioned—for example questionnaires—few details were provided of sample sizes, questions asked, etc. In contrast, a feature of NAO reports in the mid-1990s has been the increased amount of space given over to outlining methodology. Many reports now provide a brief summary of the approach and tools used in the introductory paragraphs, and the trend has also been to include a table listing the work carried out in some detail. Despite this, some still consider that it is not always clear how auditors reached their conclusions (Keen 1999).

Explanations of the methods used in studies do not appear to be given the same prominence in the other SAIs. At the Cour des Comptes details of techniques used are generally not included in reports, and the Algemene Rekenkamer's Board has not encouraged the inclusion of methodological details, although there are brief references to the work undertaken in some reports. At the VTV, methodology has been explicitly addressed in only a few reports, although in the 1990s some have discussed methods and sources of data, and in some cases even the validity of the results. In general, though, there has been little information about the structure and content of interviews, and in only a few cases were details of questionnaires, such as sample sizes, stated.

Overall, the evidence suggests that SAIs vary significantly in the extent to which they explain their methodology, although there has been a tendency in some SAIs in recent years to provide more information. In the case of the NAO, this has been encouraged by the academics who undertake the report review process referred to earlier. In trying to explain the paucity of information, we should perhaps remember the role of the reports and at whom they are aimed. In the UK, for example, they are aimed primarily at a committee of MPs, most, if not all, of whom will have little prior knowledge of the subject and insufficient time to digest much technical material. In the past, these MPs have indicated that they require material in a summarized format and, as a result, the NAO has tended to produce shorter reports, more readily comprehensible to the lay reader. In these circumstances there has been limited space to include extensive discussion of methods. Equally, some have suggested there has been little incentive to do so, arguing that limited interest among MPs has led 'the NAO to excise the kind of technical or methodological detail which would "turn off" an audience of lay MPs (though this could presumably be circumvented if the NAO published more than one version of its reports)' (Roberts and Pollitt 1994, p. 547).

8.13 Conclusion: What the Analysis of Methods Employed Suggests about the Nature of Performance Audit

We conclude this chapter by making three observations about the light our analysis of methods has cast on the nature of performance audit itself.

1. While performance has become a more hybrid form of enquiry, it nevertheless retains the audit tradition at its core.
2. While performance auditors have become more sophisticated in their work, there is still a debate about whether performance audit is a scientific discipline.
3. The heavy reliance on official documentary evidence and interviews with key players underlines the accountability role of performance audit work.

The rhetoric of our SAIs presents performance audit as very much a hybrid form of enquiry, happy to draw on other disciplines for methods as necessary. There is, as we have seen, no prescribed list of performance audit methods; instead, auditors have started to scan the horizon for whatever appears helpful in enabling them to address the new issues they face. An indication of this continuing search for new ideas can be seen, for example, in the interest at the NAO during 1997 in presentations on the work of risk management professionals and on asymmetric information, and in the ongoing work at the Rekenkamer into meta-evaluation. Such interest re-emphasizes that performance audit is a new discipline, still finding its feet, and displaying a healthy aptitude for learning. Yet, while SAIs demonstrate some willingness to be tempted into experimentation, they tend also to approach new methods with circumspection and a belief in their proven approaches that makes it hard for them to eschew old ways and take up new ones which they fear may have less rigour and pedigree. As a result, notwithstanding the developments described above, performance audit still has audit very much at its core.

Our second observation is that, despite this interest in the work of other specialists, and the adaptation of certain methods from them, there is still much debate among and between practitioners and observers about whether performance audit can claim to be a scientific discipline. Several views were advanced during the course of our study. Some have pointed to the absence in most reports of the kind of methodological discussions that feature in the work of many academic researchers, and have noted how performance auditors tend to make little reference to the work of others, again a common feature of the work of many researchers. Two members of our team have suggested elsewhere that auditors 'will plan their audits in a fairly pragmatic fashion, selecting on a more-or-less ad hoc basis whatever tools and methods seem potentially useful for shedding light on the chosen program or institution' (Pollitt and Summa 1996, p. 42). A similar view is held by Keen, who, on the basis of a substantial amount of time spent working with NAO auditors, has commented on the 'essentially atheoretical' nature of value-for-money examinations, noting that 'different findings were not fitted into an explicit theoretical framework, and questions of causation were not considered' (Keen 1999).

Others we spoke to took issue with such views. A number of practitioners at the NAO argued that developments mean that many recent studies do have a theoretical or conceptual framework behind them, even if they are not necessarily on display. Recent RRV studies on social security matters have clearly been undertaken using an explicit model linking policy intentions and end results (Swedish National Audit Office 1995b). In addition, there has been growing international contact and exchange of ideas on performance audit, increased specialization among those carrying out the work (to the extent that many performance auditors would not see themselves returning to financial audit work), and the development of an increasingly sophisticated technical literature. A distinct cadre of performance auditors has emerged, but the debate over whether theirs is a scientific discipline seems unresolved.

Finally, the heavy reliance on document examination, interviews, and secondary data discussed above appears to underline the importance of the 'guardianship' and accountability role of the performance auditor's work. Chelimsky (1985, p. 497) has emphasized that auditors are concerned with tracking down authoritative documents and with verification. While this comment applied primarily to financial audit, the emphasis on obtaining and making use of key documents—'the Crown Jewels', as one auditor put it to us—clearly remains as important as ever in performance audit. The view that the verification role is strongly present in performance audit is supported by Keen (1999), who suggests that 'VFM work is, then, a form of audit . . . concerned with checking on processes (whether something has happened), rather than asking more open questions about the nature of things or why they happen, which would be characteristic of many types of evaluation and social science research'.

Again, not all those we spoke to agreed with these views. Some at the NAO argued that they had shifted from verification to assessment some years ago; others saw different reports featuring at different places along a continuum which stretched between verification and assessment. However, even at the assessment end of the scale, we should not be surprised that Supreme Audit Institutions remain concerned with establishing *what* occurred as much as *why*. Despite the developments that have occurred and been described above, nothing in their founding legislation, or in the expectations of those they work for, has changed to allow performance auditors to abandon their important role as guardians of the taxpayer's interests. And, no other bodies have been created to take on the role of establishing that public funds have been used as intended.

9

Products

Marit Waerness

9.1 The Plan of the Chapter

This chapter will deal with the *outputs* of performance audit, the products that normally appear at the end of performance audit investigations (Figure 1.1 above). Previous chapters have analysed the role and development of performance audit and have studied how auditors work. Consideration of output should, however, be separated from that of craft and method. One cannot always deduce from the audit work itself what the outputs will be, and what they will look like. Consequently, we must first define more precisely what we mean by performance audit 'output' and describe the main outputs of the five SAIs in our study. Thereafter the following questions are addressed:

1. What types of performance audit product were produced by the five SAIs during the period studied?
2. What are the characteristics of these outputs (number, size, structure, appearance, communication process, etc.)?
3. Have there been significant changes during the period studied?

The chapter concludes with a discussion of whether there is any general trend concerning SAIs' performance audit output over time, and if so, how it may be related to the public management reforms described in Chapter 3.

9.2 What Is Meant by Performance Audit 'Products'?

By performance audit products, we mean *those information outputs that are directed towards one or more external audiences and are the result of the SAIs' performance audit work*. Often this will mean written performance audit reports. However, there are also other kinds of outputs: summaries and extracts, handbooks, newsletters, information brochures, memoranda, notes, seminar papers, and annual reports which summarize and justify the performance audit work of the institution concerned. The development of these other information products will be taken into consideration later in the chapter.

Note that by this definition we exclude the main products emanating from financial or regularity audit, except where there is no strict division between performance audit and other types of audit and the products contain a mixture of audit information.

9.3 Why Study Output?

The audit reports are important for several reasons. They are the main record of what the SAIs have found in their fieldwork and the principal means by which the auditors communicate with their main audience/s. They also give away (intentionally or unintentionally) quite a bit about what kind of organization the SAI is. And they have become one way in which the SAI can put figures to how much work it has completed—what it has achieved.

As Chapter 3 made clear, one important aspect of the public management reforms of the 1980s and 1990s has been the increasing orientation towards performance or results in the public sector. A growing assumption has been that all public bodies should produce, and be able to demonstrate, results so as to legitimize their existence. On this dimension, the five countries in our study appear to vary from a high degree of results in Sweden and the UK to a lower degree in France. The question for us in this chapter is: how far have SAIs applied this assumption not only to the audited bodies, but also to themselves? Or, to put the question differently: how 'output-oriented' have the SAIs themselves become?

One important aspect of the 'output orientation' of an institution is that it defines its own results. Most of our SAIs have started thinking of performance audit as an input–output production process and the reports as constituting the *result, 'product'*, or output of audit. In this sense, at least, SAIs have begun to take on the kind of conceptual vocabulary that is characteristic of the wider sweep of public management reforms (e.g. OECD 1995, 1997b).

For the Riksrevisionsverket, performance audit developed as a special audit activity in the era of programme budgeting in the late 1960s and early 1970s. The audit activities were from the beginning understood as a kind of production process. The project management handbook from 1975 described performance audit as a systematic *step-by-step process* containing certain necessary elements. The process should begin with a careful overview of a certain sector as a method to decide what to audit, and should end with a special follow-up audit project. The process was seen as a logical and connected whole. The RRV of the 1990s envisages audit as a much more open and communicative process—but still a production process. Audit reports are described as outputs being received and having impacts in the surrounding world. The follow-up in the audit process is a follow-up of the audit reports (Riksrevisionsverket 1987, 1993).

At the Valtiontalouden tarkastusvirasto, there has been a continuous conceptual and methodological discussion since the early 1970s concerning the purposes and models of audit. In the early 1990s a consultant's study triggered off a new discussion about the future development of the performance audit. A model of the performance audit process was presented, containing four broad guidelines for improvement. One of the points made was that each project must be based on an open communication between the auditor and the auditee to ensure a broad view of the goal, and that the resulting report must be understood and accepted by the auditee.

The National Audit Office describes its approach to value-for-money work as a 'study cycle' comprising nine stages, starting with the value-for-money strategy and ending with follow-up (NAO 1997c). Stage 6 in the cycle is the publication of the report, and the subsequent steps are what happens in Parliament and the government after the report has been published. The VFM examinations are 'designed to cover the key aspects of a subject so as to produce focused and interesting reports which add value' (pp. 5–6). The reports are described as the NAO's 'main output'.

The Algemene Rekenkamer refers to the reports containing the audits' findings as the 'results of its audit activities' (Algemene Rekenkamer 1991, p. 41). It uses the analogy of reports as the 'products' of their labours. Continuing the metaphor, it is noted that a past president of the Rekenkamer had 'drawn attention to the lesson from industry that a splendid product can prove unmarketable because it is indifferently packaged and poorly presented'.

The Cour des Comptes refers to a large range of products, among which the audit reports play a crucial role, especially as regards those audits that are most performance-related, such as the public firm audits.

As we can see from these examples, SAIs regard the written performance audit reports as a very important—if not the *most* important—output of the audit process. Each report is itself a kind of a *result*. It demonstrates that an audit has been undertaken and completed. It contains the auditors' description, analysis, and judgement of the audited matter. It summarizes the fieldwork in an accessible form. It is also the main means by which the audit institution provides information to its audiences—whether they be parliament, government, the audited body, the media, or the public in general.

This focus on reports does not mean, though, that the SAIs define the reports as the only, or final, result of audit. The reports are elements of a much wider process, including the forming of the audit mandate, strategic planning and pre-studies, conduct of examinations, information and communication with auditee, responses, follow-up of impacts, and outcome. It is the process as a whole that has the function to control and improve public-sector performance (see Figure 1.1 above). More important than producing a number of reports is the actual effectiveness of the audit, that is, the impact and influence of performance audit in the public sector. (This will be examined in the next chapter.)

A second aspect of the 'output orientation' of an institution is its effort to define and consider its clients or consumers. In the case of our five SAIs, there seem to have been some interesting developments in their relationships with their various audiences. During our interviews, a VTV representative explained that their attitude towards the audience had changed during the 1980s. The taxpayer came to be seen as the 'customer' for audit, and the auditors increased their efforts to make audit reports comprehensible and clear for all parties concerned. Within the Cour des Comptes the attitude towards the public opinion has also changed. Traditionally the Cour had seen it as an advantage to be as discrete as possible about its own activities, to keep a good relationship with the auditees. More recently, the Cour appears to be paying more attention than previously to demonstrating the impacts of its work. A new kind of activity report, which describes the work of the Cour, has for the first time been included in the 1997 public report. The president of the Algemene Rekenkamer has on a number of occasions drawn attention to the importance of packaging and presentation of products (Algemene Rekenkamer 1991, p. 1). The message is clear: audiences do matter.

Given that the 'output orientation' of the SAIs has increased in two important respects (definition of results and client/consumer orientation), we should analyse the likely consequences of this orientation for the actual output. One guess would be that an increasing output orientation leads to a larger production of output. Another guess would be that it gives the institution an impulse to change the form of its output. A third guess is that the communication and marketing of the products will be intensified. All these changes or various combinations of them may happen at the same time. We can now explore these expectations by turning to the actual output of our five SAIs.

9.4 The Main Performance Audit Outputs

Our examination of outputs will take several forms. First, in this section a short description will be given of the main performance audit products for each of the SAIs. We will then examine the number and frequency of the outputs, to see if the production has changed over the time period studied (Section 9.5). Thereafter we will discuss three important aspects of the output:

1. the *composition* of audit reports: has the SAI created new information products? (Section 9.6)
2. the *characteristics* of the audit reports: has their appearance, design and structure, printing quality, etc., changed? (Section 9.7)
3. the *communication and presentation* of the reports: have there been changes in the information and publication procedures, in the SAI's use of media, etc.? (Section 9.8)

The National Audit Office

Within the NAO, five of its six units prepare value-for-money (VFM) reports. Since 1984 all such reports have been issued in a single series of 'green glossy' reports, published as House of Commons papers. The reports are publicly available and the most prominent of the NAO's publications. They are published throughout most of the year (in total about fifty per year), and are laid in Parliament prior to publication. The reports are now stand-alone products, whereas prior to the 1983 National Audit Act the forerunners of the current VFM reports were published with the accounts of the departments and bodies under examination.

The Valtiontalouden tarkastusvirasto (VTV)

In the first of the two periods (1985–7) audit work at VTV was a combination of financial audit and what could be called performance audit, with the reports as integrated products. But since the reorganization of the late 1980s, the VTV has two product lines, categorized as 'performance audits' and 'financial audits', resulting in two different types of report. All performance audit reports, approximately twenty per year, are public and are published separately. They are submitted to the ministry of finance, with copies sent to the parliamentary state auditors (the legislature's own audit body) as well as to the audited body itself and/or its supervising ministry.

The Riksrevisionsverket (RRV)

Each performance audit is published in a separate report, directed to the audited body and/or the government. Most performance audits are planned and initiated by RRV itself, resulting in about twenty performance audit reports a year. Audit reports are sent with an official letter to the agency concerned and, in many cases, to the appropriate ministry. They also go automatically to other agencies and interested parties, including parliament, the cabinet office, and the media.

The Algemene Rekenkamer

The names and descriptions being used by the Rekenkamer to label its various audit activities have multiplied significantly during the 1990s. The many labels reflect extensions of its audit mandate and structural changes within the court, the type of audited object, the reason lying behind the audit, and the scope of the audit. One may distinguish between financial and performance audit products. The performance audit reports have changed several times during the 1980s and 1990s. Historically, the Rekenkamer produced one annual report each year, containing both performance audits and regularity audits. Only a few 'interim reports' were published separately. The number of such reports has increased during the 1990s. Between 1990 and 1995 a twice-yearly compendium was produced containing almost all performance audits from the previous half-year period (usually around fifteen). Since 1996, instead of a six-monthly compendium, each performance audit is published as a separate report, addressing either parliament or the minister in question. All reports are publicly available.

The Cour des Comptes

The Cour des Comptes makes no strict distinction between performance audit and other kinds of audit activity, either in its organization or concerning its written reports. The published 'report' (*rapport*) does not occupy quite the same place in the Cour's range of products as reports do for the other four SAIs in our set. The preamble to the 1995 annual report to the president of the Republic, for example, refers to the Cour having produced 757 reports, 388 judgements, and 692 communications during the preceding year (Cour des Comptes 1995, p. 7). The *published* reports are a special category. They are considered through a specific and strict procedure within the Cour before being sent for publication, and are specially edited extracts of 'normal' reports. The judgements that are contained within the Cour's reports, published or not, have to be responded to by the auditees or the responsible ministers. The whole procedure around the writing, clearing, and finishing of reports is based on the process of contradiction which takes place between the auditor and the auditee, and which allows the auditee to contest the Cour's analysis.

There are therefore the following main types of written report:

1. *the 'normal' audit reports*, containing considerations about financial and legal matters, and good management ('*contrôle des comptes et de la gestion de. . . .*'). These reports are not published, but are presented to the chairman of the audited body. The most significant elements found are also reported to the minister in question. Extracts from some of the audit reports may be published in the annual Public Report. Moreover, some *rapports publics particuliers* are published, based on audits that are very often performance-oriented;
2. *the Public Report*: since 1807, an annual report containing extracts from the audit reports and the answers from the auditees is submitted to the head of state. It is also submitted to parliament. It has been published since 1938 and is frequently given coverage in the newspapers. The Cour makes a short summary of the report, which is published separately and intended for use by the press;
3. *specific public reports*: since 1991 the Cour has published two or three reports a year about specific items, called *rapports publics particuliers*. They are concerned with performance issues. The reports are addressed to the ministers concerned, to the head of the audited body, or to the appropriate legal authorities. The final decisions to publish the reports are taken along the same lines as for the annual public report. Copies are sent to the president of the Republic and parliament. These special reports are probably the most similar to the other SAIs' performance audit reports.

9.5 The Number and Frequency of Audit Reports

It would be a mistake to assume that a high number of audit reports is in itself a good thing. The number of reports is only an indication of the number of completed projects, each of them varying in size and complexity, and in terms of the time taken and the impacts eventually achieved.

TABLE 9.1 The number of audit reports

	Period 1	Period 2
NAO	86	137
RRV	54	66
VTV	125	49
Rekenkamer	151	111

However, establishing how many reports have been produced is a natural starting point for our analysis.

Counting the performance audit reports for the chosen three-year periods, we arrive at the figures in Table 9.1.

For the NAO, the number of reports produced each year has grown significantly between the two periods as it has developed its value-for-money work and become more experienced in report preparation. Since the early 1990s the NAO has aimed to meet a corporate target of publishing 50 reports per year. More recently, this has been seen as a ceiling figure, reflecting the attention it is giving to other aspects of its remit, in particular, financial audit work. The figure of 50 reports is also broadly in line with the number that the Public Accounts Committee is able to examine, given the Committee's interest, for example, in looking at the reports on some of the most problematic sets of accounts.

For the RRV, too, there is a slight increase in the number of reports from the first to the second period. But if we look at the number of reports per year in the years *between* the two periods, the trend reveals itself to be fragile. The number of self-initiated performance audits has remained fairly stable at around 20 per year.

For the VTV the number of reports has gone down quite dramatically from the first to the second period. This decline in numbers reflects a change in the nature of the performance audit work. After 1987 performance audit developed as a distinct product line, and each performance audit project became more time-consuming and research-like (with between 150 to 250 days allowed for one single project).

At the Algemene Rekenkamer the number of reports issued has fallen from period 1 to period 2. Here too, the decline can be explained by the different character of the later reports. In the first period the reports were in the form of contributions to the annual report, ranging in length from a single paragraph to a few pages. In the second period most of the performance audits were reported in the June or December compendium. During this period each report was about eight pages long. A few reports were published separately as interim reports. In 1988 a new model of how to undertake performance audit was set by the Rekenkamer, leading to more time being spent on each project.

Since the reports of the Cour des Comptes are, in our terms, a mixture of performance audit and financial audit, we have not included them in the table. But the total number of audit reports (including performance audits) in the two periods may be of interest, because it gives an impression of the total amount of work. For the first three years (1985–7) the numbers were 1281, 926, and 726; for the second period (1993–5) they were 783, 694, and 613. Some audits were transferred to the newly created regional courts (*chambres régionales des comptes*). This may be part of the explanation. Also, there was a change in context—one directly due to public management reforms. The numbers of reports on public firms fell from 265 (1980–3) to 188 (1993–5), partly because of privatization. Finally, some of the reports have changed character in a way that suggests that the audit projects may have grown in size. In interview, a representative of the Cour said that the public reports are longer nowadays, and include more recommendations.

On the basis of this evidence, therefore, we cannot find support for a general thesis that there are more performance audit reports in the mid-1990s than there were in the early 1980s. For three of the five SAIs the tendency is quite the opposite—and part of the explanation for that appears to be that the SAIs concerned have refined or redesigned their products. Nevertheless, all the SAIs exhibit an interest in their own production of reports. The numbers produced are used by the SAIs both as a target and as a measure of their work.

In the NAO 1997 Annual Report, for example, the number of VFM reports is used as both a measure and a future target. The report begins with a list of eight 'Highlights of the NAO's work'. One of the eight is that '50 value for money studies have been produced' (NAO 1997b, p. 2). The report goes on to say that, in spite of reduced resources per audit, this level of output is being maintained.

Similarly, since 1993, when the RRV for the first time produced an annual report, it has presented the number of performance audit reports as a key performance indicator for the performance audit department. The VTV and the Cour include broadly similar types of measure in their annual reports (e.g. State Audit Office of Finland 1994a; Cour des Comptes 1995, p. 7).

9.6 Other Information Products

Another important aspect of the SAIs' output orientation has been to create new products or new forms of existing products, to reach new audiences or adapt better to the needs and wants of the audience. The principal developments are now discussed separately.

Audit reports have been produced in *new formats*. From 1995, the Algemene Rekenkamer created an entity called 'Letter to the Minister'. Each such letter contains a performance audit addressing problems of the internal functions of the auditee. Between 1990 and 1994 seven or eight letters were produced each year; in 1995 the number was 13 and in 1996 it was 24. The RRV has begun to publish some of its reports in English translation, obviously with the aim of reaching a wider audience. The Cour des Comptes has developed a CD-ROM containing the Cour's published reports, and a similar piece of software is now issued by the NAO.

Performance audits have also provided the basis for producing '*spin-off*' *products*. Examples of this include the NAO's 'good practice guides'. Each guide is generated by work for specific VFM examinations, for example on space utilization in further education colleges in Wales. The guide contains short descriptions of the examinations being made, some comparisons, general judgements, and lessons to be learned. It is circulated to relevant bodies, in this case all universities and colleges. The initiative reflects the NAO's desire to 'add value' and be constructive in its work. The guides are seen as a way of bringing the lessons from specific audits to a wider audience and making the most use of the material gathered during the examinations.

Two other examples are from the Algemene Rekenkamer. From the normal investigations on subsidies in 1990, the Rekenkamer formulated a set of recommendations and gave them the form of a practical 'manual' concerning state subsidies. This new product was in line with the general policy within the Rekenkamer to indicate how a situation has arisen and how it might be tackled more effectively in the future. The aim of the manual has been to improve the administration of subsidies and to contribute towards a more efficient and effective use of subsidies as an instrument of policy. Similarly, in 1989, the Rekenkamer drew up a 'checklist' from the audit of the privatization of the pilot system. The checklist contains criteria for careful future privatization.

Some aspects of performance audit work have laid the ground for creating *new types of publication*. Between 1993 and 1995, the performance audit division within the RRV generated nine publications other than performance audit reports themselves. Three were 'strategy studies', containing descriptions and analyses of a new audit field and suggesting audit questions that could be posed within each field. The first dealt with health and medical care (1993), the second with the social security system (1995), and the third with the pensions system (1995). Three other publications are general descriptions of the development of performance audit (including Swedish National Audit Bureau 1993, and Swedish National Audit Office 1995a); two reports are follow-up reports of former performance audits, and the final report deals with cluster analysis as a useful audit method.

Performance auditors have engaged in other types of activities and produced other kinds of reports and publications. Performance auditors play an important role in writing the 'official responses' of the RRV. This type of work is a part of the long established Swedish system in which the state agencies have the opportunity to comment on various public commission or government reports. Between 1993 and 1995, RRV gave 475 such responses.

The number of official responses has gone up during the last five years, and they were highlighted by the new auditor general in 1993 as one very important channel through which the RRV can present the auditors' special knowledge and opinion on different subject matters 'already during the decision making process'.

RRV staff also undertook special audit assignments for the government (until mid-1998, when a new agency was created for this purpose). During the 1990s the number of such assignments grew, and eventually represented as much as one-third the work of the entire office. These studies were not defined as performance audits, but they often entailed very similar approaches and methods.

Since 1993, the performance auditors at the RRV have also been taking part in the auditing of the annual reports which are now produced by government agencies. They audit the performance follow-up sections of these reports and in doing so generate roughly 200 audit memoranda per annum.

Finally, individual auditors in a number of SAIs have been encouraged to prepare articles for publication in academic or other specialist journals, and/or to present papers at conferences (e.g. Goldsworthy 1996, 1997; Mul and van Westing 1996).

The SAIs produce *annual reports*. While these cover the whole of their remits, not just performance audit, they are nevertheless significant publications in terms of the way they enable SAIs to 'showcase' their activities. Their precise purposes and formats vary considerably, and have changed over time (Pollitt and Summa 1997b). The NAO Annual Report shows 'how we manage our own resources to ensure good value for money' (NAO 1997b, p. ii). The chapters that deal with financial audit and VFM audit contain performance information under headings like 'results and impacts' and 'costs and quality'. The report is attractively presented and is obviously intended to appeal to a broad and general audience.

The annual report from the RRV is a statutory publication which is required from all Swedish government agencies. The purpose of the report is similar to that of the NAO. In the chapter on performance audit, the effectiveness of audit is measured by the percentage of observations and remarks that have led to measures being taken by the responsible authorities. The VTV is similarly obliged to produce an annual report. The emphasis in the report is not so much on performance in terms of impacts as on the costs of the audits and the time it takes to conduct them (i.e. input and process measures).

The annual report of the Rekenkamer has undergone radical changes during the last decade. At the time of writing it covers information on government-wide and follow-up audits; in addition, it gives an outline of the developments within the Rekenkamer in the field of audit, and information on personnel, financial, and organizational matters. The format is colourful and accessible.

The Cour des Comptes has for a long time published a lengthy annual report (typically about 500 pages) containing summaries of audit findings and comments from the auditees. Traditionally, the report has not contained any self-reflexive performance information, except for the total number of examinations and decisions. But in 1997, for the first time, the report included an activity report, describing the work of the Cour.

Thus, there does seem to be a trend for annual reports to develop into products that demonstrate and 'explain' the activities of the SAIs—very much including performance audit—to a general public. The annual reports contain more and more information about the audit activities themselves, rather than simply summarizing audit findings. In many cases they also relate changes in audit activity to reforms and restructurings in the wider public sector.

On the basis of this overview, we can conclude that the portfolio of performance audit publications and associated products in the 1990s is clearly more varied than that of the 1980s. This seems to be the case even where performance audit work has been restricted by limited resources and recruitment. It seems to be the result of a conscious strategy by the SAIs to adapt to new audiences and changing circumstances. All the SAIs are concerned to adapt the various information products to specific audiences and to make the most out of the performance audit work by letting the work result in different products. They have developed the format of their reports. Increasingly, they have separated audit information (directed to the different stakeholders) from other types of information of more general interest.

9.7 Characteristics of the Audit Reports

What is a 'good' performance audit report?

Having established the nature of the product range, we now turn to consider what SAIs themselves see as making a 'good' report. One important characteristic of the SAIs' performance audit reports that makes them special in the public policy arena is their authoritative status. This is the result of the SAIs' privileged access to information, and the fact that they are expected to give an authoritative view on the particular subject matter. This status brings with it special quality requirements, especially concerning balance and the reliability of the SAIs' information sources. As a result, all SAIs have developed systems for assuring, or formulated criteria for assessing, the quality of their performance audit reports.

In the VTV there has been an internal quality group working with the question of quality of audit reports. Four quality criteria have been formulated:

1. The reports should be equal and fair, neutral, and objective.
2. The reports should be credible.
3. The reports should have usability.
4. The reports should be interactive and open.

From 1997 it is intended that these quality criteria should become VTV policy.

Within the RRV, the responsibility for output quality has traditionally belonged to the heads of sections and the individual audit teams. The assurance of quality has been a part of the normal audit process. To assess the quality afterwards, the RRV has turned to external groups—including researchers, politicians, public servants, experts, and interest groups—which are given the opportunity to give their opinion (Riksrevisionsverket 1993). But quality belongs to the 'eternal' questions. Several times quality policies have been formulated and criteria have been discussed. Various groups of performance auditors and senior staff have been working to develop the concept of quality, including a move to come in to line with the general quality concepts in the public sector. Some quality criteria have been reiterated: the chosen subject should be of strategic importance on government and agency level; the audit should be thorough, analytic, impartial and balanced; the audit team must communicate well through the process; the recommendations must be feasible, and the text well structured and well written (Riksrevisionsverket 1993).

Similarly, the Algemene Rekenkamer has formulated the following quality criteria: the reports should be distinctive from all other parliamentary documents; they must be reliable, objective, sober but stylish, just and wise, resolute, expert, and independent (Algemene Rekenkamer 1991, p. 41). The style of the report must support the desire for openness. The reports should also be published on time, and have a clear message.

At the Cour, the public reports are expected to have the following features: the chosen subject must be of a generally interesting and strategic kind, and the magistrates may use the opportunity to make more detailed descriptions and express themselves more freely to make the reports interesting to a wide audience (interview).

Finally, in the early 1990s the UK comptroller and auditor general gave an indication of what he considered were the key features of a successful NAO report. The work should

1. succeed at the Public Accounts Committee (PAC);
2. go to the heart of the matter;
3. say something new;
4. not be 'political' in the sense of encouraging party division at PAC hearings;
5. be understandable by people who know nothing about the subject;
6. be relevant to departments in managing the real world;
7. be interesting and significant to the media; and
8. be valuable and defensible to knowledgeable outsiders (NAO internal paper).

In our discussions, NAO staff indicated that these criteria remained valid. In addition, staff suggested that the NAO's senior management was looking for reports to include, where appropriate, an innovative methodology, and in all cases regarded the appearance of the report and the presentation of the material as very important.

In seeking to ensure quality, SAIs have taken a number of steps. Some have begun to use outside assessors to check the quality of their reports. Since 1993, the NAO has contracted with a number of academics in the field of public administration, initially from Brunel University and later from the London School of Economics, to review each published VFM report. The external assessors apply a set of quality criteria such as the quality of the presentation, the adequacy of the methodology, and the soundness of the conclusions, and they give each report a quality mark. The reviewers have also been asked to provide constructive advice on improvements. More recently, the VTV has adopted a broadly similar system. The RRV does not have an assessment of each single report, but quality seminars are held regularly where external interest groups and stakeholders are asked to comment on the quality of the reports and on the performance audit work as a whole.

Thus, all the SAIs have committed themselves to demanding objectives and quality criteria for their output. All their ambitions seem admirable, but can they be fulfilled simultaneously and for all kinds of output? Opinion about what is a good audit report will vary between different stakeholders. The auditor and the auditee may have different views. Sometimes there may be a difference of opinion between the senior managers within the SAIs and the single audit team. Laypersons may view a report differently from specialists within the field, and practitioners will probably view the audit text differently from academics.

How, then, can performance audits hope to satisfy such formidable lists of criteria? One solution would be to do what most of the SAIs have already begun to do, namely, produce different kinds of report for different audiences, with different quality criteria. It might be easier to focus on one audience at a time instead of producing reports that try to satisfy all groups simultaneously. But at the same time, the main output—the audit reports—will probably always be of more than single-dimensional interest.

Who speaks to whom, and how

This raises the interesting question of who is speaking to whom when SAIs publish their performance audit reports. Do these reports, for example, express the voice of those who designed and conducted the audit, or do they express a more synthetic, corporate view—or some mixture of the two?

The reports of the Cour des Comptes are first sent to the head of the audited body and the minister involved. Moreover, the most striking points are usually stressed in *référés* sent by the *premier président* to the ministers involved or in *lettres du président*, which are communications sent by the *président de chambre* to the most senior civil servants and the head of the audited body. If the Cour does not receive a substantial and satisfactory answer within six months, the *référés*' are sent to parliament. In some cases (when legal concerns have emerged from the audit) a *note du Parquet* is sent, which is a communication addressed by the *procureur général* (who provides legal advice on matters related to the Cour) to the head of the audited body or to the relevant minister. The head of the audited body may also be judged by the budget and finance Cour (Cour de Discipline Budgétaire et Financière). The reports are written in a formal and strictly impersonal way. No individual names of auditors are mentioned, and it is clearly the institution as a whole, the Cour, that has taken the decisions and that speaks in the reports. In the published reports the opinion of the auditee is presented in a separate part.

The VTV sends its reports to the auditee and the Ministry of Finance, with a copy to the Finnish Parliamentary State Auditors. The auditee is given the opportunity to comment on draft reports and such comments are usually included in the text. The reports are available to the public and are issued with a press release. They are quite neutral and impersonal in tone. The names of auditors or decision-makers are not mentioned.

Since 1996, all performance audits within the Algemene Rekenkamer are published separately, addressing either parliament or the minister. Most of the audit reports are submitted to the States General. They are official parliamentary documents. Any parliamentary committee can discuss the reports, but they are usually considered by the State Expenditure Committee. The alternative is to present the findings in the form of a special 'letter to the minister'. These letters are regarded as official reports and are, upon request, available for parliament, but they are not given large-scale external distribution. Both types of report include the comments of the responsible minister.

The Rekenkamer has for a long time followed the practice of submitting its findings for comments to the minister. Upon receipt of the comments, the Rekenkamer decides on the final report and publication. This means that it does not have complete control over the timing of publication of its reports (Algemene Rekenkamer 1991, p. 43). Rekenkamer reports, too, are impersonal and institutionally oriented, with no individual auditors or decision-makers mentioned. The opinions of the auditee are presented separately.

The reports that result from the examinations of the NAO are presented to parliament in the name of the comptroller and auditor general. The names of the staff that worked on them are not referred to anywhere in the text. Parliament, and especially the Public Accounts Committee, is the main audience, although there is an assumption that the report will be of interest to others such as the examined body, specialists in the field, and, to a lesser extent, the general public. Reports are written in a language understood by the non-specialist. They attempt to describe matters in simple terms, using a language free from jargon and explaining technical matters wherever necessary. The tone that the NAO tries to achieve is one of balance and fairness, although some critics have suggested that this can mean that the reports give little indication of what the auditors really think on the subject matter.

The RRV performance audit reports are written for the ministry and/or the government agency in question. But interested members of the public, the mass media, and similar bodies in other countries should be able to read the reports and learn something from them. This means that reports normally include general background information, thorough and well documented analysis, descriptions of methods, and any reservations (e.g. time and resource limitations). At the same time, they must highlight key points, provide a short summary and sharp conclusions, and include recommendations for the future.

In RRV reports, the individual audit team and the person who has finally taken the decision to approve the report (the auditor general or some of the directors) are mentioned by name in the introduction to the report. This is common for all state agency reports in Sweden and may be seen as part of the general public-sector culture of openness.

Although describing the various SAIs' reports in a text such as this is no substitute for actually reading them, there are a number of aspects of performance audit reports that can be considered in a more general way. These include the length of the reports, their structure, appearance, and modes of dissemination and presentation. We comment briefly on these aspects in the paragraphs below.

Length

The NAO's value-for-money reports vary significantly in length. The standard length of a report is probably in the region of 30 to 40 pages, with an executive summary of perhaps 6 pages. At one extreme, a report on the regulators of the privatized utilities that appeared in 1996 was around 300 pages long, much of this being made up of completed questionnaires; at the other extreme, the first report on how government bodies were managing the Year 2000 computer problem was 15 pages long. Staff are encouraged to write focused reports, and senior management to play a role in cutting down draft reports. The overall aim is to end up with a report that deals only with the key issues, and these should be summarized further in the executive summary which is intended as a stand-alone document. Members of the Public Accounts Committee have advised that they consider this a key part of the report, as they may be able to read only this section prior to attending a hearing of the report.

RRV reports vary from 25–30 pages up to several hundred. The average for reports from the first period examined is 70 pages, and in the second period 80 pages. The variation in length is even more significant in the second period, with a number of quite short reports but also some very long ones. There is no official policy setting strict targets for length: it depends on the audit theme, team, and the available time.

A typical audit report from the Cour des Comptes will be about 100 pages long when it is presented to the Chamber. In the case of public firms, the final and official ('blue') report will be between 20 and 30 pages long. The tendency is towards shortening these reports. The public reports, on the other hand, are often longer (up to 200 pages). For these reports the tendency seems to be the opposite; the reports include more and more recommendations, and the magistrates are given room to develop their arguments.

The average length of the reports from the Algemene Rekenkamer varies both within a single year and between different years. Concerning the June and December compendia, the thinnest one in the period 1990–5 had 64 pages covering six different topics, and the thickest one had 168 pages covering twenty-four topics. The separately published audit reports in the period 1990–4 were about 7 pages long, in 1995 about 13 pages, and in 1996 about 24 pages. The tendency for these reports is towards making them more extensive. This seems to go well with an increasing orientation towards publicity and openness.

VTV performance audit reports also vary in length. Generally, they are substantial documents. In recent years it has not been unusual for them to be 100 or more pages in all.

Structure

The structure of the NAO value-for-money reports has clearly changed. A VFM report from the 1980s (e.g. NAO 1988) contained a short summary-and-conclusions chapter followed by two or more subject chapters analysing different aspects of the audited body. Descriptions, analysis, conclusions, and recommendations were mixed in the running chapter texts. A typical concluding formulation is 'The National Audit Office welcome the prospect of further action . . .' (NAO 1988, p. 3).

By contrast, a typical report from the 1990s (e.g. NAO 1993) is different. The opening summary is likely to be succinct and to spell out the main messages in a more pointed or recommendatory style; more information may be given on the methods used by the audit team; diagrams, boxed examples, and photographs are more likely to be used; contextual information may appear in appendices. The formulations tend to be: 'The National Audit Office recommend that . . .' or 'The National Audit Office conclude that . . .' In the reports from 1996 onwards the summary is now termed the 'Executive Summary'. The recommendations are given special prominence. They are presented in green squares under their own headings as 'Recommendation 1', Recommendation 2', etc. Thus, NAO value-for-money reports now separate description from analysis, methodological reflection from subject matter, and main points from minor details. The summary and conclusions are written so that they offer the reader a short-cut to the 'whole story' and the most interesting audit points.

The structure and style of the RRV reports have also changed, even if the tendency is not as clear as for the NAO. A typical report from 1984 starts with a summary, then has an introduction describing the audit field, the background, earlier audits, the political goals, etc., before entering into the audit itself. Normally the report contains few appendices. The recommendations are presented as part of the running text in the summary and in the different chapters. In a typical report from the 1990s, the recommendations are given more prominence. The summary may contain formulations like 'RRV recommends . . .', italicized or listed as points. The last chapter in the reports will normally be called something like 'RRV's conclusions and recommendations'. In a report on nuclear waste disposal from 1995 there is an English summary as well as the Swedish one. In the last chapter ('Conclusions and Recommendations') there is a special section for suggestions. Over the period as a whole, the structure of the performance audit reports from the RRV has shifted. First and foremost, the recommendations are presented in a new way and the reports have gradually come to resemble consultant's reports.

A typical *rapport particulier* of the Cour des Comptes contains the most crucial conclusions that have emerged from the audit. Many of the descriptive parts that are included in the first reports are deleted from the public version. Appendices may be included only if there are technical points that require such a presentation.

Between the first and second periods there was some shift towards a more standardized structure for VTV reports; for example, by 1995 the inclusion of an executive summary had become fairly universal. In other respects, however, there was still significant variation between reports. Most of them contained sets of conclusions, but it did not appear that these were usually expressed as 'recommendations'. (The closer an SAI saw itself to the 'management consultant' pole in Figure 7.1, the more one might expect 'recommendations' rather than 'conclusions'.) Interestingly, in Finland the executive summaries of all performance audit reports are now published as a separate, annual volume (as well as appearing in the individual reports themselves).

Since the mid-1980s the SAIs all seem to have developed structures for their audit reports that reflect more overtly their functions of helping the decision-making process and bringing about changes.

Appearance

The presentational aspects of the reports have become a central issue for the SAIs. At a glance one can see that, for all the SAIs, the audit reports have changed appearance over time, becoming more colourful, with better paper quality and layout. All the SAIs have developed routines for presenting their reports to the audiences. When describing the usefulness of their own work, they assume that their reports are disseminated, read, and reacted upon. This of course puts pressure on them to improve the appearance of the reports.

The NAO states in its 1995 Annual Report that 'We are continually striving to improve the quality of our reports and respond to the demands of the environment in which we operate' (NAO 1995a). The value-for-money reports in the 1980s were fairly dull in appearance, with dense text and few illustrations, graphics, etc. In the 1990s there have been several changes to format, most recently in 1997, to make the reports more attractive. Advice has been taken on the design of page layouts, and greater use has been made of photographs and graphics, as well as shaded, illustrative boxes and sign-posting within the report. The presentation of information in reports is one of the criteria that external assessors have been asked to look at.

The Algemene Rekenkamer has accepted that its publications and recommendations will be scrutinized with a more critical eye than before. This has increased the pressure to operate more professionally and to produce top-quality reports (Mul and van Westing 1996). Before 1987, when the annual report contained most of the audits, it had a very modest layout, and there were no illustrations. Today, the annual report gives an outline of the general development within the Algemene Rekenkamer and its field of control. A new colour is chosen annually. The content includes graphics and illustrations, and the structure and layout make the report easy to read.

The June and December compendia looked the same throughout the period 1990–6. The separately published reports have their own style: they have a black and white photo on the front relating to the audit object/theme, and follow a structure and layout that makes them easy to read.

The appearance of the performance audit reports from the RRV developed dramatically during the 1980s. Each audit team would choose a special colour, cover page, printing quality, illustrations, graphics, etc. The reports gradually became quite luxurious and lacked a common style. This trend was arrested in 1993. The new auditor general decided that each report should follow the RRV's official graphical profile, and have a much more modest appearance. This new trend of the 1990s is perhaps a consequence of the resources being tighter, but also it can be said to be more in line with RRV policy and culture not to waste public money.

Since 1993, the practice of the VTV has been to publish the performance audit reports in reasonably elegant booklets and with coloured covers bearing a standard design. The distribution is fairly broad. In the 1980s audit reports were produced in mimeographed form, only with a few copies available.

For the Cour des Comptes, the appearance of the public report has changed over the last ten years. Now it has a multi-colour cover sheet and good paper quality. Titles and subtitles make the reports easy to read. The specific public reports resemble small books, with a high print quality.

In general, there are some common characteristics concerning the appearance of the reports. All the SAIs have started publishing 'series' of audit reports, with set styles and structures. Their reports have been consciously developed to be easy to read, to recognize, and to refer to. Where referred to, the methodology for the audit work and other background information are often placed in appendices, and it has become the norm to include a summary.

9.8 Communication and Presentation of Reports

The SAIs have different communication practices, but each has developed its practice in recent years. Since 1992 the VTV has had a declared communication policy for the office. For each report there is a press release. The press release is sometimes contracted out to professional information organizations, for example to the Ministry of Finance Press Unit or to an expert public relations company. The distribution of the reports is fairly broad. This contrasts with the 1980s, when only a few mimeographed copies were made available.

In recent years the NAO has given increased attention to relations with the press. The strategy for publishing a report is worked out by the Press Office, aimed at maximizing the coverage received, or at least at giving each report the best chance of attracting the interest of journalists. NAO reports have long been issued with press releases, which like the reports are agreed with the auditee, and a press officer has been available to discuss the reports with journalists. In the past, the NAO has not tended to give interviews to radio or television, but this appears to have changed in recent years. Those staff members who are likely to need it are now given media skills training.

Even if most reports from the Cour des Comptes are not published, the number of published reports is growing. The main public report is addressed to the president, delivered to parliament and distributed to the press. A press conference is organized, where the content and aims of the report is presented. A summary of the report is distributed to journalists and other interested parties. Since 1994 there is also an annual public report concerning social protection. The *rapports publics particuliers* are also sent to the newspapers, and a press conference is organized. In 1993 a special unit was created and dedicated to the task of external communication, to relieve the magistrates from this task and make the process of communication more professional.

For the RRV, the regular procedure is for about 1,000 copies to be printed. The report is addressed to the government or the ministry in question and/or the government agency, which gets a pre-publication version. Then it is sent to parliament and to the most relevant standing committees, and to each of the main political parties, public libraries, local government authorities, the other Nordic countries, and the mass media. A press release follows each report. A few reports each year are translated into English, to reach an even wider audience.

Within the Algemene Rekenkamer, it used to be that the sector director, together with the project manager, made a proposal for publication which the board approved or disapproved. Since 1996, however, all performance audits are supposed to be published. The reports are sent to the minister, parliament, and the press one day before publication. Sometimes the project manager accompanied by a member of the board gives a presentation of the report to the parliamentary committee or the ministry. The publication is then accompanied by a press statement and the press is offered the opportunity to put questions to the board about the report. One day before publication of the annual report, a press conference is given by the president or other members of the Rekenkamer.

It can be seen from the above paragraphs that all the SAIs work actively to create attention for their products, to secure dissemination, and to develop contacts with the press. The ambition is to 'sell' the reports to a wide audience, and to do that each SAI has attempted, to greater or lesser degree, to professionalize the presentation of its work.

9.9 Discussion of Output Trends

Overall, all five SAIs have clearly made efforts to improve the adaptation of their products for different audiences. The number of audit reports has increased for some of the SAIs. The size of each report has increased for others. And the variation and composition of products has changed for all SAIs: there are more public reports and a greater variety of information products. Shorter versions of the reports for the general reader have been introduced. The NAO and the Rekenkamer have developed practical guides directed at certain target groups based on some of the normal performance audits. The Cour des Comptes has published reports in CD-ROM format to reach new audiences. Performance audit reports from a non-English-speaking country (Sweden) have been published in English. The appearance of the main audit reports has been improved. The reports have become easier to read and to identify. The output of the performance audit work is also more actively communicated, through more professionalized channels. Furthermore, SAI annual reports have begun to include more material about the SAIs' own activities, very much including performance audits.

We can now return to one of the main questions that was raised in the beginning of this chapter: how output-oriented have SAIs become? Bearing in mind that an increased emphasis on outputs and 'results' is one of the hallmarks of contemporary public management reform (Chapter 3), we can say that all five SAIs are now very concerned about the quantity and quality of their output. In some respects, their products have obviously improved over the period studied. More performance audits have become public reports;

popular versions of the reports have been produced. The opinions of the readers are seen to matter, and the accessibility of the texts has improved accordingly. The SAIs care about the appearance of the reports, which has improved. All of them may be said to have become more or less professional producers of information. The increasing output orientation can therefore plausibly be seen as a part of the general managerialist trend discussed in Chapter 3. SAIs have in this respect become somewhat more like other public-sector organizations.

9.10 Why Has Output Orientation Increased?

Given the conclusion of the previous section, an explanation is called for. One is quite obvious and is specifically related to the role of the SAIs as audit institutions. SAIs are seeking to make impact. With more reports, better adapted to their audiences, the chances of making impact are probably higher. The notion of 'impact' is discussed at length in the next chapter.

A second explanation is more general. The SAIs supply information within a huge information market. The amount of written information in general is increasing, and so is the competition among the information-producing institutions. SAIs must at least hold their own position in the market-place for public-sector information and news. To achieve this, they have felt obliged to enhance the attractiveness of their products.

A third explanation takes the general 'output ideology' as its starting point. The SAIs, like other public-sector bodies, wish to demonstrate that they are productive and are making impact. To be output-oriented is a way of justifying your institutional existence. The SAIs produce audit reports as their main output, and they have to do this in a quick and efficient manner if they are to be able to publish a decent number of reports each year, be able to respond to requests for information, and be able to take part in various decision-making processes. Crudely, to justify their own use of public money, they have to show some credible outputs.

A fourth reason is more technical and contributory. Like many other public-sector organizations, SAIs have introduced and developed new information technology during the period. This has made it possible to produce more reports, more attractively and more quickly.

Finally, we can only guess at the relation between the output orientation, the outputs themselves, and the actual impacts or effectiveness of performance audit. One view might be that some SAIs are now nearing the borderline of becoming too narrowly 'product-minded'. There is a risk that, when an authoritative audit body puts too much effort into its own products and presentation of products, it may forget its other role. The main function of the audit institution is to 'be there' intensively and extensively; to be awake and critically to follow public money and the performance of public bodies, but not necessarily to aim at being a 'performer' itself.

An alternative perspective—one certainly held by some of our interviewees—is that there is no real tension between, on the one hand, a smooth, professional presentation and, on the other, rigorous and critical independence in audit practice. Indeed, the first could be argued to be necessary if the full influence of the second is to be felt.

To some extent these differences of view could be said to be matters of taste. (To some, an SAI may be more trustworthy if it remains august and distant, and a tiny bit old fashioned!) What would be a warning sign, however, would be if evidence were to emerge that the selection of audit topics, or the inclusion of substantive and relevant material in the texts of public reports, had been affected by considerations of 'image'. No such evidence has come to our notice, but the issue is one that merits periodic re-investigation.

10

Impacts

Jeremy Lonsdale

10.1 Introduction

We now turn to consider the 'impact' of performance audit work undertaken by the five SAIs in our study. By impact we mean primarily the direct and indirect effect or influence that an SAI can have on the practices, performance, and culture of the audited entity as a result of its performance audit work. Impact may arise from recommendations made by the SAI which result in the strengthening of weak administrative procedures and practices or lead to financial savings. Alternatively, it may involve influencing or, in some cases, instigating debate on a particular subject. And, lest we assume that SAIs can have impact only when they bring about change, we should not also forget the reinforcement value of positive assurance provided by performance auditors where they find good practice.

The issue of impact raises a number of fundamental questions about the nature and role of SAIs. How are they able to have their impact? What impact do they want to have? Are they, and should they want to be, agents for change, or do they have a more limited role as providers of information? Can they be both at the same time? What might reasonably be expected of SAIs, in terms of their ability to instigate change, given their constitutional positions? This chapter attempts to provide some answers to these questions.

In very simple theoretical terms, the performance audit process may be seen as a basic knowledge-driven model, where in linear sequence the audit examination generates information which, following consideration, is designed to stimulate action where considered necessary. More specifically, SAIs select what they consider to be significant topics for examination, or else agree to undertake particular projects suggested by others that they consider are worthwhile. They carry out research work, before preparing a report of findings which draws attention to shortcomings and offers recommendations for improvement. Their reports are considered by a number of third parties, including the auditees and wider government authorities and, to varying degrees, legislatures. On the basis of the evidence presented by the SAI, decisions may be taken within government to alter existing practices or policies. Subsequently, to ensure that promises of change are implemented, SAIs may undertake follow-up work.

Some have questioned how likely it is that such a model will produce worthwhile improvements in performance. Power (1997, p. 119) suggests that 'Typically the audit feedback process embodied in a formal management control system reflects a naively mechanistic and self-corrective view of organizational change, with levels of often highly ritualized calculative specificity.' Leeuw (1996, p. 56) refers to the 'auditors' implicit feedback theory', which assumes that 'feedback from the auditor is needed, that the auditee will listen and will take follow up action, that this action will lead to the realization of formal goals and there will be no unintended and undesired side effects'. In Leeuw's opinion, such a model also leaves out the possibility that an auditee may take no strategic action—e.g. that an auditee may make a merely symbolic response, so as to appear to be taking action.

On the basis of our work, we would agree that the reality is a lot messier than the theory, and that the ability of SAIs to have an impact through their performance audit work is far less straightforward than a simple model might imply. There may be a number of reasons for this. For example, an SAI's ability to have impact, and the kind of impact achieved, is likely to depend to a great extent on the questions it asks, as well as the types of method it employs, important points when considering the most appropriate combination of skills required for performance audit. The extent of any impact may also depend on the prime purpose of the examination. Where a study is designed principally to describe a sequence of events for the purposes of holding a body accountable for its actions, it is less likely to have demonstrable impacts compared with a study designed to analyse a problem and suggest practical recommendations. Equally, there may be a number of different impacts, occurring at different stages of the audit process—before, during, and after the work—and different effects felt at different levels of an organization.

Despite this, we would argue that there is considerable evidence of beneficial impact from performance audit work, as well as signs of sensitivity within SAIs to the potential drawbacks of their role and the need to work with auditees, where possible, to effect beneficial change. We also consider that there is evidence that their impact has increased over the period under examination as SAIs have taken action in different ways to enhance the impact of their work. This chapter, therefore, considers:

1. what SAIs say about the impact of their work;
2. the evidence of the impact of performance audit reports, and the nature of these impacts;
3. whether and how SAIs measure the impacts;
4. independent assessment of impact;
5. any negative effects of performance audit work;
6. the efforts SAIs make to enhance the impact their work has; and
7. other influences on the impact of performance audit.

10.2 What SAIs Say about the Impact of their Work

All the SAIs in our sample profess to be seeking to encourage beneficial change of some kind by undertaking performance audit work. For the Riksrevisionsverket performance auditing is 'an independent force for change' (Swedish National Audit Office 1995a, p. 5) and 'achieving results is of fundamental importance' (Swedish National Audit Bureau 1993, p. 44). Its aim 'is to improve efficiency and effectiveness by means of investigation and evaluation', and the job of performance auditors is 'to discover efficiency problems throughout the government administration and, by analysing these problems, provide well-founded proposals for change' (Swedish National Audit Office 1995a, p. 5). Similarly, Sir John Bourn, the head of the National Audit Office, has commented that the aim of his office 'is to undertake studies where we can provide "added value", for example, by concentrating on performance actually achieved and by making positive, constructive recommendations for improvements' (Bourn 1994, p. 73). For the Valtiontalouden tarkastusvirasto, 'auditing activities produce such new information that can be put to practical use and that can be expected to result in considerable economic benefits' (State Audit Office of Finland 1994a, p. 6).

SAIs also argue strongly that aiming to have an impact underpins how they execute their work at all stages. We observed in Chapter 7 that, in assessing potential subjects for examination, they consider issues such as the risk to value for money of particular activities, the likelihood of being able to make worthwhile recommendations, the political and public interest in the subject, and the financial importance of the area. With a wide audit field to choose from, and demanding audiences, SAIs seek to undertake work that will have beneficial results. A strong report, providing new information and analysis and making recommendations that are implemented, contributes to the overall goal of improving the value for money from public activities. In addition, it underlines to outside observers the value and worth of the work of the SAI.

Thus, auditors appear increasingly to plan at the outset how they will undertake their work to ensure that it has the best chance of achieving the results intended. In the NAO a review of the 'likely impact' of an examination is carried out at an early stage (see Section 7.5 above), and a poor assessment may result in the study being abandoned or refocused (Goldsworthy 1997, p. 6). Similarly, in the VTV a prestudy is undertaken to check the 'auditability' of a performance audit study object. One element in such a prestudy is to form a view as to the likely findings, although this preliminary hypothesis is not intended to constrain subsequent fieldwork. Later in the audit process, having issued their reports, some SAIs draw attention to the impact of their work in their annual reports and in discussions with their paymasters to justify future budgets. The NAO and the RRV, for example, report publicly on the number of changes to government administrative practices for which they claim to be responsible —a point we will examine later.

It is also clear that the same SAIs consider it vital that the value and impact of their work is recognized by others. A recent NAO guide stated that 'It is important that we can demonstrate to Parliament the impact of our work and that departments see a difference from what we do' (NAO 1997a, p. 23). The RRV has emphasized the importance of its work producing 'demonstrable results in the approximately 350 government agencies it deals with, and also in the Government's efforts to bring about change. The RRV's work, therefore, extends beyond the process of control, to encompass giving assistance and speeding up these processes in various ways', describing the 'dual nature of this assignment [as] an essential aspect of the RRV culture' (Swedish National Audit Bureau 1993, p. 23). During interviews at the VTV, senior staff told us that the auditor general had proposed that more concrete information about results and impacts should be given in its Annual Report.

However valid these official assertions, the question of how much impact their performance audit reports have had was a difficult one for many of the experienced auditors we interviewed to answer. There was a natural tendency to assert the importance of their work, and a genuine belief that it had impact, including a directly educational role in encouraging bodies to think more critically about why they undertake certain activities. At the same time, there was a widespread recognition that measuring such impact was difficult, if not impossible. Some (at the NAO) felt that attempts to quantify impact were worth attempting, if only to avoid unsubstantiated assertions that their work was successful. Others, elsewhere, doubted that such counting had any real meaning. Some auditors were concerned that they should not overstate their claims, recognizing that it was often very difficult to be sure whether an action by a department was really due to their work or to other influences. On the other hand, there was a belief that there was a natural tendency for auditees to claim that they would have taken remedial action anyway, even though, subsequently, auditors often became aware that their work had had more impact than they had been led to believe.

Overall, though, staff within the SAIs considered they had a general deterrent effect—an impact in discouraging bad practice simply because they existed, and could and did undertake performance audits—as well as a more specific effect in the areas in which they carried out their examinations. The RRV has distinguished between the direct effects of its work, which it has described as 'somewhat easier to measure', and other effects, which it considers are harder to assess, including preventative and attitude-changing impacts and the long-term effects of implemented recommendations (Swedish National Audit Bureau 1993, p. 77). The NAO sees things in a similar way, explaining that

> firstly, there is the general stimulus to provide better value for money that comes from departments' awareness that the NAO carries out a selective, systematic

programme of investigations over all programmes of expenditure, and that examinations will be followed up by a hearing of the PAC. It is not possible to quantify in money terms this general effect. However, if the impact of the combined examinations of the NAO and PAC were to improve the value for money provided by departments by no more than a fraction of one per cent more than it otherwise would be, there would be benefits running into many millions . . . and . . . secondly, there are specific improvements to value for money which flow from changes made to procedures on the specific programmes investigated by the NAO or on similar programmes. (NAO 1994a, p. 19)

The former effect cannot, by its nature, be quantified, but I have seen plenty of references in the course of audit work to the need for activities to be seen to be good value for money in view of the likely interest of the NAO, or the Public Accounts Committee. The possibility of an NAO report being considered in a committee hearing is widely seen by commentators and officials alike as a strong incentive to ensure that the value for money of activities is assessed thoroughly early on. One commentator has noted that:

The knowledge that, on its day, the PAC could put the most seasoned permanent secretary, in his role as departmental accounting officer, through the wringer over some aspect of procurement, expenditure, and increasingly, value for money, inspired a high degree of preparation at the highest level in a ministry prior to a PAC appearance even if, in the event, the committee concentrated on minnow-matters instead of sharks and whales. (Hennessy 1990, p. 332)

This prospect is very likely to have an effect during policy development and implementation.

While confident that their work is worthwhile and effective, staff at several SAIs recognized that the impact varied considerably from study to study. At the RRV, one senior official suggested that perhaps two or three reports a year out of twenty raised subjects for the first time; a further ten or so dealt with subjects that were new, but where other parties had also contributed to the impulse for change; and in the remainder the RRV had contributed to a debate started by others. SAIs also appear to consider that the impact of their work has increased in recent years. The Rekenkamer's opinion, expressed at the start of the decade, was that the effects of their audits had grown during the 1980s. One publication stated that:

In the 1970s ministers and members of parliament did little with the results of Court of Audit audits. The Lower House displayed little interest, posing certain written questions to ministers that were dutifully answered. No further attention was paid to those responses. As recently as 1984 the Court of Audit reports relating to the years from 1979 up to and including 1982 were dealt with in a summary fashion. (Algemene Rekenkamer 1991, p. 49)

Since the mid-1980s, when they had expressed concerns that the Lower House was not adequately supervising government policy, the Rekenkamer's view has been that this body has taken a more active interest and has done more with its findings. In 1996 a senior official of the Rekenkamer noted that:

> There has been a marked increase in the attention paid to the Court's reports at the political level. They are dealt with quickly and thoroughly. Ministers are compelled to make pledges. Appreciation for the Court of Audit's work has patently increased, even if the contents of its reports are by no means always welcome from the political point of view. (Witteveen 1996, p. 28)

This view was repeated in our interviews at the Rekenkamer during 1997. Staff at the RRV noted that the government in Sweden has been increasingly keen to show that it uses bodies such as the RRV in preparing its work, and the Minister of Finance now informs the Riksdag annually on the action taken on the basis of the RRV's comments. At the Cour, staff considered that their constitutional position and the quality of their staff had ensured that they had had a strong influence in the past. More recently, these strengths were being augmented by increased professionalism, greater publicity for their work, and new competences.

10.3 Evidence of the Impact of Reports

Having examined what SAIs and some of their staff say about the impacts of their work, we now turn to the evidence for their assertions. In our view, it is not difficult to identify individual performance audit reports, or sequences of audits in a particular area, that have had an impact at an operational and policy level. The RRV's recent work on fraud and abuse in the welfare system has attracted considerable interest in the Swedish parliament, government, and media (Sandberg and Ivarsson 1996, p. 32), with studies of housing benefit and maintenance allowance systems bringing administrative changes that are expected to save at least three billion kronor a year. Stiffer penalties have been introduced against those working while claiming benefit, and in the 1996 supplementary budget bill, the Swedish government proposed that parliament allot 350 million kronor over three years to counter-fraud measures. An RRV study of the Swedish Forestry Administration made a series of recommendations that were taken up by a government commission on the future of the forestry industry. Subsequently, the government presented a Forestry Bill to the Riksdag and proposed that the RRV's recommendations be implemented (Swedish National Audit Office 1995a, p. 19).

In the Netherlands, the Rekenkamer's 1994 report on the police force caused considerable public reaction, and as a result the government announced that it would take measures to improve performance (NAO 1996a). Interestingly the Rekenkamer has the ability to make an impact very early on in the life of a project, interpreting its powers as giving it the ability to examine a subject as soon as a decision with financial implications has been taken.

In 1986, for example, the Lower House responded to a critical report of the Rekenkamer about the privatization of the State Fishing Port Authority by cancelling an agreement and ensuring that the renegotiated agreement secured a better price and greater protection for the taxpayer (NAO 1996a, p. 148). When the Rekenkamer investigated the new agreement, it established that the Authority had been sold at a much better price and that after-sale financial risks had been better covered by the ministry (Algemene Rekenkamer 1991, p. 37).

In France, a study by the Cour des Comptes of the administrative and financial framework of the social policies to assist handicapped adults led to the reform of the provision of grants to handicapped adults. The report was delivered by the Cour's *premier président* and two presidents of chambers to the members of two committees of the National Assembly, over the period when MPs had examined a disposition of the financial act reforming these grants (Lamarque 1997). In 1995 an examination of the Association de Recherche contre le Cancer resulted in a complete reorganization of the body and the removal of its head, while in the same year an audit of the bank Credit Lyonnais revealed serious mismanagement and fraud, which provoked a major public debate about internal and external controls.

In 1995 the VTV audited the system for rating the financial capacities of municipalities. This system provided the basis by which hundreds of billions of finmarks were allocated to the municipalities as state grants (Valtiontalouden tarkastusvirasto 1995). The audit showed that the system was highly complicated and opaque, that it resulted in unequal treatment for different municipalities, and that recent changes in the system had further aggravated the distortions, giving multiple and overlapping compensations for certain types of municipality and disadvantaging others without any apparent economic justification. In its report, the VTV sketched a model for an improved system, and proposed that the present arrangements should be replaced as soon as possible because of their wasteful and unjust character. It even proposed that responsibility for preparing the change should be transferred from the Ministry of the Interior to the prime minister. Unsurprisingly, this report captured much media attention. It was fiercely criticized by the responsible minister (again, unsurprisingly). A new coalition government entered office soon afterwards, and brought in reforms that were fairly much in line with the VTV's recommendations.

The NAO distinguishes between different types of impact. Some are classed as 'quantifiable financial' impacts, with 'real and readily accessible changes in the financing of the area in question' (NAO 1997a, p. 23). A good example is that of privatization audits, where in recent years the Office has drawn attention to the risks to value for money when government departments have decided to sell shares in a company all at once rather than in stages. Having regard to this, recent privatizations of National Power and PowerGen were conducted in stages, and as a result the taxpayer benefited from additional proceeds of £2.3 billion, £1.15 billion in 1996 alone. Another example is an examination of the management of accommodation by higher education institutions in Wales, which led to quantified financial savings; for example, two of the institutions visited by the NAO made changes that resulted in reductions in planned expenditure of £15 million (NAO 1997b, p. 30) Another examination—of university purchasing arrangements—led to savings of £78 million between 1994 and 1996, while improvements to procedures for identifying, evaluating, and countering VAT avoidance contributed to the collection of £100 million of additional revenue in 1995–6 by HM Customs and Excise (NAO 1997a, p. 25). The NAO also refers to quantified non-financial impacts such as improvements in customer satisfaction, reductions in waiting times, or shorter construction periods. Qualitative impacts are also recognized, these being 'actions which improve government operations or provide better service to the public but for which there is no discernible measurable benefit' (NAO 1997a, p. 26). Finally, senior NAO staff pointed out that another impact of their work could be direct savings to the citizen, for example in the case of lower car insurance prices for the disabled (following a recent report on the subject).

In general, SAIs tend to steer clear of highly political matters, but in a small number of cases performance audit reports have had an impact at the political level. In France at the end of 1997, members of the cabinet of M. Dumas (a former minister for foreign affairs and the current president of the constitutional council) were fined by the Cour de Discipline Budgétaire et Financière following evidence gathered during an audit by the Cour des Comptes. In the UK, the NAO's report on the government's sale of Rover Group to British Aerospace in 1988 concluded that the selling price of £150 million undervalued the real market value of the company by between £50 million and £400 million pounds. A leaked memorandum to the Public Accounts Committee revealed that the government had paid £38 million of 'sweetners' to aid the sale. According to observers, the report embarrassed the government 'very severely' (Glynn *et al.* 1992, p. 56), and was instrumental in leading to the European Commission's demand for the side payments to be repaid. Another NAO report, on aid to build the Pergau Dam in Malaysia, set off a train of events that led ultimately to political controversy involving the overseas aid minister, the secretary of state for defence, the foreign secretary, and the prime minister of the day. The NAO report concentrated on the value for money of the deal and on whether it stuck to aid guidelines, but politicians asked 'more political questions' (Pollitt and Summa 1996, p. 39), and uncovered a more controversial story. Then there was the case of the VTV audit of the allocative system for municipal subsidies, referred to earlier in this section. In that instance the responsible minister went as far as publicly accusing the VTV of politicking, by publishing a report on a sensitive political issue close to an election. The office did not change its position (or enter into public argument) in response to this attack. A few months later the new government's reform proposals seemed to have been influenced by the VTV's recommendations. One might also note that, by suggesting that responsibility for the reform of this system be transferred from one minister to another, the VTV seemed clearly to have entered the political arena. This part of their report, however, was not implemented.

10.4 Measuring Impact

Although there is little doubt that the performance audit work of SAIs can and does have an impact, measuring the precise scale of this impact is far more difficult. This is not, of course, a problem confined to audit work. In the area of health services research, for example, there has been considerable discussion about how to assess the payback from research (see Buxton and Hanney 1995). As we noted earlier, some results, such as the alteration of practices recommended by an SAI, may be obvious, but others, like the influencing of political debate, are less clear. As has been observed elsewhere, 'In many cases it must be extremely difficult confidently to identify, quantify and separate out the specific contribution made by an audit investigation (as opposed to a host of other influences) to an administrative innovation that incurs expenditure' (Pollitt and Summa 1997b, p. 321). Explicit systems (of varying degrees of refinement) for measuring the impacts of performance audits were seen in four of the five SAIs at the time of our study, the exception being the VTV; in that organization staff advised us that procedures had been in place for discussing reports internally, but had now stopped.

At the SAIs that did have procedures for recording changes, greater attention to measuring the impact of performance audits appears to have been shown in recent years than in the 1980s. The most recent development has been at the Cour, where from 1997 the annual public report presented an analysis of the impact of the SAI's activity, including performance audit, an indication of the greater attention that is being paid to the impact of reporting. At the Rekenkamer senior staff suggested that a more systematic approach began in about 1992, whereas previously there had been no procedures for assessing impacts other than examining the press coverage that reports received. Follow-up audits began in the mid-1980s. At the NAO, as well, greater emphasis has been placed on demonstrating the value of the Office's work during the 1990s and particularly in recent years, with the Office recently stating that 'Following up and measuring the impact of vfm examinations is an integral part of our standard procedures' (National Audit Office 1997c, p. 50).

The most common means of measuring impact, both at the NAO and elsewhere, are discussed in the following subsections.

Changes made by government

Influencing practices in government is a professed aim of all the SAIs in this study. As a result, the most common measure of impact—used by the Rekenkamer, NAO, and the RRV—is the proportion of recommendations in performance audit reports accepted by government. There are, of course, drawbacks to such a crude measure of impact. It gives no weighting to the relative importance of the changes, in terms of the benefits to the taxpayer or financial impact. Nor does it indicate whether effecting the change is a straightforward task for the auditee, with few wider implications, or one requiring major reform, a point also raised in discussions about recommendations arising from the work of evaluators (Weiss 1987). And, of course, there is a big difference between an organization's promising to introduce particular measures, and its actually doing so once the focus of attention has moved on. Despite this, counting the number of recommendations accepted is perhaps an inevitable starting point.

The Rekenkamer has estimated that some 70 per cent of its recommendations are accepted by the government, although the extent to which remedial action has actually been taken is less clear (NAO 1996a, p. 149). One of its own reports (Algemene Rekenkamer 1991, p. 47) cast doubt on this figure, suggesting that 'Not infrequently [these undertakings to take action] lack substance or are not complied with. In these circumstances the Court of Audit is unable to do any more than to persist in exposing undesirable developments.' However, in our more recent discussions, staff considered that the office's impact had increased in recent years and repeated the figure of around 70 per cent.

The RRV has an operational goal of reporting 'on the extent to which the latest years' observations and proposals have resulted in the government and the agencies taking appropriate measures for action'. Its annual publication, *The Results of Three Years' Performance Auditing*, describes what action has been taken as a result of their proposals. Overall, the RRV has suggested that about two-thirds of its performance audits provide demonstrable results within three years, and that only 'a few proposals have not been acted on at all' (Riksrevisionsverket 1997a, p. 20). For example, a total of 61 per cent of proposals made in audits undertaken between 1991–2 and 1993–4 had been completely or partly implemented, 35 per cent were under consideration or partly implemented, and just 4 per cent had not been implemented.

The NAO's measure is slightly different, in that its Annual Report records the proportion of recommendations made by the Public Accounts Committee—based on NAO reports—that have been accepted by the government. Figures for recent years indicate a success rate of over 90 per cent per annum. The NAO also uses the total number of significant changes made by audited bodies as a result of its examinations as a measure of success. Recent figures suggest that the recorded impact has grown sharply—from

249 in 1993, 'including 101 improvements in economy, efficiency and effectiveness and 17 in quality of service' (NAO 1994a, p. 12), to 'over 2,600 significant changes to [audited bodies] procedures' in 1996 (NAO 1997b, p. 29). Part of this considerable increase may be explained by what some staff suggested was the greater importance attached, in recent years, to following up and identifying such changes—a strong indication of the influence of New Public Management (NPM) ideas within the NAO. Others suggested that it indicated that NAO recommendations had become more specific, making it easier for reports to lead to longer lists of proposals.

As we noted earlier, much of the Cour's work is not published. What appears in the public domain, therefore, is a carefully selected subset of the organization's reports, many of which remain confidential between the Cour and the auditee concerned (Pollitt and Summa 1997b, p. 322, and interviews). Indeed, much of the Cour's impact appears to be behind the scenes, making it very difficult to compare it with the other SAIs. The Cour does not systematically survey the implementation of recommendations arising from its work, but the Annual Public Report now includes details of the follow-up of previous evaluations, and within each chamber (the subdivisions within the Cour), staff keep in touch with auditees and gather information on the reforms implemented following recommendations by the Cour. On occasion, details of these may be publicly cited, as when the *premier président* introduced the annual report to members of parliament on 26 November 1997; he pointed to various cases, including the collective resignation of members of the board following an audit of the Mutualité Sociale Agricole. However, citing examples in this way is clearly somewhat different from the kind of regular counting and publication of overall impact indicators, which is the practice at the NAO, the Rekenkamer, and the RRV.

Whatever the levels of success highlighted above, the figures do indicate that not all recommendations made by SAIs are accepted. After publication, proposals in SAI reports can be, and on occasion are, 'vigorously contested—and effectively rejected—by the auditees, or by the government ministers representing them' (Pollitt and Summa 1996, p. 45). The example of the VTV report on municipal subsidies has already been mentioned. In another case the Minister of Transport used a press conference to criticize a VTV report on the system of subsidies to the shipping industry.

Financial savings

Uniquely among our set of SAIs (although not within the wider world of audit, where, for example, the GAO in the United States and the Audit Commission in the United Kingdom undertake similar exercises), the NAO has taken the measurement of impact one stage further by attempting systematically to attach a financial value to the changes for which it can claim responsibility. The details of administrative changes with possible financial implications are identified by the audit teams responsible for each report as part of their routine follow-up. The figures are discussed and agreed with the audited body, a process that one member of our team has described elsewhere (in Weekes 1996, p. 19) as resulting in 'one of the most conservative formulae for calculating savings used in Europe'. This approach is designed to make the figures less speculative than might otherwise be the case.

In recent years the NAO has claimed 'savings' arising from its work in excess of seven times its own running costs, the majority from performance audit work. For example, in 1993 the figure quoted was £229 million, while in 1997 the NAO reported that 'Over the past three years these savings have totalled some £858 million in addition to on-going savings arising from earlier recommendations' (NAO 1997b, p. 29). Staff told us that the figure for financial savings had now become a key target and indicator of the impact of the NAO—as well as a driver of study design and an important factor in the NAO's bid to Parliament for resources. While some staff in other SAIs were sceptical about the validity of this kind of exercise, the size of the claims made by the NAO could, if anything, be understated, given that the audited bodies have no reason to exaggerate the impact of the NAO's work. In the future, we were told, the quantified savings claimed by the NAO might be externally validated.

Although they have not implemented a system exactly the same as that at the NAO, the RRV's most recent annual report (Riksrevisionsverket 1997a, pp. 21–2) included examples of audits that had led to quantifiable savings. The study of maintenance allowances mentioned above is reckoned to have led to savings of SEK 500 million, while the RRV has stated that 'it has been estimated that several audits performed during the last two years have provided significant effects for government finances, in several cases exceeding SEK 100 million each year and in some cases considerably more'. A number of other studies have resulted in recommendations for savings which, they believe, may accrue after further examination.

Impact on parliament

Another key indicator of impact considered by SAIs is the amount of attention their work gains in parliament. At the RRV, staff told us they examined whether the office's work was mentioned in the Budget Bill and each head of unit checked this document and the supporting background material. Another reflection of whether a report had had impact was for the auditors to be invited to give a presentation to the relevant standing committee of the Riksdag. At the Rekenkamer, too, staff considered that how their reports were received in parliament was important, in particular whether members were pressing ministries to take the action recommended in their reports. Staff pay attention, for example, to the number of questions asked of the government about their reports by the States General.

Those interviewed at the NAO also indicated that one measure of success for their reports was whether they led to productive hearings of the Public Accounts Committee, i.e. that led to worthwhile recommendations, and, as we have seen above, the proportion of the Committee's recommendations accepted is a key measure of impact. At the Cour the position differs, as parliament is not the main recipient of audit reports, but despite this links are growing, especially in the area of social security, where regular meetings are arranged between members of parliament and senior members of the Cour. Moreover, members of parliament frequently refer to the reports of the Cour.

Internal measures

The measures above are publicly stated indicators of impact. In addition, SAIs use internal measures to assess the success of their work in influencing others (as was noted in Chapter 7). One aspect of the post-audit review at the NAO is to seek comments from the audited body in a questionnaire. This asks, among other things, whether the auditee considers that the examination provided it with any new insights into its work. The NAO also seeks the views of senior officials in the bodies subject to its audit on the value of its work. The RRV's performance auditors have tried other ways of obtaining feedback on the quality and worth of their work, in the form of seminars and conferences attended by the external recipients of audit reports and other interested parties. Staff at the Rekenkamer advised us that a similar approach was likely to be introduced within their office.

All SAIs have sought press coverage in recent years, having previously tended to avoid such contact, and all monitor the amount of coverage obtained by their work. Some staff still considered that the press often distort their work and findings and do not cover the more difficult subjects very well. In general, however, SAIs welcomed good coverage in newspapers and specialist journals as an indicator of the worth of their work. Articles reporting the NAO's work (both performance and financial audit) appear most weeks in the broadsheet press, and an assessment of the media coverage is included in the post-publication scrutiny carried out by audit teams. Press attention is monitored and analysed at most, if not all, SAIs.

10.5 Independent Assessment of Impact

Up to now, our discussion of the impact of performance audit has been based almost entirely on what SAIs have reported about themselves. Assessing whether these views are reasonable is not easy, as there is little independent information available. As a starting point, it is perhaps worth suggesting that if SAIs' work were entirely without merit or value they would have been found out by now, given the level of concern expressed in all countries about the use to which public funds are put. To our knowledge, none of the SAIs under examination is subject to sustained public criticism about the value of its work. Indeed, the contrary appears to be the case. For example, in 1997 the president of the Finance Committee of the French parliament described the annual report of the Cour as a 'crucial instrument in the control of the public finances' and praised the growing relationship between the Cour and parliament. In the UK senior politicians have spoken publicly of their admiration for the work of the NAO (see e.g. Weekes 1996, p. 17), and the (admittedly rather set-piece) annual parliamentary debate on the work of the Public Accounts Committee has been used as an opportunity for MPs to comment favourably on the work of the Committee and the NAO.

One relatively favourable external assessment came in a study of an NAO report (Roberts and Pollitt 1994) which concluded (p. 547) that 'NAO VFM work can have an impact on parliamentary debate, and on the procedures of government departments and agencies. It can and does enhance democratic accountability.' A recent specialist review (Tulip 1997) of an area where the NAO had undertaken work—university purchasing—concluded (p. 24) that a 1993 report had been 'a major stimulus' to much of the sector, leading to significant savings over a number of years. A study of the role of the NAO in examining privatizations in recent years (Hodges 1997, p. 35) begins with the statement that 'The National Audit Office has played an important role throughout this period in examining the conduct of the privatization process.'

In Sweden, the Swedish parliament's views on the RRV's performance audit work were collected by a political scientist commissioned by the SAI. RRV reported that the review had established that the 'Swedish Parliament has great confidence in the RRV's reports and the RRV has enjoyed the confidence of Parliament for many years. There is a predominant feeling in Parliament that the RRV's performance audit maintains consistently high standards and that its reports are reliable' (Riksrevisionsverket 1997a, p. 23). However, RRV noted that, 'In view of the great amount of information from different sources received by Parliament, it is not always the case that the RRV's reports have a visible impact in the form of references.'

At a political level, the potential importance of performance audit reports does not go unnoticed. In the UK one unnamed department confirmed in 1996 that 'Our ministers get very excited about the press coverage of NAO reports and PAC hearings' (Weekes 1996, p. 16). In the Netherlands the Algemene Rekenkamer was criticized by a number of former ministers (still politically active) after an audit report on a programme partly carried out during their time in office was cleared only with the then current minister (Mul 1996). In both examples politicians had been concerned at the impact of the reports of SAIs, and in the latter case were keen to have the opportunity to make their comments on findings.

However, there has also been criticism of the value of performance audit and what some see as its limited impact. Certain critics consider that SAIs 'pull their punches', saying less than they could. In considering the NAO, Power compares it to the Audit Commission (the UK's local government audit institution), judging that the latter can be more 'up front' in its recommendations, largely because it is not a servant of Parliament. And, he adds, 'The NAO tends to pull back from open-ended evaluations which would divide the Public Accounts Committee on party lines and undermine its credibility' (Power 1997, p. 48). One former member of the committee, Tim Smith, suggested that the NAO's impact and its ability to make its observations clearly had been affected by the process of clearing reports (Smith 1993).

A number of writers (e.g. McEldowney 1994, and Glynn *et al.* 1992) have suggested that the impact of SAIs (and other auditors) has also been reduced by the difficulties associated with assessing the effectiveness of government activities, an area into which SAIs have, as we saw in Chapter 6, ventured only infrequently. Despite the public management changes discussed in Chapter 3, the problems SAIs face in doing such work include the lack of clear objectives in many policies, the difficulties of drawing clear links between intentions and outcomes of decisions within government, poor information on which to make assessments, and the perceived danger of straying into criticism of the policy itself, rather than its execution. This final point has not been lost on auditees. According to reports, after the NAO's report on the sale of Rover Group to British Aerospace at the end of the 1980s, senior civil servants became concerned at the NAO's interest in the effectiveness of policy. According to one source (quoted in Glynn *et al.* 1992, p. 56), a number of permanent secretaries issued a publicly reported warning in 1991 about the way they felt the NAO was entering the policy arena and becoming political.

10.6 Negative Impacts

These criticisms lead us on to consider the potentially negative impacts of performance audit work. It is, of course, very difficult to assess the scale of any negative effects. They may pass unnoticed and unmeasured, or be only vaguely understood, and SAIs do not report on them. However, there is a recognition within most SAIs that audit can have unpredictable and even adverse impacts within audited bodies and that, consequently, they have a responsibility to minimize these impacts.

From the point of view of some auditees, the most obvious drawback is the cost to them of being subject to a performance audit, although this is very rarely monitored by the body under examination (or, indeed, by the auditor). The potential importance of the end product of the audit (perhaps a report to parliament critical of its activities) to the reputation of the audited body usually ensures that auditees take care to provide requested material and make staff available for interviews, as well as to monitor the progress of the auditors. Such efforts inevitably disrupt work programmes to some extent (Hogwood *et al.* 1998). In the UK, the report clearance process—often taking three months, but in extreme cases lasting much longer—adds to this, with senior staff carefully scrutinizing draft reports in order to make comments. Similarly, the inclusion of the study in the programme of PAC hearings will, given the importance attached to it, add considerably to the cost to the auditee and involve the most senior staff in time-consuming familiarization of the subject under consideration. Despite this effort, some have questioned whether a committee hearing is the best forum for identifying improvements and securing change. One former member of the Committee, who participated in many such hearings until 1997, stated: 'There is a tendency for the PAC during the course of its hearings to place too much emphasis on the search for a scapegoat for past errors and too little on the lessons to be learnt for the future' (in Smith 1993).

There may be also other impacts on the auditee. Although very difficult to prove, there may well be cases of bodies introducing administrative changes in advance of, or during, investigations. This may not always be a bad thing. One auditor told us about an organization that revised its guidance on the risks associated with particular activities within weeks of a presentation on provisional audit findings. However, the same person noted, with some concern, that another organization had introduced a, perhaps unnecessary, administrative system simply as a result of an innocent enquiry he had made. There may also be cases of bodies distorting their work programmes to ensure that they 'tidy up' particular areas of responsibility prior to an audit.

Some consider that there is also a pyschological impact of being subject to a performance audit. One observer has suggested, without giving any examples, that,

> based on recent Dutch experiences, auditors are sometimes confronted with the question of why they don't pay attention to the negative impact of their fault-finding approach on the audited organization's human and social capital. Sometimes the commitment of employees to an organization declines after a performance audit is published, even when the findings of the report cover only side-aspects of the organization. This in turn may reduce the motivation of employees. (Leeuw 1996, p. 55)

Other commentators have expressed concerns about the constraining impact of performance audit on the culture of greater risk-taking associated with many of the New Public Management changes discussed in Chapter 3. Auditors have traditionally been concerned about compliance with procedures, and some consider that they find it hard to change their approach. Sir Peter Kemp, architect of the 'Next Steps' initiative which created the system of executive agencies in the UK, claimed in 1997 that 'today in government, for instance, the private finance initiative is being strangled by fears of upsetting the National Audit Office or Public Accounts Committee' (Kemp 1997). Such views were rebutted by the NAO. The director responsible for the examination of these projects (who has considerable experience in the private sector) stated in a published interview that 'within the rules civil servants should "think and innovate"' (Timmins 1997), and suggested that the reason some were not doing so was that no one quite believed that the NAO was recommending this.

10.7 Enhancing the Impact

Many of the developments in performance audit outlined in earlier chapters have been implemented by SAIs with the aim of increasing the impact of their work. Thus we have seen, for example, the introduction of a variety of new methods at the NAO; the recruitment of staff with new skills at several SAIs; the development of better planned studies in all SAIs; longer-term audit strategies at the RRV; efforts to work more closely with auditees at the NAO; the development of greater publicity for reports in all SAIs; the move from consolidated reports to single, stand-alone publications in the Rekenkamer; and efforts to obtain broader and deeper rights of access to bodies spending public money in the RRV and NAO.

Publicizing reports has been particularly important in enhancing the impact of reports and the reputations of SAIs as bodies with influence. In 1995 a senior figure in public-sector audit in the UK commented that recent developments have suggested that 'the ability of the auditor to act wholly independently is a function of the auditor's ability to use the media. The greater the ability of the auditor to do this, the more independently he or she can operate, for neither government nor opposition can afford to ignore the impact of the media' (Hepworth 1995, p. 42). Thus, while SAIs publicize their work to try to ensure that it reaches the widest audience, they also appear to do so in the belief that external publicity is perhaps the strongest lever they have to ensure that they are listened to and their recommendations implemented.

As Chapter 9 showed, there have been many signs of SAIs increasing their efforts to influence the media and gain attention for their work. All SAIs issue press releases with their reports, but some have taken their efforts further. The Cour des Comptes' *premier président* has established a team with public relations expertise to enhance the SAI's media profile, and press briefings are organized on all public reports. The Rekenkamer has established a new unit for its editorial function to ensure high-quality reports, and has developed a higher media profile to push its message. The VTV has made use of a public relations company in recent years and in some cases has contracted out the preparation of its press releases. The NAO has upgraded the post of press officer and introduced strategies for gaining media coverage for individual reports.

In seeking greater impact in the media, SAIs are aware of the importance of balancing attempts to increase publicity for their findings with a need to avoid antagonizing those with whom they must maintain an ongoing relationship—the auditees. As Pollitt and Summa put it, 'In general politicians and the lay public may want a diet of dramatic stories—tales of waste, corruption, and inefficiency, replete with good guys and bad guys. However, the audited bodies themselves may respond best to careful, modulated presentations that make recommendations for non-dramatic, incremental improvements' (Pollitt and Summa 1996, p. 44). Where this is not seen to be the case, there can be a reaction. In the Netherlands, the former prime minister, Mr Lubbers, criticized the Rekenkamer for publishing press statements which were stronger than the actual reports justified (Mul 1996).

In interviews, staff at all SAIs also indicated that there had also been increased efforts made to court and influence parliament and government. At the RRV, staff spoke of trying to play a part in setting the political agenda rather than just fit in with it, in particular by examining in detail key issues of concern, such as the labour market and the quality of schools and universities. At the Rekenkamer, increased efforts have been made to choose subjects for examination that were considered to be 'of interest and relevance to Parliament and society in general', rather than more narrow and technical matters that had been studied in the past. There was greater contact with parliamentarians over the choice of subjects for examination, and since 1996 the Rekenkamer has offered and undertakes regular briefings for parliament. At the Cour, as we have seen, considerable emphasis is currently being laid on developing closer links with parliament, especially but not exclusively in the field of social security.

Efforts have also been made by SAIs to increase the impact of reports in other ways. Calls by the RRV and the NAO for an extension of their powers so as to follow European Community funds through to final recipients, and the NAO's efforts to be granted access to social housing providers and a number of other bodies (NAO 1995a, p. 3), reflect a desire to get 'closer to the action', as one NAO director put it. In this way, the impact can be enhanced as auditors have a greater chance of finding dissonance between claimed and actual performance. In Chapter 8 we described how SAIs had strengthened the efforts put into designing studies, and in some cases were looking for more innovative approaches in order to produce what they hope will be more penetrative studies. The move by the Rekenkamer to publish reports separately rather than in compendium form, which was referred to in Chapter 9, has also been driven by the desire for greater, and more regular, impact.

We have also seen evidence of SAIs making greater efforts to gain acceptance for their findings among auditees and seeking ways of spreading lessons from their work beyond the confines of the formal accountability processes. Much of the literature on the utilization of evaluation findings stresses the importance of working with, and involving, the evaluated body. SAIs appear to have followed this line. Presentations of provisional findings, regular meetings, and closer contact during audit fieldwork are all designed to increase auditees' receptiveness to their messages and so increase the impact of the performance audit work. Several SAIs also attempt to spread their word more widely. The RRV has made efforts 'to pass on experience, verify observations and gain acceptance for conclusions' by organizing seminars, training courses, and other activities in cooperation with the cabinet office and RRV's financial management division. The NAO has also sought to disseminate more widely the information gathered during its work, issuing good practice guides after a number of audits, and circulating a newsletter with key findings from performance audit reports.

10.8 Other Influences on Impact

In the introduction, we referred to the theoretical model of how performance audit reports are intended to have their impact. We reported comments that this model was too simplistic and, to some extent, seemed to assume that SAIs operated in a vacuum. So far, we have placed the emphasis on how SAIs themselves try to ensure that their work is successful. However, ultimately, things do not rest in their hands alone. Performance audit reports are not guaranteed a warm reception and, as we have seen, may be resisted, a situation not dissimilar to that faced by evaluators and other researchers working in a political environment. The reports may pass into the public domain largely unnoticed except by those responsible for them or subject to the audit. The impact of some reports may be negligible, either because they were not particularly successful pieces of work and contain methodological shortcomings, or because, ultimately, they concluded that arrangements or activities examined were largely sound. While this latter point should perhaps be the cause for some celebration from all concerned for the good use of public money, from the auditors' point of view, there may ultimately be a sense of disappointment that they have not found reason to make recommendations.

Many high-level environmental factors condition the success of individual performance audit reports. Our conclusions in a number of places in this book hint at an ambiguity in the role of SAIs which we might expect would affect the impact of their work. On the one hand, there are a number of strengths to their constitutional position. They have official status and an ability to raise issues at the highest levels of government. They have powers of access which ensure they can unearth sensitive material, as well as independent means of reporting that enable them to draw that information to public attention. In addition, in most countries there are mechanisms that ensure their work is given consideration. On the other hand, SAIs operate in political environments in which they are not, in most cases, among the biggest players. Nor do they have legal powers to enforce their recommendations (with the partial exception here of the Cour's powers to fine and discipline). In addition, they have limited resources, but a potentially endless list of topics to examine, thus having to spread their attention widely. There are limits to the SAI's ability to comment on the merits of policy decisions, and the need to take into account, either formally or informally, the views of auditees, leading at times to an element of compromise in their work. SAIs must also balance concerns to protect their independence and professionalism with a recognition that their ability to continue to do their job requires an ongoing relationship with auditees. Thus, if SAIs are powerful weapons—and we consider that they are—they are perhaps weapons designed to be used in fairly controlled circumstances.

The response of auditees to audit findings is also a lot less certain than the model suggests. In some cases they may refuse to accept findings and recommendations, or else may pay only lipservice to them. On occasions, an SAI's impact can be rapid, with steps taken swiftly by government to make changes to obvious weaknesses, often before a report has been published. At other times change is slow and reform longer-term and incremental, perhaps necessarily so in complex areas. There is also the question of the extent to which auditees consider implementation of recommendations made by auditors to be in their interest. Where financial savings that might accrue do not benefit them, for example because they must be returned to the Treasury, the incentives are limited and making changes may be seen to be more trouble than they are worth. Equally, the sometimes confrontational nature of the performance audit process, where auditors may be trying to impose recommendations on organizations at the end of a process that has highlighted major shortcomings, does not always help to maximize the chances of the auditee 'owning' the proposals.

The response of other participants in the audit process is also of great importance. For example, where there is interest or concern within the legislature, and findings in a report are considered impossible to ignore, there may be great public pressure for change in response to performance audit findings. Some subjects are more likely to accord with the broad concerns of parliament—issues of obvious waste or impropriety, for example, or high-profile cases of poorly implemented projects are 'meat and drink' to politicians—whereas other matters may be considered too technical and dry to excite interest, despite their importance. The ability of legislators is also significant and, in the view of some, not always to be taken for granted. Ten years ago some observers in the UK commented on the 'highly variable nature of the scrutiny' brought to bear by the Public Accounts Committee, and on the 'lack of skill or inclination on the part of some of its members' (Robinson 1988). Similar sentiments were expressed earlier about the use made of the Rekenkamer's work by the States General prior to the mid-1980s.

In addition, luck may play a big part in determining the impact of a report. Despite all the planning that goes into undertaking performance audits, there appears to be much truth in the suggestion that a report's impact 'will often depend partly on the chance factor of what other news is current at that particular time. If the topic the auditors set off to investigate (sometimes long ago) is now fashionable, their report may have great public impact. If, however, the political and media spotlight has meanwhile moved on to other topics, then their report may have little public effect' (Pollitt and Summa 1996, p. 43).

Timing of publication is inevitably a part of this. The appearance of the NAO's study on the performance of the Meteorological Office during a summer heatwave in 1995, when there was little other news, ensured it, perhaps, disproportionate attention (NAO 1995b). The change of senior personnel at one organization during the course of another NAO study meant that the new chief executive, not feeling responsible for mistakes in the past, took a positive view of the examination (Goldsworthy 1997, p. 9).

In their dealings with the press, SAIs are helped by the fact that they are seen as 'official' and 'independent' carriers of what is often bad or scandalous news about fairly easily understood issues such as fraud, waste, or incompetence, subjects that make for strong press stories. To a very great extent, media coverage of performance audit reports takes the SAIs' position as authoritative, resulting in coverage that reinforces the impression that they are bodies with 'clout'. In reporting the results of performance audits, journalists have little or no time to question what SAIs have done or said, or to make an independent assessment of what has been concluded. Such reflection can and does occur later, perhaps in more academic considerations of audit, but, in general, the world has moved on by then. The need to compress complex issues into short stories also leads journalists to make simplifications that, in many cases, reflect well on SAIs. Many of these factors seem to enable some SAIs to 'punch above their weight'—to have greater impact than they might otherwise have.

10.9 Conclusions

The evidence gathered for this chapter suggests that performance audit work can and does have an impact. In each of the countries examined, performance audits have led to changes to government activities—some significant, others small but, nevertheless, important. In many cases the responses to recommendations in audit reports have led to substantial savings in public funds. There has also been an unknown, but possibly extensive, deterrent effect arising simply from the fact that SAIs exist, as well as a more general educational impact on those organizations and activities examined, and on the wider government sector. In addition, our evidence suggests that the impact of SAIs' work, and SAIs' concern to demonstrate their impact, have both increased over the periods we have considered.

Performance audits appear to have a range of impacts. This can, perhaps, be likened to a ripple effect, with the intensity of the impact strongest at the point of contact, where the stone hits the water—the body or bodies examined—but becoming weaker as the waves spread outwards. At the centre, the audit examination may influence the actual procedures of the body examined, with recommendations resulting in changes to practices in place at the time of the audit. There may also be an impact on particular policies, for example in terms of encouraging a rethinking of an entire service. A subtler effect is on the auditee's own future thinking. An audit may encourage the body to think more clearly about its objectives, priorities, and the measurement of its own performance, perhaps leading to more structured approaches, where instinctive ones might previously have been the norm. Outside the immediate focus of the audit—as the waves spread outwards—an SAI may influence other bodies undertaking similar work (e.g. schools or health authorities beyond those visited for an audit) or having similar features (e.g. bodies with similar treasury or personnel functions, but not necessarily in the same sector), or else may influence how public bodies as a whole deal with particular aspects of their work (e.g. in influencing what is acceptable behaviour for public servants).

Assessing exactly how much impact performance audit has had is a formidable, if not an impossible, task. Those SAIs that have taken the most managerialist stances—the NAO, the RRV, and the Rekenkamer—have, to varying degrees, taken to advertising their own assessments of the impact of their work in their annual reports; but these are not independently verified, and may be subject either to underestimation or exaggeration. It is even harder to identify and assess the negative impacts of their work, which some consider occur. In these circumstances it is very difficult to assess whether performance audits undertaken by our SAIs are worth the resources employed on them short of suggesting that in many cases they most certainly are, and that in others the payback is less obvious or perhaps non-existent. There is, perhaps, scope for further research to follow up a number of audit reports to establish exactly how many potential readers were reached and what use they made of the reports.

In any final assessment, the question remains of how far SAIs, as currently constituted, staffed, and positioned, are likely to be able to effect change and improvements within government. In our view SAIs are clearly agents for change, if that means they recommend improvements in government practices, and act as a catalyst by highlighting poor performance and providing information that is a starting point for consideration of change. Beyond that, we suggest that SAIs are constrained by their status and constitutional positions, by their lack of executive power, and by expectations of how they should conduct themselves. While much of the literature in the field suggests that evaluators can maximize their impact by working with the subjects of their work to bring about change, efforts by SAIs along these lines appear to be constrained by their primary role in holding public bodies accountable, in public, for their use of taxpayers' money, as well as by the expectation (both inside and outside the SAIs) that they will remain independent of their auditees. And, while the existence of formal arrangements for considering SAIs' reports enhances the likelihood that they will be given proper consideration, these procedures—which can be confrontational—tend to generate a defensiveness among auditees which is not necessarily conducive to ensuring that effective change takes place.

11

Overview

Christopher Pollitt

11.1 Hindsight and Foresight

Conventionally, it falls to the final chapter to deliver upon the promises made at a book's beginning. Not infrequently, in the sobering light of hindsight, those promises appear, to a degree at least, rash. In Chapter 1 we set out nine central questions and promised to provide answers to them. Ten chapters later, those questions still appear to be significant and worthwhile, although the responses to some of them are more oblique or conditional than we may have hoped at the outset. Most of this final chapter will be structured according to those nine questions, but we will also go beyond them by permitting ourselves some limited speculations about the future of performance audit. In doing this, our aim, as indicated earlier, is not to prescribe some particular direction or reform, but rather to identify certain strategic choices and constraints which we believe will face those who wish to develop performance audit further.

Of course, most of our answers to each of the central questions have already been elaborated in the previous, more detailed, chapters. The task here is therefore to summarize, to integrate the separate answers (so far as seems possible), and to draw out any overall implications. For convenience, the original questions will be repeated as section headings.

11.2 What is Performance Audit, as Practised by the SAIs in our Study?

The brief answer here is that 'performance audit' has been somewhat differently defined, and also somewhat differently practised, in the five SAIs we have surveyed. Furthermore (see next section), the practice of performance audit has developed within individual countries over time, so that the actual activities of auditors have varied from one period to another, and between one audit and another. These differences were documented in earlier chapters, especially Chapter 2, and there is no need to repeat that detail here. The main point is that performance audit is not a standardized product (though there are some who hope, through guidelines or standards or training, to make it more of one than it has been in the past). While there is an agreed INTOSAI definition of performance audit, there is no single, timeless methodology or set of practices that 'really is' performance audit. Instead, we are examining a developing and only loosely defined set of practices and associated rhetorics or discourses. Thus, the very *identity* of performance audit is neither precise nor entirely stabilized. This makes matters more complicated, but also more interesting, than if we were examining some simpler and more strictly prescribed activity.

To say that there is variance between studies, between countries, and over time is not, however, to suggest that we are dealing with an indecipherable chaos. On the contrary, there are some key patterns and definitional elements. One might say, first, that the *values* that drive performance audit are different from those that inform traditional, financial audit. For the latter, the notion of conformance to a prescribed pattern or process or set of rules is crucial. The auditor verifies the degree of conformance with these pre-defined 'requirements' (Barzelay 1996; Chelimsky 1985). By contrast, the connections between performance audit and the public management reforms described in Chapter 3 are most obvious. Most of the public management reform initiatives emphasized a shift from the control of inputs and processes to new forms of control based on the measurement of outputs and outcomes. The previous administrative systems stressed the correct allocation of finance to the appropriate budgetary 'lines', the economical use of inputs, and the conformity of actions with prescribed procedures. The new approaches claimed to give more flexibility with respect to inputs and processes ('letting managers manage' and 'making managers manage'), in return for stronger monitoring and evaluation of *performance*, i.e. outputs and outcomes. Put another way, the main priority within control and monitoring systems was supposed to migrate from the values of economy and regularity towards the values of efficiency and effectiveness (see Figure 1.2 above; and see Hood 1991 for a discussion of the value shifts involved).

These shifts in the foci for public management are mirrored in the express concerns of performance auditing. It is performance auditors who can assess whether public agencies are succeeding in providing more for less (efficiency), whether the quality of public services is being improved, whether staff are being deployed rationally in relation to tasks, whether programmes are achieving their goals, and so on. It is performance audit that is concerned with good management, value for money and the 'three Es'. This at least is the claim—the rhetorical strategy—of performance audit, even if, on occasion, the practice is less ambitious.

However, there is no suggestion that performance audit is intended to *replace* financial audit. Rather, it has been developed as a complement to traditional audit, just as the New Public Management claims to add managerial efficiency and effectiveness to the traditional bureaucratic values of prudence and procedural correctness. The parallels between the development of public-sector managerialism and the development of performance audit are intimate: both proceed from the same set of values, both are entwined within the same reform ethic, both first tentatively manifested themselves during the 1960s and 1970s, but put their roots down more deeply and widely during the fiscally more austere 1980s (Power 1997, pp. 44–9).

A second distinguishing feature of performance audit is that, unlike traditional audit, it is carried out *almost entirely within the public sector*. Indeed, this may even become a factor in the career calculations of some staff within certain SAIs. Working as financial auditors, particularly within the accruals-type accounting systems that are being or have been introduced in, for example, Sweden and the UK, staff have a better chance of finding alternative employment with commercial audit companies than if they are working as performance auditors, practising skills and techniques for which there is much less demand in the private sector. It is tempting to go further and claim that performance audit is an activity unique to SAIs. However, that is not the case. To begin with, there are important public-sector audit bodies which are not, technically SAIs, but which practice performance audit—sometimes on a considerable scale. Examples would include some of the French inspectorates, the Audit Commission in the UK, the parliamentary audit organizations in Finland and Sweden, and the EU Court of Auditors in Luxembourg. Beyond that, however, some countries have witnessed a spread of performance audit-like practices to public-sector bodies which, although not audit organizations in the usual sense, have taken on audit-type functions, including the assessment of the performance of other public-sector organizations, or of their own organization. Power (1997, pp. 98–109) cites the recent and rapid growth of 'audits' in the fields of academic research and teaching and in medical practice. These new sproutings, though interesting in themselves, have not been the focus of our research. We may, however, note *en passant* that much of the activity under these headings has gravitated towards either procedural concerns or the kinds of systems approaches that we have found important within the performance audit practices of SAIs. It seems that professors and doctors also fight shy of the 'hard stuff'—that is, of attempting directly to measure efficiency or cost effectiveness (Kerrison *et al.* 1994).

11.3 What Have Been the Main Trends in the Development of Performance Audit since the Mid-1980s?

The first point to acknowledge here is that the trends have been different in different countries. This might have been expected because, in so far as the development of performance audit has been intimately linked to the introduction of new approaches to public-sector management, it would be an obvious working hypothesis that, in countries where public management reform had been especially vigorous or radical, the development of performance audit would also have been most rapid. One can take this point further back: the speed, scope, and character of management reforms were themselves strongly related to the underlying character of the politico-administrative systems in each country (see Chapter 3). Very broadly, performance audit has been more energetically adopted by those countries with a 'public interest' tradition of public administration (especially those with more majoritarian, less consensual, styles of executive government) than by those with a strong *rechsstaat* or administrative law tradition. These differences were introduced in Chapters 3 and 4, and seem to hold not only for the five countries in our set, but also for other major European states, such as Germany and Italy, as well as for majoritarian, public interest-type regimes such as Australia and New Zealand (Pollitt and Bouckaert 1999). However, the connection is not a strict, black-and-white one, because the *rechsstaat*–public interest distinction is itself only approximate. Among our set of five countries, the Netherlands and, to a slightly lesser extent, Finland and Sweden constitute intermediate cases. Each of these countries mixes a relatively strong development of an administrative law tradition with a positive orientation to the Anglo-Australasian-American ideas of performance management. Each has supported an explicit and separate development of the practice of performance audit, and of the open (public) reporting of such audits.

However, the postulated positive relationship between the intensity of public management reform and the development of performance audit holds only in some particular ways, and not in others. Many commentators would agree that the UK (together with Australia and New Zealand) has pushed furthest with the particular 'NPM-ish' types of reform (see Table 2.3 above). The other countries in our study fall into a 'middling' category, in which the volume of management reform has been considerable, but where its sheer pace and scope have not attained the intensity experienced in the UK and Australasia. Sweden is perhaps a borderline case, and harder to assess. The rhetoric of management reform there has been quite radical and insistent, but the actual achievements appear more modest. Thus, Hood (1996a) places Sweden in his 'high reform emphasis' category, alongside the UK and Australasia. Also, it is important to remember that the *content* of reform in France, Finland, the Netherlands, and Sweden has been balanced more in favour of modernizing and less on the side of minimizing the state apparatus than in the UK (Hood 1996a; Jones 1993; Pollitt and Summa 1997a; Trosa 1995b).

Building upon this picture, therefore, one might predict a particularly powerful and far-reaching development of performance audit in the UK, a fairly sophisticated development of it in Sweden, and a moderate growth of it in the other three countries. What we actually find depends on which indicators we choose to measure the development of performance audit. Here we will recap just two: the volume or weight of studies (Chapter 2), and the degree of diversity and sophistication in methods (Chapter 8). Unfortunately, the evidence produced in Chapter 2 does not reveal any very striking connection between the depth of management reform and the volume or topic selection of performance audit. What is demonstrably the case, however, is that by the mid-1990s the resources devoted to performance audit (in its various manifestations) were very substantial in all the SAIs covered by this study. But on the very rough measures available (each on a somewhat different base from the others), it could not be said that a greater fraction of resources was being allocated to performance audit (*vis à vis* other activities) by the NAO or the RRV than by other SAIs.

Other measures, such as the numbers of reports issued or the proportion of them that directly addressed public management reform issues, also require extremely careful interpretation. The annual number of value-for-money (VFM) studies conducted by the NAO effectively doubled from the mid-1980s to the mid-1990s, while the RRV's output also rose, though by a smaller percentage. Over the same period, the numbers of performance audit reports published by the VTV and the Algemene Rekenkamer apparently fell, but this is deceptive, since in both cases the complexity and length of individual reports tended to increase (i.e. they were fewer but 'heavier'). Furthermore, we do not have a consistent measure of the proportion of all performance audits that directly address management reform issues. Again, therefore, the conclusion would be that these measures do not show any totally convincing or uniformly positive correlation with the scope and intensity of management reforms in the countries concerned.

We may now turn to the question of technical developments within performance audit (Chapter 8). Here it does seem to be the case that the tools of performance audit have undergone significant development in the SAI of the most intensively 'management-reformed' state. At the NAO, consumer surveys and analyses of performance indicator data have both become established as 'normal' and accepted parts of the auditors' armoury. Occasionally, also, economic analysis (cost effectiveness, deadweight, displacement, supplier effects, etc.) may be used, and more recently focus groups have appeared on the agenda (although one must be careful not to suggest that the adoption of a technique in one or two studies amounts to a new practice norm). Furthermore, the increasing sophistication of performance audit in this technical sense has been largely shared by the SAI in the second most 'management-reformed' country, Sweden. Perhaps one could say that, since the mid-1980s, the Swedish and UK SAIs have each given some prominence to increasing their methodological self-consciousness and sophistication, whereas the Dutch, Finnish, and the French SAIs have, in different ways and degrees, been somewhat more reticent. That is not to imply that the RRV, VTV, and Cour are in some sense lagging behind in a race. (Indeed, each of these has attempted some ambitious studies, as Chapter 5 in particular indicated.) However, they seem to have made less of a public or professional issue out of 'tools and techniques'. There is less evidence, in their cases, of descriptions of their methods in their reports, of technical handbooks or mandatory training courses or any of the other paraphernalia of self-conscious technical self-improvement. For example, the Cour has given increased attention to training, but the courses that have been devised are offered on a voluntary basis; i.e., magistrates may choose to attend but are under no obligation to do so.

In sum, it might be said that the rank order of SAIs in terms of the elaboration of special tools and methods for performance audit roughly corresponds with the rank order of the corresponding governments in terms of the intensity of its public management reforms. However, it would need swiftly to be added that, like all correlations, this is neither a judgement nor an explanation.

There are other ways of approaching the question of the possible connections between intensity of management reform and the depth of development of performance audit. One could, for example, concentrate more on the content of reform rhetoric, and argue that a positive correlation should be sought not so much with the overall volume of management reform as with the extent to which such reform has embraced the Anglo-American-Australasian doctrines specific to the idea of a New Public Management (NPM) or the 're-invention' of government. The NPM has tended to lay particular stress on privatization, contracting-out, and increasing the 'consumer responsiveness' of public services. This is perhaps a more fruitful line of interpretation, since NPM rhetoric has probably been strongest in the UK and Sweden and weakest in France (where the preoccupation of the early 1980s was much more with decentralization than with privatization, contractualization, or consumerism). Similarly, it could be argued that the *rhetoric* of performance audit has been strongest in the RRV and the NAO, and least evident in the Cour. However, even this pattern can easily be overstated, for there has not been that much difference between the NAO and RRV, on the one hand, and, say, the Rekenkamer on the other. Furthermore, other variables may have played an important part in the willingness of individual SAIs to adopt the language and concepts of performance audit. To the extent that an SAI was already powerful and secure (as was the Cour), it may have felt less need to identify itself with the latest management fashions than its less prominent or influential counterparts in other countries (the VTV springs to mind—see Pollitt and Summa, 1997b).

The selection of tools for performance audit is necessarily somewhat related to the selection of topics. For example, when the NAO decided, in a number of studies during the early 1990s, to investigate issues of public service quality, the need for ways of measuring user/customer satisfaction with services became obvious. This led directly to an increase in the use of customer surveys as a tool. When we examined topic selection, further differences between our five countries emerged (Chapter 5). From the late 1980s or early 1990s, some SAIs (especially the Rekenkamer and the VTV) decided to prioritize broad and systemic rather than narrow and substantial types of study—those embracing more than one audited body or even more than one policy sector. To some extent in recent years the Cour also seems to be developing a stronger emphasis on thematic or cross-sectoral investigations, such as in social protection or the administration of charities or museums (personal interviews). By contrast, the NAO seemed to shift *away* from these types of study in the early 1990s, although by 1996 there were signs of a renewed enthusiasm for a thematic approach. Overall, it might be said that there is definite evidence of an interest in management reforms as topics for audit in all five of our SAIs, but that each approached the matter somewhat differently, particularly in terms of the preferred scope of studies, the range of tools they were comfortable using, and the extent to which they saw the need to explain their investigatory methodologies in their published reports.

11.4 What Have Been the Interactions between Performance Audit and the Public Management Reforms?

As was made clear in Chapters 3 and 4, and in numerous examples in subsequent chapters, the interface is both intimate and complex. The shared value-emphasis has already been referred to (Section 11.2 above). At a more mundane level, some management reforms are such obvious 'targets' that it would be hard for any self-respecting SAI to resist making investigations of them. Examples here include privatization and then public utility regulation in the UK, the multiplication of quangos in the Netherlands, the repeated efforts at decentralization in Sweden, or the restructuring of Finland's national administrative agencies which took place between 1993 and 1996.

However, the interactions in question have often been more subtle than the simple equation of a particular reform generating an obvious topic for performance audit. The growing emphasis on 'managing for results' in many public sectors creates an ever-larger space for 'auditing for results', i.e. performance audit (OECD 1997b). New outpourings of performance indicators and other performance data offer SAIs rich opportunities, but opportunities that require both new auditing skills and a reconsideration of what is most appropriate to internal management and what to external audit (NAO 1998b). Nor is it easy, given the volume of reorganizations and management change in all five of the countries under study, for an SAI, limited in its own available resources, to decide which of the new opportunities are the most important or, to put it more dramatically, which to seize first.

The international popularity of public-sector management reform also encourages an atmosphere of public debate in which all public-sector institutions—even SAIs—are more likely to be asked to justify themselves by demonstrable 'products' or achievements. This can be seen most clearly in the annual reports of the SAIs in those countries where the rhetoric of performance management has taken deepest hold (Pollitt and Summa 1997b). Thus, for example, the reports of the NAO and RRV dwell at length on the *usefulness* of their activities and on the *results* they have achieved. By contrast, the annual public report of the Cour has not normally indulged in such self-justifications. In 1997, however, *Le Rapport Public* contained more detail and discussion of the Cour's activities than it had done previously, indicating a wish to inform and convince a wider audience of the range and volume of its work.

Finally, it could be said, building on the point about common values, that the fundamental ethic of performance audit is closely intertwined with the ethic of performance management reform. The two activities are frequently conceptualized as 'being about the same business'. Both make frequent use of the input–output model, as described in Chapter 1 (see Figure 1.2). Both participate in the same community of discourse, which features efficiency, effectiveness, and productivity as key values. A recent OECD publication entitled *In Search of Results: Performance Management Practices* recognizes this connection:

> A key element for the sustainability of reforms is coherence in internal and external performance management initiatives, including performance auditing. (OECD 1997b, pp. 20–1)

11.5 What is the Nature of the Performance Auditor's Craft?

There is something of a paradox concerning the situation of the performance auditor, about to set out upon a new study. On the one hand, he or she enjoys greater scope for creativity in study design and tool selection than would be the case for a typical financial audit. The guidelines are not so tightly prescriptive. The scope for crafting something original and even innovative is larger. And yet the practical constraints—time, resources, clearance requirements—are often very demanding indeed.

In one way, therefore, the craft of the individual auditor or audit team lies in reconciling these conflicting sets of demands: on the one hand to be more 'professional', more technically sophisticated, more creative in study design, more focused on the crucial but difficult issues of efficiency and effectiveness, and on the other to produce studies more quickly, more cheaply, and in formats that will make them accessible to a range of different audiences (auditees, politicians, the mass media, and so on). This is a difficult challenge indeed, and responding to it has brought additional tasks in its train.

One main direction in the effort to meet these demands has been to make performance auditors more expert, and also to use more specialists who are not necessarily auditors. As we have seen, most SAIs have, to greater or lesser degree, employed contracted experts to contribute to particular studies—doctors to advise on investigations in the health care sector, professional valuers to advise on studies of the sale of government land and facilities, and so on (personal interviews; and see Pollitt and Summa 1997c, pp. 92–3).

One effect of this on the craft of the auditor has been to increase the significance of team management skills. In the Netherlands, Sweden, and the UK performance audit has now become routinely a team activity. Only in Finland and France is the stress still (usually, but by no means always) on the individual auditor as the sole investigator and author of a particular report. Even in these two cases, there are distinct signs that more cooperative and collective modes of working are on the increase. At the Cour, for example, there has been the recent creation of a 'skills exchange' network (hotline) between the magistrates, and the experience of working in teams (e.g. eleven auditors working on the study of policies to assist handicapped adults: Lamarque 1997, and personal interviews). At the VTV the study of the restructuring of central administrative agencies (1994–5) was a large-scale team effort involving a number of auditors (Valtiontalouden tarkatusvirasto 1994).

Another vital element in the craft of the successful performance auditor is the ability to negotiate with the staff of the audited body (Pollitt and Summa 1997c). While the complexity of this aspect varies somewhat with the precise clearance arrangements in force in a particular country at a particular time, all five of our SAIs currently stress the need to communicate carefully with the auditee before attempting to deliver and/or publish any final report. Our interviews at the Cour left us in no doubt of the importance of the process of *contradiction*, in which the auditee comments on the provisional findings of the Cour's magistrate. The willingness of auditees to argue over even small details is attested in the appendices to some of the *rapports particuliers*, where lengthy point-scoring and self-justification are hardly unknown (e.g. Cour des Comptes 1997a, pp. 161–234). At the NAO the clearance process is structured in such a way that the audited body is asked to agree to the text of the report that is to go to Parliament, and this can sometimes take a long time (Roberts and Pollitt 1994, pp. 534–5). One experienced VFM auditor expressed his philosophy of dealing with audited bodies to us as one of 'no surprises', i.e. exhaustive consultation, not only on the final text, but on methods, interim drafts, and many other aspects. However, by the late 1990s there were some straws in the wind indicating that this doctrine, as it became more publicly understood, was beginning to be questioned because of the opportunities it seemed to provide for auditees to delay and obfuscate unwelcome findings (Kelly 1997; Wighton 1998).

The clearance process can therefore have an important influence on what eventually finds its way into the final report and the public domain. However, the details of this process are normally hidden from public view. This opacity is lessened somewhat in those instances where an SAI's reports may include the dissenting comments of auditees (as is the case in France, Finland, and the Netherlands). The other important feature of the clearance process is the way in which drafts are subjected to intense internal scrutiny within the SAI. This is the point at which the 'product' passes beyond the hands of the auditor or audit team that conducted the study and is laid before senior collegues for comment and amendment. Considerable changes may ensue; for example, both scrutiny by assistant auditors general within the NAO and discussion by the other magistrates within a *chambre* at the Cour are known to be demanding occasions.

11.6 What Methods Are Used in Performance Audit?

The short answer to this question is that many different methods are used—quantitative, qualitative, economic, social scientific, traditional audit practices, and so on. However, as Chapter 8 showed, this apparent diversity cloaks the fact that most of the time, in most countries, performance auditors fall back upon a few tried and trusted techniques, especially the study of the documents of the audited bodies and the questioning of their staff. The analysis also indicated that, despite the existence in some SAIs of special reviews of methods, and despite official enthusiasm ('the guide is intended to encourage you to be innovative in your work': *Designing VFM Studies*, NAO 1997a), in practice, developments in the use of tools has been incremental. 'Occasional experiments' is a more accurate description than 'a great leap forward'.

This observed pattern raises a number of further questions. In those untypical instances where some rare method is applied—a multiple regression analysis, say, or a focus group—what has happened to make the innovation appear possible and desirable? Equally, if a technique has been used successfully once, why is it not taken up regularly thereafter? None of the documents published by SAIs offer much clue on these points. Our interviews did, however, hint at some plausible answers. To begin with, it would be a mistake to underestimate the conservatism of SAIs. Most of them have developed strong and distinctive organizational cultures. Their senior and most influential members are likely to be the most heavily steeped in these cultures, which include 'taken-for-granted' ways of doing things. A new method may appear to be risky in a number of different ways. First, it may be challenged as unusual, unreliable, or unfair by the auditee. (For example, there is anecdotal evidence that benchmarking against other organizations has on occasion been fiercely resisted by some auditees in the UK, despite the government's own conversion to it in respect of executive agencies: Next Steps Team 1998). Second, the SAI itself may possess only small knowledge of the technique, so that the possibility that it may be implemented inappropriately may seem too great.

There is also a rather more blunt perspective on the issue of tool development: namely, that existing tools are 'good enough' for the SAIs' main audiences. If there is no great dissatisfaction with the methodological *status quo*, why change? From an SAI's point of view, occasional sniping by a few academic critics hardly constitutes a major problem requiring urgent action. (Of course, both the NAO and the VTV have recently taken on board academic advice offered within the context of consultancy work, but that is a slightly different case.) We found little evidence of governments or parliaments pressing hard for the use of more sophisticated analytical tools by performance auditors, and, indeed, we would have been surprised if we had.

None the less, innovations do take place. When we asked about particular studies that seemed to us to be unorthodox or novel in their designs, the typical answers involved a combination of factors—the nature of particular study topics, the assignment of particular auditors with special skills or interests, the willingness of senior members of SAIs to countenance limited 'experiments' at particular times, and so on.

Thus, the lack of a standardized approach to performance audits means that there are in principle many opportunities for creative auditors to introduce new tools and approaches. In practice, however, these opportunities are quite sharply constrained by cost and time factors, the strength of tradition, and the high degree of aversion to the risk of the SAI's reports being attacked on the grounds of reliability. The image of audit reports as firmly factual and, in effect, the final word on a topic is not one that SAIs are readily prepared to sacrifice, and in practice there is little sustained pressure for them to rush to adopt new methods.

Yet, to the (varying) extent to which SAIs are methodologically 'traditionalist', there is a price to be paid. Certain kinds of issue, especially those of policy or programme effectiveness, are difficult to address if auditors confine themselves to the standard paths of interviews and documentary analysis (Keen 1998). This is an interaction to which we will return a little later.

11.7 What Criteria Are Applied within Performance Audit?

The central message of Chapter 6 was that, while the 'three Es' have been important, it has not been those criteria that have occupied the largest share of the time of practising performance auditors. In all five countries, both in the mid-1980s and more recently, the most frequent and dominant criterion actually applied has been that of some notion of good management practice. This is a finding of some significance. Clearly, it connects with the pattern of methods used (see the preceding section and Chapter 8). Clearly, also, it has enabled the development of performance audit out of financial audit to be a relatively gradual, low-risk one, in the sense that a performance audit that seeks to establish whether prescribed administrative procedures within an audited body have been followed is conceptually not so strikingly different from a financial audit that seeks to establish whether prescribed financial and accounting rules have been followed. At base, both are procedures for checking conformity with a set of pre-established standards, a very familiar situation for auditors (Chelimsky 1985).

Yet, sensible though this trajectory for the development of performance audit may seem, contained within it there is a puzzle. This may be encapsulated in the question: where do the standards for good management practice come from? When we put this question to members of staff in the SAIs, the response was typically that the standards of good management practice were taken from the audited bodies themselves—that auditees would have their own standards and that it was then the job of the auditor to see to what extent these were being followed. Did this mean, then, that 'good management practice' varied from one context to another, and that there was no general model? Responses to this further question diverged. Some interviewees thought that there *were* generic standards, such as articulating clear objectives and having systems in place to measure the extent of their achievement and the cost of achieving them. Others suggested that there was no need for a general model (except possibly in the most abstract terms) because it was self-evident that, for example, managing a small, local, specialized museum had little in common with managing a huge national museum (and even less with, say, contracting for a new European fighter aircraft). What is clear is that the source and nature of models of 'good management practice' are less clear and uniform than the source of models for correct accounting practice or financial administration. Audited bodies by no means always possess (still less publish) authoritative statements of their management practices which are sufficiently detailed to be used operationally as templates for audit. Nor is there any general agreement on the extent to which, or in what way, the nature of 'good management' should vary between different contexts.

In short, the basis for performance auditors' judgements about good management practice may not be as firm as the basis for the judgements made by financial auditors concerning the presence or absence of good financial and accountancy practice. Audit may have 'become the benchmark for securing the legitimacy of organizational action' (Power 1997, p. 10), but the models of what constitutes 'good' organization, and even more the question of why one form of management is to be preferred to another, tend to remain opaque.

Beyond this lies a further question: how close is the connection between the presence of good management practice and the efficiency and effectiveness of policies and programmes? Our research will not answer this question, but it does suggest that SAIs are not entirely confident of the answer either. Conceptually, it is not difficult to show that an efficiently managed programme may be ineffective, or, conversely, that a poorly managed programme may sometimes be effective. Most people who have worked in government are familiar with the possibility of a badly designed policy being implemented as best as can be by a group of stoical but sometimes-despairing civil servants. To take another example, a weakly run university may nevertheless have excellent professors who teach very effectively, while an efficiently managed university may have low unit costs, low drop-out rates, efficient use of buildings and facilities, and a host of other administrative virtues, yet provide teaching which leaves the students poorly educated. The point of this argument is that, if the connection between good management practices and the 'three Es' is less than sure, then performance auditors will need to go beyond the former in order directly to investigate the latter. Systems audits of auditable good practice will not substitute for substantive audits of effectiveness. (This message is elaborated at greater length in Power 1997.)

Another way of approaching the issue of the criteria used in performance audit is to ask what role they play in the reports that SAIs produce. In this respect one might say that, for all the SAIs we looked at, the role of criteria was often implicit rather than explicit, a taken-for-granted thread in a descriptive narrative rather than (as might be the case in, say, an economic or experimental evaluation) a central feature of the design of the study concerned. Individual studies often contained, in effect, a mixture of criteria —common-sense notions of 'good management', peer-referenced standards of 'good practice', and economic concepts of economy and/or efficiency. It was rare for this *mélange* of criteria to receive any explicit discussion or acknowledgement in performance audit reports. If one thinks of a spectrum of approaches to criteria-setting, running from an external/prescriptive/criterion-referenced pole to an internal/descriptive/peer-referenced pole, then most performance audit work would come nearer the latter than the former end of the range (Dowie, forthcoming).

11.8 What Kinds of Product are Generated by Performance Audit?

Here there has been a clear trend between the mid 1980s and more recent times—one of an increase in the variety, and sophistication of SAI products reaching the public domain. Chapter 9 identified the particular manifestations of this general process in each of the five countries. Even where there is no expectation or requirement for most of an SAI's work to be available to the public—as is the case for the French Cour—the volume, variety, and presentational standards of published materials have increased and the public relations function has been reorganized along more professional lines. Well produced audit reports (often illustrated), professionally crafted press releases, and even CD-ROMs of an SAI's work constitute the new norm. The SAIs in some countries—especially the NAO, but to a lesser extent also the VTV and RRV—go beyond this and offer annual reports which contain not merely summary descriptions of the work done but also some performance data about the audit body itself (Pollitt and Summa 1997b).

The significance of these developments is considerable. They represent a kind of 'coming out' by SAIs, a recognition that they need to be proactive in communicating their work and explaining its value. In a very general sense, this trend is probably linked to the broader sweep of management reform. It could be argued that one element within the international growth of managerialism has been the belief that a well managed organization, whether in the public or the private sector, will be one which, *inter alia*, has a public 'mission statement', loses no opportunity to publicize its successes, and uses professional advice to help it sustain and improve its external 'image'. These are exactly the things that in a more-or-less gradual and sober manner, our five SAIs have been attending to.

11.9 How and To Whom is Performance Audit Work Presented, and With What Effects?

Each of the five SAIs had more than one potential 'customer' for their work. The specifics of the politico-administrative regime (Chapter 3) and the legal mandate (Appendix 2) determine the identity of the principal recipient of performance audit reports. The range runs from the mainly executive-oriented RRV to the mainly legislature-oriented NAO, but all SAIs hope to win wider, more general attention. Thus, the NAO lays considerable emphasis on also helping departments, agencies, and other audited bodies (NAO 1997b, p. 9), while the RRV draws the attention of the Swedish parliament to its usefulness (Riksrevisionsverket 1997a, p. 23). The Rekenkamer has enhanced its salience to the Estates General (Witteveen 1996) and reformed its regular publications. The Cour, even if it still makes most of its reports outside the public domain, has in recent years clearly given greater attention to its more public outputs, both in terms of increasing the number of regular publications and by strengthening its press office. The VTV, though possibly the SAI in our set with the least close and concrete relationship with an identifiable 'customer', has nevertheless begun to 'glossify' its publications and take a more professional approach to media relations. Many of our interviewees mentioned internal debates about clarifying the audiences for different types of SAI 'product', and communicating more effectively with those so identified.

The impacts of performance audit work are, as Chapter 10 demonstrates, difficult to attribute, to measure, or even fully to conceptualize. Should one measure only financial effects? Over how long a time period? How far down the chain of presumed cause and effect? Should the costs of audit be set against the measured benefits, and if so should this be done in a disaggregated way or only as a global calculation, right across the whole field of the SAI's performance audit activities? In a way, the problem of measuring the true effects of performance auditing is a microcosmic echo of the problem of measuring the impacts of the macrocosmic public management reforms discussed in Chapter 3 (see also Pollitt 1995). In both cases there are obvious risks in under-measuring and in over-measuring; there are also both cognitive and motivational threats to validity and reliability. Cognitively, how much can be attributed to performance audit, as opposed to the many other parallel developments that influence the course of government action (budgetary pressures, interest group lobbying, media pressures, technological change, and so on)? Very occasionally the answer is clear: there may be a definite and acknowledged cause-and-effect relationship between a specific audit and a specific change. More often, however, the audit is only one ingredient in the stew. Then there is the even greater difficulty of making sensible allowance for the deterrence effect—the extent to which public bodies do or refrain from doing things because they anticipate the possibility of being audited (whether or not that anticipation is eventually fulfilled). To our knowledge, no one has proposed an operationally reliable way of measuring this effect, though many commentators agree that it exists.

Motivational circumstances frequently further complicate the cognitive difficulties. Not to put too fine a point on it, it is usually in the interests of auditees to present a picture of the world that minimizes the extent to which changes are due to audit (often claiming that such changes were in the pipeline anyway). At the same time, it is in the interest of auditors to maximize their estimates of the impacts of their own work. The more SAIs seek to present measures of their achievements, the more this attribution problem is likely to be a focus for argument. The reverse holds for the actual or alleged negative effects of audit—auditees will tend to exaggerate 'compliance' costs, and audit bodies have an interest in offering the rosiest possible picture of this aspect of their operations.

Despite these multiple difficulties, there is evidence that all the SAIs in our set have become more concerned publicly to demonstrate that their work makes an impact. The attempt to 'price' the achievements of performance audit has gone furthest in the most managerialist regime—the UK—but a concern for the identifiability of 'results' is audible in much less 'NPM-ish' contexts. At the VTV, for example, we were told that there was a determination to put better information into the annual report about results and impacts—'something really concrete must happen'. And at the Cour we found a good deal of work in progress on the new annual activity report, the first issue of which appeared as this book was being written (Cour des Comptes 1997b). During our interviews at the Cour it was stressed to us that there was a need to demonstrate the breadth and consequentiality of the Cour's work to the public, and it was pointed out that this represented something of a departure from the previous tradition of conducting audits in a very discreet way.

Yet there are risks in this trend—risks of which senior members of the SAIs are very well aware. As was described in Chapter 10, SAIs have in general tended to enjoy a 'good press'. In particular, their independence, status, and authority are seldom challenged. In the past this authority has derived from history and position, not from any publicly displayed rigour of method or measurement of results. The danger is that, the further an SAI goes down the road of measuring its own performance, the more it will be seen as 'just another' public organization, to be judged against a narrow cost–result yardstick and not accorded any special reverance or status. The strategy, therefore, seems everywhere to be to move cautiously, tip-toeing into reflexive performance measurement while holding firmly to the distinctive identity of a Supreme Audit Institution.

11.10 The Identity of Performance Audit

Roles and 'truths'

There is a sense in which the tale we have told in the preceding pages can be likened to the development of a character in a story. The period since the mid-1980s has been one in which the identity of performance audit has become better defined. In many countries the statutory basis for it has been clarified, reinforced, or extended. INTOSAI has formulated an agreed international description of its essential character. Within individual SAIs it has been increasingly recognized, in a variety of procedural and organizational ways, as a distinct activity. Guidebooks and training courses have appeared. In some cases the character of performance audit has been even exposed to 'therapy' in the form of internal or external reviews or assessments. In others the approach has been more cautious and gradual, but none the less, the need to audit management practice and pay attention to 'results' is widely acknowledged. In the five countries we have examined (though not in all other European countries) performance audit has therefore definitely 'arrived'. It has become a known quantity, a familiar presence in the process of governance.

Yet, beneath this apparent maturity, performance audit still carries some of the unresolved problems of its youth. As the environment for SAIs continues to change, these tensions or contradictions will need to be managed, and, depending upon the skill with which that is undertaken, may turn out to be serious character defects, minor difficulties, or even positive advantages.

Rhetorics and cultures

So what is the character of performance audit, and what do we mean by 'tensions and contradictions'? The nature of this identity can be sought in at least two different ways. One obvious strategy is to examine the tools used by performance auditors and the criteria they appear to apply. From this it may be possible to infer the identity of the set of practices concerned. Chapters 6 (criteria) and 8 (methods) in particular pursued this route, and we will return to their findings in a moment. An alternative strategy, however, is to look at the backgrounds of performance auditors, at their training and socialization, and at the general aspirations expressed in documents such as annual reports or speeches by senior members of SAIs (i.e. the rhetorics of identity). This kind of approach was begun in Chapter 7 (the auditor's craft). There it was demonstrated that performance auditors came from a variety of backgrounds and that, even if there were elements of convergence,

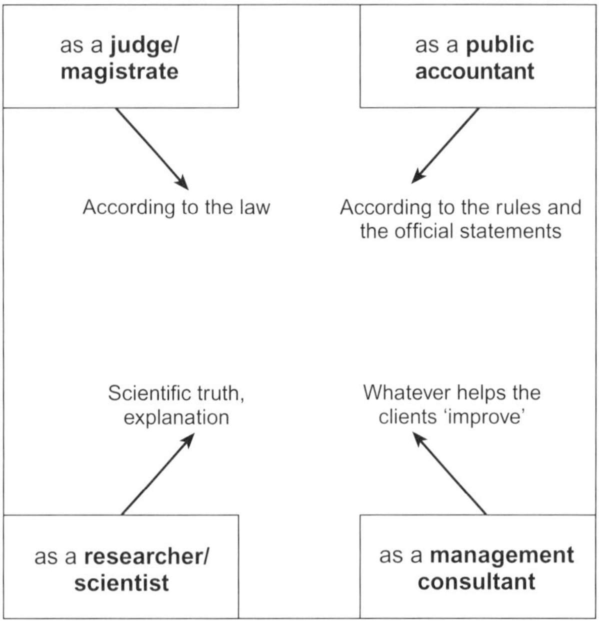

FIGURE 11.1 Some 'truths' for performance auditors

there remained substantial differences of training and culture between the five SAIs covered by this study. One way of conceptualizing these differences was to think in terms of four possible roles for performance auditors: as judges/magistrates, as public accountants, as researchers/scientists, or as management consultant/improvers. Each of these was an 'ideal type' or 'polar extreme' . None of our five SAIs was a pure example of a single role—all were mixtures. Nevertheless, Figure 7.1 was useful in representing some of the ideals or aspirations that have characterized the discourse surrounding the recent development of performance audit, and showing how any particular SAI might opt to 'pitch its tent' in a position that represented a different combination of the four roles from that chosen by other SAIs.

Taking this approach to the identity of performance audit one step further, one might suggest that each of the four roles incorporates a distinctive version of the 'truths' that performance auditors are seeking. This notion is displayed in Figure 11.1.

The role of *judge or magistrate* carries with it the assumption that the prime focus of the auditor is on the compliance of the actions of public bodies with the law. The law is the absolute, the source of the norms and standards by which action and inaction may be interpreted and assessed. Such norms and standards may be quite various, and may lead the auditor into very challenging interpretations of 'performance' (for example if a law specifies equality of opportunity as a requirement of a policy, or specifies a particular concept of service quality). Nevertheless, a general concept of compliance underlies this 'version' of auditing—actions must be tested from the point of view of their conformity with the law of the time. Clearly, among the five SAIs covered by our study, the Cour offers the example closest to this pole. As an advocate general of the Cour wrote,

> Even if the activities of the Cour are only partially jurisdictional, its organization and functioning are essentially shaped by its statute of jurisdiction. (Descheenmaeker 1992, p. 25; translated from the French original)

By contrast, the role of auditor as *public accountant* sees truth as being established through the exposure of actions to public scrutiny and debate. The focus is on transparency, and on the processes of openness and publication by which transparency can be brought about. Public authorities should do what they say they will do, and the public should be able to check this against a full and accurate account of what they actually have done. As the UK comptroller and auditor general says in his forward to the NAO's Annual Report, the first key task is 'to examine and report to Parliament on whether public money is spent properly and wisely' (NAO 1997b, p. 1). The job of the performance auditor is to facilitate the provision of this information, digging it out where it has not yet been provided and verifying and validating it where it has. As with the role of judge/magistrate, there is a strong thread of compliance-checking in this approach. However, the compliance in this case is not so much conformity to the law (though this may certainly be part of what is assessed) as compliance to a wider, looser notion of democratic processes and 'holding up to the light'.

The role of *researcher/scientist* is a more recent addition to the range of self-images for auditors than either the magistrate or the public accountant. Here the emphasis is on scientific standards of procedure and method, and on the generation of new knowledge. Scientific accuracy is the aim, where the auditor's pronouncements will be accepted not so much because of his/her status as because it can be seen that the best and most appropriate analytic methods have been employed to generate an objective picture. As the Swedish Auditor General put it,

> The Swedish National Audit Office is an important producer of analyses, and many of those analyses could be called evaluations. (Ahlenius 1997, p. 83)

A similar perspective comes from the (then) director of policy evaluation at the Rekenkamer:

> I believe that combining the strong points of evaluation (the methodology applied and attention paid to theories and theory-driven evaluations) with the strong points of audit (the orientation towards management, the focus on following the money, and the attention paid to documentary evidence) may well lead to a new interdiscipline in the twenty-first century. (Leeuw 1996, p. 59)

Notions of compliance are much less to the fore at this pole. Instead the task of the performance auditor is to produce explanations which can be defended in terms of their analytic rigour and methodological sophistication.

Finally, there is the role of the *management consultant*. Again, this is something of a newcomer to the hallowed portals of Supreme Audit Institutions. Within this role, both the scientific niceties and the demands for tranparency are less to the fore than securing improvements in the management of public agencies:

> In its work the RRV shall provide a transfer of know-how, advisory services and support to the Cabinet Office and government agencies to ensure that appropriate measures are taken. (Riksrevisionsverket 1997a, p. 4)

Or, as the NAO puts it,

> to work with the bodies we audit to secure beneficial change' (NAO 1997b, p. 1)

Here usefulness is a greater focus of attention than either legal correctness or scientific truth. And to be useful, one needs to be close to the auditee, to understand its problems and work with its members to achieve reform.

To repeat, we are certainly not suggesting that any of our five SAIs neatly fits into one of these four roles. Neither are we suggesting that one of these really *is* performance audit whereas the others are not. (All four roles can include a focus on the 'performance' of an audited body, though what is meant by this will vary from one to another.) What we are proposing, however, is that different strategic choices are available to SAIs between the extremes (i.e. within the 'boxes' of Figures 7.1 and 11.1). And we are also making the basic point that no institution can perform all four roles—seek all four kinds of 'truth'—equally well. To move closer to one of the four poles inevitably places a strain on an institution's ability to meet the requirements of any of the other three.

Tools and criteria

Now let us step down from these broad questions of role and self-image, and go back to the other way of exploring the identity of performance audit. That is, what can be inferred about this matter from an analyis of the criteria and methods that auditors have used? As Chapters 6 and 8 demonstrated, a wide range of approaches, methods, and tools have paraded under the banner of performance audit. Some are used over and over again (documentary study, informal interviews) while others have (to date) been used but rarely (multiple regression analysis, econometrics, focus groups). It would be difficult for any one person to master this entire portfolio of possibilities. Equally, this diversity makes it difficult to answer the question, 'what do performance auditors actually do?' in any simple or straightforward way. Power expresses part of the problem thus:

VFM audits do not follow a common pattern and reflect different emphases and values. In general the mix of emphasis on the three Es varies almost by assignment, a function of the specific programmatic demands made of the audit and of the routines and experts which can be readily assembled in its name. (Power 1997, p. 51)

In our view, the issue is even more complex, not least because the criterion of 'good management practice' is at least as important, and probably even more difficult to operationalize in any standardized way, than the 'three Es'. Thus, both tool use and criteria applied vary considerably. In this regard, one finding common to both the criteria chapter (6) and the methods chapter (8) was that, although innovation had certainly taken place, the 'normal' performance audit had changed only gradually. In other words in practice, many performance audits still investigate conformity to some notion of good procedure (rather than applying the criteria of efficiency or effectiveness), and many still overwhelmingly rely upon interviews and the inspection of documents (rather than the use of sophisticated analytical techniques). The more analytical studies of efficiency and effectiveness were the exceptions rather than the rule. In terms of Figure 11.1, one might say that the day-to-day practical identity of most performance auditors continues to lie more in the upper half of the box than the lower, although more 'expeditions' into the lower half appear to have been made by the RRV and the NAO than by the Cour or the VTV.

11.11 Identity and Strategic Choice

It is possible to imagine scenarios in which this uncertainty about 'standard practice' could be exploited to the disadvantage of performance auditors in particular, or SAIs in general. It could be argued (indeed, it has been argued, by Barzclay and others) that performance audit isn't really audit at all, and—to go beyond Barzelay—that it should be decomposed into its elements and distributed to the 'real experts'. Along this line of logic, one might see economic analysis being undertaken by specialized economic units or institutes, assessments of business success going to management consultancies, social surveys being given to sociologists, and studies of programme effectiveness being conducted by generic evaluation units staffed by suitably trained social scientists. Lawyers and accountants (the backbone of most European SAIs) would have little part in any of this. To them would be left the traditional forms of regularity audit plus new and developing elements of financial analysis (risk audits, accruals work, and so on).

On the other hand, the uncertain identity of performance audit could be turned to its own advantage. SAIs could become the envelope institutions within which creative designs for the external analysis of the efficiency and effectiveness of government programmes and projects could be developed, protected by the immense benefits of the statutory independence and historically earned authority which only SAIs can wield (Pollitt and Summa

1997c). They could even become a 'central purchaser and coordinator' of the skills of other bodies, acting in this capacity on behalf of the legislature or the executive, depending on the constitutional arrangements in the country concerned. In this scenario the epistemological diversity of performance audit becomes an advantage rather than a flaw; it constitutes a flexible space (the 'box' of Figure 11.1) within which approaches can be developed to address the new problems thrown up by the restructured and reformed public sectors of increasingly managerialist states. Ministers, parliamentarians, and publics are all interested in whether financial accounts are fair and accurate, but they are also most certainly interested in whether programmes actually work, and in whether they do so in the most efficient possible way. A substantial part of the attractiveness of performance audit has lain in its promise to answer some of these big questions. Our research has shown that sometimes it delivers on this promise, but that often it stops in the foothills (possibly because of a lack of time, skills, or information), contenting itself with the useful but essentially preliminary issues of good management practice. It could be argued that, now that performance audit has enjoyed a decade or so of maturation it is time for a renewed focus on the second and third of the 'three Es'—efficiency and effectiveness.

There is at least one more step in this line of speculation. This concerns the fact that there is a big difference between the second 'E' (efficiency) and the third (effectiveness). Increasingly, public-sector organizations are themselves measuring efficiency (input–output ratios—see Figure 1.1). This is a fundamental feature of the maturation of the public management reforms described in Chapter 3. To the extent that this comes about, the need for *ad hoc* external efficiency audits by SAIs should decline. SAIs may well still wish to validate the auditees' own measurement systems (we have noted evidence of this as a trend in several countries), but in principle such validation should be a relatively straightforward type of work, conceptually akin to 'checking the books' in traditional, financial audit. Effectiveness, however, is a different matter entirely, as many SAIs have found. This is an area that has, in effect, long been claimed by SAIs as part of the territory of performance audit, but which has only seldom been actively settled and cultivated. This, therefore, could be one direction for further development in the medium term.

However, to take an 'effectiveness turn' would mean increasing the gap between performance audit and financial audit (since effectiveness studies are the least similar type of performance audit to financial audit). It might also imply a shift towards the audit of policies and programmes rather than specific institutions (because the most sensible units of analysis for effectiveness are policies or programmes with reasonably coherent sets of objectives). In terms of approaches, methods, and criteria, a heavier concentration on the effectiveness criterion would necessitate a shift towards more explanatory and analytical types of study (i.e. towards the researcher/scientist role in the bottom left-hand corner of Figure 7.1). There would be a need to explain *why* observed results (whether 'good' or 'bad') had been obtained, and this would point towards a greater need to build causal models or spell out programme or policy logics. Alongside this, there would be a need to treat the issue of criteria (i.e. what was meant by 'effective') in a more explicit manner. In very general terms, it might be said that effectiveness-oriented performance audits would look more like economic analyses, or like experimental evaluations, than most performance audits have done until now.

The two scenarios outlined thus far might be thought of as limiting, or, at least, as 'low' and 'high' cases. In the first (low case), performance audit virtually disappears as a distinct type of activity, as its 'manifesto' is taken over by other organizations and groups. In the second, performance audit rapidly increases its emphasis on the effectiveness criterion and, in consequence, is obliged routinely to expand its range of approaches and tools, and more generally to take its leave of the comfortable shelter of compliance-based criteria. Naturally, there are also 'middle ways'. One would be to continue, incrementally, to develop the *status quo*, concentrating on assessments of management practice but perhaps sharpening the models of 'good management' that are currently in play. In many ways this strategy might be thought to suit the hitherto cautious nature of SAIs. The practice of performance audit would then continue to resemble the practice of financial audit; it would be a process of checking reality against standards, and the work could be divided up along sectoral or institutional lines which fitted the sectorally based internal structures that most SAIs continue to use.

At first sight this appears to be the lowest-risk scenario of the three. The full implications, however, are not necessarily so attractive. It is a strategy that would require, implicitly or explicitly, SAIs to give up the claim that they could serve as prime sources of assurance about the effectiveness of government programmes and policies. Indeed, it would even weaken their claim to report directly on issues of efficiency, since good management practice is not yet efficiency, even if it may be one of the prerequisites for efficiency.

All of which brings us directly to a further major issue. This concerns *the identity of the object* of performance audit. This is perhaps a less obvious or controversial question than that of the content of practice or the choice of criteria, but it none the less confronts SAIs with a strategic choice. To put it briefly, performance audits can focus on policies, programmes, institutions, or projects. If they are designed with *policies* as the basic unit of analysis, then they will tend to emphasize the effectiveness criterion: has the policy achieved its objectives? These types of study are usually methodologically the most challenging and politically the most sensitive. If audits focus on *programmes* or on specific *projects*, then a range of criteria may be brought to bear—effectiveness, efficiency, or good management practice, though our research indicates that the second and third of these are considerably more common than the first. Where *institutions* are the prime foci of concern, then the tendency will probably be to address issues of good management together, possibly, with those of efficiency. None of our five SAIs is limited to only one kind of object for its performance audit, but there do seem to be differences in priority between one country and another. Thus, the VTV and the Rekenkamer have proclaimed their preference for broad-scope audits of programmes and policies, looking at systems and levels of coordination and not confining themselves to the boundaries of particular institutions or even sectors. The RRV was once enthusiastic about these more ambitious types of study, but then seemed to move somewhat away from them, undertaking more smaller-scale practical studies of efficiency and good management practice in individual institutions or types of institution. More recently still the emphasis has shifted again—this time towards studies of state obligations and whole programmes in the welfare sector, education, and the labour market. In France the Cour is showing some signs of an incremental shift towards broader-scope investigations, but this has not gone as far and is not as explicit as in the cases of its Finnish and Dutch counterparts. However, when the Cour does address a broad field of policy, it does not hesitate directly to criticize the state for failing to define objectives with sufficient clarity (e.g. Cour des Comptes 1997a, pp. 128–9). By contrast, the NAO has usually concentrated on the workings of individual organizations (payments in the Department of Education and Employment, National Health Service supplies) or the success of particular projects (the completion of the British Library, the sale of various previously nationalized enterprises).

The point here is that the methods used and the criteria of judgement applied both tend to be influenced by the types of topic chosen. When an SAI chooses its objects of study—using financial weight, risk, political salience, and whatever other selection criteria seem appropriate—it is also to some extent determining the kind of performance audit it will be engaged in.

The third and final issue is that of the nature of the *relationships with other institutions and groups* that performance auditors wish to create and sustain. Again, in this respect the mature identity of performance audit is not yet entirely clear. There is a danger that, like over-enthusiastic adolescents, performance auditors may try to represent themselves as simultaneously all things to everyone. More specifically, one may ask whether or how it is possible for one report or even one institution fearlessly to account to the public, usefully to report to politicians, scientifically to advance knowledge of public programmes, *and* sympathetically to advise civil servants and programme managers on how to manage better (i.e. to occupy all four corners of Figure 11.1 simultaneously). Of course, our different SAIs work within different politico-administrative regimes, and under different sets of constitutional provisions (Chapter 3 and Appendix 2). Some were set up mainly to serve parliaments, some mainly to serve governments, some both.

It is not surprising that our research found many instances of SAIs seeking to identify the specific needs of particular audiences more closely, and to design their performance audit products accordingly. Once more, we do not wish to suggest that there is 'one best way'. But, though the question of relationships may manifest itself in different contexts in different countries, in a generic sense it is a basic issue in each case.

One easy answer would be to say that the audience is defined in the founding statutes and mandates of each SAI, but that is true only up to a point. In practice, it is clear that such provisions, though immensely important, are commonly cast in such general terms that they leave the SAIs with significant room for manoeuvre to shape their day-to-day relations with a variety of actors. To take an obvious example, none of the founding statutes in any country specifies how the SAI should deal with the general public or the mass media.

Another easy answer would be to say that, whatever the details of the surrounding regime, SAIs and their auditors have, above all else, to be *independent*. This was quite a popular answer among auditors themselves, in our interviews with them, and also features in the SAIs' official publications (Pollitt and Summa 1997b, pp. 329–30; Witteveen 1996, p. 26). However, independence is quite a complex notion, and one that quickly dissolves into a number of different components or dimensions. In practice, it is by no means the case that every SAI in every aspect of its work is totally independent of all external influences—indeed, such a scenario is neither feasible nor even necessarily desirable. In the recent UK debate over the 'public audit model', a representative of the Chartered Institute of Public Finance and Accountancy argued that those performing public audits needed to be independent in five different respects:

1. Auditors should not be appointed by the bodies they audit.
2. Auditors should have security of tenure.
3. Auditors should be able to carry out other, non-audit, work only under specific and carefully monitored circumstances (to prevent clashes of interest arising).
4. Auditors should be financially independent so that price competition does not pose less a threat to quality.
5. Public audit bodies themselves should be publicly accountable (Evans 1998, p. 72).

Two points may be made about this list. First, it omits discussion of certain aspects of the performance auditors' role. For example, when auditors accept (as they often do) the audited body's or a peer group's definition of 'good practice' or 'sound management', how independent are they being in terms of criteria? More tellingly, perhaps, we have seen that widely different practices obtain in different countries in relation to the clearance of draft reports with auditees. At least some of these practices appear to give considerable opportunities to audited bodies to delay or challenge the contents of audit reports. Second, even within its own terms, the CIPFA list describes an ideal state rather than the messy and varying circumstances of real life.

It would be inappropriate, in this concluding chapter, to go through each of CIPFA's five points in detail, but a pair of illustrations may suffice to show that independence, though real and substantial for each of our five SAIs, is construed differently in each country and is never entirely 'pure'. Thus, if we take the issue of tenure, auditors within an SAI may enjoy a strong form of tenure yet be relatively poorly paid, so that the attractions of private-sector practice result in the kind of 'brain drain' that can threaten the independence of an SAI in a less direct sense than seems to have been envisaged by CIPFA. For example, in its Annual Report for 1995/6 the RRV says that it 'has been able to establish that the question of salaries has become an increasingly important factor if we are to retain qualified members of staff' (Riksrevisionsverket 1997a, p. 34). Or, if we look at the public accountability of SAIs, we can see that there are variations in transparency (Pollitt and Summa 1997b). Some give less information than others about the methods they use. Some do not publish the results of all (or even most) of their investigations. Some have strong and others more tenuous relationships with their legislatures (see e.g. Lumijarvi and Salo 1997, pp. 119–21). Some have undertaken parts of their work in very close cooperation with their executives. So, while we would fully accept that 'independence' is a crucial issue, it is not a concept that will straightforwardly provide a simple key to how the possible relationships between performance auditors and other institutions and groups either are or should be articulated.

Before we leave the issue of relationships with other institutions, we should also record that relations *between* SAIs appear to be becoming increasingly important. While we argue that it would be premature to propose the existence of some globalizing trend towards uniformity, it *is* the case that a network of SAIs exists and that mutual borrowings and loans (of ideas, techniques, personnel) are already taking place. INTOSAI and EUROSAI provide forums in which issues of common interest can be identified and discussed. As we have noted, EUROSAI has set up working groups on performance audit and on evaluation. The development of EU institutions is also beginning to have an effect, with national SAIs consulting with each other about how to respond to initiatives coming from the European Court of Auditors. Some joint work has taken place—for example, in the defence sector between the Cour, the NAO, the German Bundesrechrungshof and the Italian Cortei dei Conti, or between the Algemene Rekenkamer, the NAO, and the RRV on overseas aid. The RRV's 1997 *Report of the Auditor General to the Government* records that:

> The RRV conducts parallel audits with other organizations in the EU to a certain extent. In 1996 the RRV started a regular exchange of information with the European

Court of Auditors in the agricultural sector and, at present, with six other national audit institutions in order to identify parallel audits. (Riksrevisionsverket 1997b, p. 23; see also NAO 1997b, pp. 9–10)

As yet, these connections cannot be described as more than *ad hoc*, but they are certainly an issue for future researchers to keep track of. Perhaps the time will come when SAIs will attempt to fashion a more collective approach to the perennial issues of their relations with (especially) audited bodies.

11.12 Final Remarks

We have suggested that there are at least three aspects of the identity of performance audit that remain less than fully clear—or, to put it another way, where SAIs face strategic choices as to which of several paths to pursue:

1. in respect of the *core practices and criteria* that henceforth are to characterize performance audit;
2. in the selection of the *principal objects* of such studies;
3. in defining their *prime intended audience* and deciding how to conduct relationships with any *secondary audiences*.

As we have sought to show, these three choices hang together; making any one choice has implications for the other two. In a previous era it might have been possible for SAIs to 'plough their own furrows', working away quietly, pursuing their specialized and respected business of traditional audit. Since the mid-1980s, however, it has become clear that this is no longer a viable option for any of the five institutions covered by our research. In different ways and at different speeds, each SAI has, through a mixture of pressure and choice, begun to emerge into the wider world. This emergence has involved dialogues with executives and legislatures, the adoption of more proactive policies towards the media, and gradually increasing cooperation with other SAIs. It is a trajectory which, sooner or later, leads to new comparisons being made and demands being put; in other words, it sharpens the question of the identity and purpose of a Supreme Audit Institution at the end of the twentieth century. The growth of performance audit has been one, crucially important, strand in the process of modernizing SAIs. The future direction of its further development will tell us much about the identity of these vital institutions.

APPENDIX I
Research Methods

Research aims

Like many academic research projects, ours began with an 'off-the-top-of the-head' perception that 'there was something to be discovered' about the nature and development of performance audit and its relation to public management reform. Initially, it simply seemed to (some of) us that this was an important but 'underdone' area for serious study. From this fairly vague and opportunistic starting point discussion among us grew and, after a process of refinement, we arrived at the nine main questions set out in Chapter 1:

1. What is performance audit, as practised by the five SAIs in our study?
2. What have been the main trends in the development of performance audit since the mid-1980s?
3. What interactions between performance audit and the public management reforms have, to a greater or lesser degree, affected most OECD countries over the same period?
4. What is the nature of the performance auditor's craft?
5. What methods are used in performance audit?
6. What criteria are applied within performance audits?
7. What kinds of 'product' are generated by performance audit?
8. How is performance audit work presented, i.e. to what audiences and with what discernible results?
9. What changes have there been in respect of each of the above over the last ten to fifteen years?

Designing the study

We knew at the beginning that, if really interesting answers were to be arrived at, a comparative design would be necessary. The fact that performance audit was being discussed and practised in a number of countries, but that, at the same time, there seemed to be some glaring differences as to how it was being conducted, cried out for a comparative treatment. The next question, therefore, was 'a comparison of which countries?'

Our eventual selection of Finland, France, the Netherlands, Sweden, and the UK was arrived at for a mixture of theoretical, methodological, and practical reasons. Methodologically, we thought that four or five countries were probably the minimum for a decent comparison; theoretically, we thought it sensible to try to include a fairly wide range, from those who, prima facie, appeared to be very enthusiastic about and ambitious in regard to their performance audits to those who approached the issue more cautiously and did not necessarily see performance audit as a new and distinct species of activity. However—and we readily acknowledge this as a limitation of our study—we did not choose a country that does little or no performance audit at all. (There would have been problems as well as possible advantages in doing so. We couldn't have counted and analysed non-existent performance audit reports, and experience suggests that it would have been difficult to discuss with auditors in such countries why they were *not* doing something, and something, moreover, about which many of them would probably have known very little.)

A second consideration was the constitutional position and powers of the SAI concerned. Previous work had led us to suppose that these factors might influence the approach taken to an activity such as performance audit. Therefore, in an effort to explore such influences, we included in our study an example of each of the main types of SAI identified in a recent survey of EU audit bodies (NAO, 1996a):

1. a monocratic SAI principally responsible to its national legislature (the NAO);
2. a monocratic SAI within the sphere of jurisdiction of its national executive (the RRV and the VTV);
3. an SAI that has the collegial form of a court, although not exercising judicial powers (the Algemene Rekenkamer);
4. an SAI that is a court with judicial authority (the Cour des Comptes).

Another variable influencing our choice was our wish to cover a range of approaches to and experiences with public management reform. In a sense this was not difficult, since virtually no two countries have taken identical or even very similar approaches to public management reform (see Chapter 3 and its references). Nevertheless, one of our intentions was to include countries that had prided themselves on having vigorously pursued certain types of managerialism along with others that had been more cautious or selective.

Finally, our choice was influenced by a number of practical and happenstance factors. At an early stage we ruled out the United States because, although the General Accounting Office (GAO) had certainly been very creative and developmental in its approach, it was also the SAI about which the most has been published already. Furthermore, we had something of a positive bias towards a European focus, and our personal networks drew us along in that direction too. Finally, those of us who started the project always wanted it to be a 'live', interactive process with discussions and meetings, not just a 'virtual team' communicating only by e-mail, fax, and telephone. Again, this pointed towards a reasonably restricted geographical focus—Northwest Europe (given a little poetic licence for the 'westernness' of Finland).

Having selected our five countries, we embarked upon research that, in terms of its approach, could be described as a set of five holistic, multiple case studies (Yin 1994). Our unit of analysis was essentially the corpus of performance audit work carried out by each of the five SAIs. Possibly the most influential contemporary writer on case study research, Yin, argues that such an approach is particularly useful where a study

(a) investigates a contemporary phenomenon within its real life context, especially when:
(b) the boundaries between phenomenon and context are not clearly evident. (Yin 1994, p. 13)

It was our view that the boundaries between performance audit and kindred activities (such as financial audit or evaluation—see Chapter 2) were far from clear, so these characteristic strengths of the case study approach were appropriate and helpful to our subject matter.

A case study approach permits *analytic* generalization and theory-testing, but not *statistical* generalization (Yin 1994, p. 10). However, there is nothing in the case study approach that prohibits the use of statistical techniques or other forms of quantification albeit in a subsidiary role. It is a misconception to suppose that case studies are always irredeemably 'qualitative'—or, indeed, that they are essentially ethnographic. Our main effort went into the study of documents, but this was not entirely number-free. On the contrary, we undertook some basic classifying and counting of performance audit reports, mainly because they offered the most obvious and accessible, if imperfect, way of measuring certain dimensions of performance audit activity (see particularly Chapters 5 and 7). Once made, these measures permitted us to compare volumes of performance audit activity at different time periods (essential if we were to offer a substantive answer to the last of the nine main questions). They also enabled us—in a broad-brush way, and with a number of important qualifications—to make some comparisons between different SAIs.

We supplemented and followed up our very extensive documentary analysis with a programme of structured interviews of senior staff at each SAI. Interviewing allowed us to explore the meanings and interpretations given to performance audit activities, and to changes in those activities, by auditors themselves. It was also useful in giving us an opportunity to test some of the interpretations and understandings we had arrived at during the earlier, document-based, phase of the project ('respondent validation'). Details of both the counting of audit reports and the conduct of the interview programme are given in the following section.

Overall, therefore, we adopted a multiple case study design which allowed us to explore varying definitions and concepts of performance audit, to investigate the borderlines between performance audit and adjacent activities, to begin to measure some broad parameters of performance audit work, and to test and extend all this through structured discussion with senior members of the SAIs concerned.

Methods

We have counted, categorized, and read a large number of performance audit reports. We have also read many other potentially relevant documents produced by SAIs (e.g. annual reports, handbooks) and surveyed the available academic literature plus some more journalistic accounts.

There were advantages and disadvantages in taking audit reports as the basis for categorizing and counting. On the benefit side, they were concrete and discrete and were used as the basis of some recording systems by the SAIs themselves. Not uncommonly, annual reports from SAIs include a 'count' of reports as one indicator of their performance. However, for us the limits of this approach included the fact that one of our SAIs—the Cour—does not lay the same emphasis on the importance of the *published* report as its main product as do the others, and that not all SAIs have always distinguished clearly between performance audit reports and other kinds of report. A third issue is that performance audit reports vary considerably in size and content, both between SAIs and within SAIs, so it would be misleading to think that behind the numbers lay a set of homogeneous 'units'. Finally, it is important to remember, more generally, that there are other important 'products' from performance audit work apart from the reports themselves (Chapter 9).

One of our ambitions was to identify trends in performance audit work over time. To help with this, we decided to look at two periods of activity for four of our five SAIs. (The Cour could not be included in this part of the analysis because most of its work is not published.) For each of the four organizations we identified as many performance audit reports as we could from the three-year period 1993–5 ('period 2'), and then read and analysed a large sample of them. For the comparison over time, we chose another three-year period from the 1980s ('period 1'). The precise periods varied slightly according to the particular circumstances of the SAI in question (1986–8 for the NAO; 1983–5 for the Rekenkamer; 1983–5 for the RRV, and 1985–7 for the VTV). In each case, we counted all the reports we could identify and then looked through them to establish their contents (see Chapter 5). The numbers of reports we examined in this way were as follows:

- *period 1*: 86 for the NAO, 49 for the Rekenkamer, 50 for the RRV, and 125 for the VTV (because of the large number of VTV reports in this first period, only every third report was read);
- *period 2*: 137 for the NAO, 58 for the Rekenkamer, 57 for the RRV, and 49 for the VTV.

When the phase of documentary study was well advanced, and we had already begun to develop some interpretations of the phenomena under scrutiny, we embarked upon the interview programme. In each of the five SAIs we conducted three or more non-attributable interviews with senior staff who possessed extensive experience of performance audit. These sessions were used both to explore in-depth questions that could not be settled by documentary study alone (e.g. issues concerning the 'craft' of performance audit, or the political sensitivity of some aspects of the work) and to validate some of our interpretations of what we had read. Most of these interviews were conducted by two members of the research team: one 'from another country' and one who was on his or her 'home ground'. In this way, we hoped that our own different perspectives would complement each other and produce some of the benefits of 'cultural triangulation'. On average, the interviews lasted about an hour—none was less than 40 minutes.

The interview schedule we used is reproduced below. Not all questions were used in every interview.

Interview schedule

General introductory questions

1. What do you think have been the most significant changes in performance audit in your SAI over the last ten years?
2. How has the balance changed between performance audit and financial audit?
3. What effects (if any) have recent public management reforms and restructuring had on performance audit?

Programming performance audit

4. How are the topics for performance audit chosen?

The auditor's craft

5. What additional skills (if any) are needed by performance auditors?
6. What training is provided?

7. What are the main time and money constraints on performance audit?
8. Are consultants/external experts used on performance audits and, if so, how and under what circumstances?

Methods used in performance audit

9. Do you think your SAI has begun to use any important new methods in performance audit over the last ten years or so (and, if so, what are they)?
10. How, in practice, are the methods to be used within a particular audit chosen? (by whom? at what stage? is there a conscious programme of designing the audit? etc.)

Criteria used in performance audit

11. When performance audit reports refer to good management practice or appropriate administrative procedures, what exactly do auditors have in mind? (Follow this question up by asking whether there are explicit models of good management or good administration and, if so, where auditors get these models from.)
12. Has there been any significant shift in the kind of criteria applied within performance audit over the last ten years or so?
13. How is the clearance procedure organized?
14. We have formed the impression that good management practice or the use of appropriate administrative procedures is a much more commonly used criterion than true efficiency or effectiveness. Do you agree, and, if so, why do you think this is?

Outputs of performance audit

15. Do you think that the attitude of your SAI towards its main audience has changed significantly over the last ten years? (If so, in what way?)
16. Have the appearances and types of product produced on the basis of performance audit changed over the last ten years and, if so, how?

Assessing the impacts of performance audit

17. How do you assess whether a particular performance audit report has been successful or not?
18. Does your SAI have a formal system for measuring the impacts of performance audit? (If so, how does this system work?)
19. Can you give examples of particular studies that you would regard as especially successful (or unsuccessful)? What are their distinguishing features?

Possible future developments

20. What do you see as being likely to be the most important new developments in performance audit over the next few years?
21. How do you see the balance of work within your SAI as between performance audit and other types of activity changing (if at all)?
22. Do you think that the performance audit work of your SAI has had much influence on the way public management changes have developed in your country? (If so, can you give examples?)

Appendix 2
Supreme Audit Institutions: A Summary of their Structure and History[1]

Valtiontalouden tarkastusvirasto (VTV), Finland

The VTV was established under the 1947 State Audit Act, although its first forerunner was established in 1824. It is 'an independent and neutral government agency responsible for ensuring the legality and soundness of the government's financial management and compliance with the national budget'. The VTV examines the revenue and expenditure of the Council of State, government bodies (including ministries, state offices, and agencies), state enterprises, and recipients of state subsidies such as local communities, public utilities, and joint stock companies in which the state holds a majority share. The VTV comes under the jurisdiction of the Ministry of Finance, but under the Finnish Constitution its work programme is independent. It has access at all times to all documents it may require, and under the 1947 Act can fine anyone failing to comply with requests.

The VTV is headed by an auditor general, appointed by the president of the Republic on a proposal of the Council of State. The appointment is for life, but with a retirement age of 65. The auditor general and three audit councillors form the Audit Council, which considers the office's financial plan and draft budget, audit planning instructions, and the guidance issued to state bodies. The office is divided into four operational units, two responsible for performance audit, one for financial audit, and the other for internal services. The VTV has around 120 staff, the vast majority of whom work in Helsinki. All audit staff have university degrees, with postgraduate qualifications in accountancy and business common.

There is no direct official contact between the VTV and the Finnish parliament; instead, relations are conducted through the parliamentary state auditors, who are responsible for overseeing the finance of the state and supervising compliance with the budget on behalf of parliament. The VTV is required by statute to provide the parliamentary state auditors with its annual plan of operations and to submit all reports to them for information.

[1] The information for these summaries is taken primarily from the National Audit Office book *State Audit in the European Union* (NAO 1996a), permission for the use of which we are grateful. The book contains detailed descriptions of the work of all 15 Supreme Audit Institutions of the European Union, and the European Court of Auditors. Copies can be obtained from the NAO.

Cour des Comptes, France

Under the French Constitution, the Cour des Comptes is charged with assisting parliament and government in supervising the implementation of the state budget. It was established in its present form in 1807, although its predecessors date back to the fourteenth century. The Cour's functions have been greatly increased in the course of the last fifty years, and its organizational structure, duties, and powers are now set out in an Act of June 1967. The audit of social security, public enterprises, and nationalized industries was added in 1976, when audit bodies previously responsible were merged with the Cour. The audit of local corporations, agencies, and companies has, since 1982, been devolved to regional *chambres des comptes*, established to carry out this role.

The main task of the Cour, according to the Constitution, is to assist parliament and government in checking the proper execution of the state budget and the annual law on social security. However, it is independent of both institutions, and ranks, together with the Council of State and the Cour de Cassation, as one of the *grands corps de l'état*, the senior administrative bodies in France. The Cour audits the accounts of the state, the state autonomous agencies (*établissements publics nationaux*) and of state-owned companies (*enterprises publiques nationales*). It may, at its discretion, audit the accounts of entities, public or private, that receive financial assistance from the state or its agencies and companies. It also audits the accounts of the independent units that run the health insurance and pensions system (*organismes de sécurité sociale*).

The Cour is headed by the *premier président*, appointed by decree from the president of the Republic. It is divided into seven *chambres*, each headed by a president. Each *chambre* adopts an annual work programme on an entirely independent basis, and the Cour's overall work programme is drawn up from these proposals by the *premier président* after discussion with the other presidents. In addition, the *parquet général*, headed by the *procureur général*, provides advice on legal matters and acts as intermediary between the government, the Cour, and the judicial authorities. The Cour consists of some 500 people, 250 of whom are magistrates appointed for life by decree of the president of the Republic. Auditors are postgraduates from the Ecole Nationale d'Administration, often with qualifications in public law, finance, and economics. Many spend a significant part of their career in other jobs and then return to the Cour later in life.

The Cour's audit work involves establishing that the accounts present a true and fair view of all transactions, as well as that these transactions have been performed according to financial regulations and in the most effective way. The latter work, known as *contrôle de la gestion* (or performance audit), has steadily developed in recent years.

Algemene Rekenkamer, the Netherlands

The Algemene Rekenkamer is an independent body, which supports the work of the States General. It has a history dating back to 1814, but state audit in the Netherlands can be traced back to the fourteenth century. Its role was most recently formulated in the 1976 Budget and Accounting Act, and it is 'responsible for auditing state revenue and expenditure'. The Rekenkamer has no judicial powers and is not a court. Its budget is set following discussions with the Ministry of the Interior and the Ministry of Finance.

The Rekenkamer's audit field is extensive, covering some 50,000 separate bodies. It can also examine public limited companies and private companies where share capital is partly or wholly owned by the state, corporate entities that have been given state loans or guarantees. The Rekenkamer reports to the States General. Any parliamentary committee can discuss its reports, but they are usually considered by the State Expenditure Committee, which has the authority to call ministers to account and seek further evidence from the Rekenkamer.

The Rekenkamer undertakes both regularity and performance audits. Its regularity audit is systems-based and relies heavily on the work of ministerial internal audit divisions. The Rekenkamer examines the divisions' audit programmes and the conclusions they have reached, and the Rekenkamer staff then undertake their own work around this.

The Rekenkamer has a board of three members, including the president, each of whom is appointed (for life or until state retirement age of 70) by the government from a selection made by the lower house of the States General. The composition of the board is politically balanced. The Rekenkamer has six audit divisions, divided into audit sections which are based in the government ministries. It has some 320 staff, of whom 200 are directly involved in audit. The majority of auditors are graduates in statistics, economics, and law.

Riksrevisionsverket (RRV), Sweden

The RRV was established in 1961 when the National Accounts Board and the Government Audit Bureau were merged, and was reorganized most recently in 1992. It is the central administrative body for government accounting and auditing and is subordinate to the Ministry of Finance. It is headed by an auditor general, appointed by the government for a six-year term which can be renewed. The RRV has discretion as to its work programme, but undertakes many government-commissioned examinations each year.

The RRV's audit mandate covers state agencies including their regional and local offices, public utilities, national subsidy transfers to households, businesses and government bodies, and certain state owned companies. The RRV does not audit parliament and associated bodies, the cabinet office, or the ministries, which are examined by parliament's own audit agency, the Riksdagens Revisorer. The RRV has access to all information it requires, and under Sweden's public access to information legislation must allow access to its completed audit files.

Until 1998 the RRV was divided into three departments—for performance audit, financial audit, and financial management and accounting—each headed by an assistant auditor general. In July 1998 the financial management department was removed from the RRV and established as a separate agency, the National Financial Management Authority. Until this change, the RRV had a staff of around 500, mostly based in Stockholm. All audit staff are graduates, predominantly in social sciences and economics.

National Audit Office (NAO), United Kingdom

The NAO was established in 1983, taking over the responsibilities of the former Exchequer and Audit Department, created in 1866. It is headed by the comptroller and auditor general (C&AG), who is appointed by the monarch on an address by the House of Commons, the motion for which is made by the prime minister. The C&AG is independent of government, and has full discretion as to his work programme. He reports to Parliament and is an officer of the House of Commons. Resources for the NAO are determined directly by Parliament.

The audit function of the C&AG is primarily in two parts: the certification of some 650 accounts, and the examination of the value for money of specific programmes, projects, and activities. He also has inspection rights to some 4,000 other bodies that receive public funds. The C&AG provides his audit opinion in a certificate published with each set of accounts. His reports are examined by a committee of the House of Commons, the Public Accounts Committee. In addition to his audit role, the C&AG undertakes a smaller comptroller function, which makes him responsible for giving authority for Treasury requests for funds.

The NAO is divided into six units, five of which undertake both financial audit and value-for-money work, and the sixth of which provides central services. Each is headed by an assistant auditor general. The NAO has a staff of 750, but in addition makes extensive use of contracted-in consultants and agency staff. Audit staff, who are mostly university graduates trained by the NAO as accountants, specialize in either financial audit or value-for-money work.

APPENDIX 3
The Development of Performance Audit

Finland

The origins of state audit in Finland can be traced back to medieval times, although the first predecessor of the VTV, the General Revision Court, was established in 1824. This body's mandate covered the auditing of the accounts of all public bodies, including military operations. In the early twentieth century, the Senate's economic committee commented on the very limited nature of state audit, which paid attention only to formal aspects of the accounts, rather than whether audited authorities had acted as 'appropriately' and 'carefully' as could have been expected. The committee recommended that the Court be given an extended mandate, but there were no changes before Finland became an independent state.

The 1919 Finnish Constitution provided for the examination of the appropriateness of financial management, as well as the legality of expenditure. Subsequently, the 1923 Audit Decree stated that the tasks of the State Revision Office (established under the Constitution) included investigating 'whether any wastefulness or unnecessary expenditure or expenses exist' (SAO 1996, p. 2). In the 1940s, the wartime requirements gave an additional impetus to these considerations. A separate unit was established to audit the accounts of state bodies, with the audits focused particularly on the 'appropriateness' of the use of public funds. After the war, the Act on the Auditing of Public Funds 1947 made audit of the appropriateness of public expenditure explicit in legislation, allowing the newly established audit office, Valtiontalouden tarkastusvirasto (VTV), to undertake what can, in a broad sense, be considered as performance audit.

The focus of attention during this period was very much on the appropriateness of expenditure, rather than the performance of public bodies. Some years later, at the beginning of the 1970s, discussions began within the VTV, focusing on the idea of auditing the activities of public bodies. In 1971 a government committee on state audit proposed that appropriateness audit be extended and redirected to look at well defined topics or projects. This work would focus on the planning and programming systems for the audited activities, their economy and efficiency, coordination with other activities, and the possibilities for development. In 1978 another committee, investigating the structure and development of central government, spoke out against 'mere numerical and legalistic' audit, advocating that the VTV examine the efficiency and effectiveness of administrative activities.

By the mid-1970s, this new approach to audit had already been adopted by the VTV, at least in its explanatory rhetoric. During the 1970s and 1980s its work—focusing on how well activities were planned, on how well they linked with broader policies, and on their efficiency, economy, and profitability—was referred to as 'activity audit' and was considered a more advanced form of audit, in contrast to more 'limited' and 'legalistic' financial audit. To begin with, it was not treated as a separate discipline, but in 1981 the distinction between 'activity audit' and financial audit was made for the first time in VTV documents, and activity audit was allocated resources separately.

In the early 1980s a further government committee examined principles for the development of state audit. It took as its starting point that activity audit needed to be developed further, to be clearer methodologically and to receive increased resources. The committee's report offered conceptual refinements to the definition of 'appropriateness audits', 'efficiency audits', 'effectiveness audits', and the criteria to be used in them, and finally proposed that a greater proportion of the VTV's resources be devoted to activity audit. Before 1987 the VTV's audits of ministries and agencies combined financial and value-for-money (VFM) work, and all audit reports included VFM observations. The VTV was organized into units according to the branches of administration, and in planning their work no distinction was made between performance-oriented and financial audits. After the reorganization in 1988, performance audit in its current, separate format was established, and increased effort was put into developing its own profile, and methods and ways of working.

During the 1990s there were a number of developments in the VTV's performance audit work. Examinations tended to focus on broader, cross-sectoral topics rather than single organizations or sub-functions. There was a greater tendency towards openness in the VTV's relations with auditees and the general public and, after 1993, greater emphasis on the appearance of published reports. During the 1990s the VTV has produced around twenty reports a year, and in 1995 it published, for the first time, a collection of summaries from all eighteen performance audit projects completed during the year, a practice now repeated annually. In 1996 the VTV underwent further organizational changes which split the performance audit unit into two.

France

Providing a description of the development of performance audit in the Cour des Comptes is made difficult by the fact that it is not treated as a separate discipline in the way that it is in the other SAIs examined in this book. The most important provision relating to the Cour des Comptes is the 22 June 1967 law on its role and organization. Articles L 111–3 and L 111–4 provide for the Cour to examine aspects of economy, efficiency, and effectiveness. The former refers to the Cour considering 'the good use of public money', and the latter states that the Cour 'audits the accounts and the management of the public firms'. This involves enquiring into the organization of the audited body, the number, level, and pay of its staff, its procurement policy, its equipment policy, its costs compared with its achievements, and the usefulness of its activities to the state or to the general public.

Since 1991 the Cour has published a series of *rapports publics particuliers*. These address particular subjects, in many cases assessing the adequacy of management and making recommendations. Up to around 200 pages long, their size allows for significant discussion of the activities under examination. From around the same time, there has been increased interest within the Cour in evaluating public policies, and from 1992 the *premier président* has chaired the INTOSAI working group on evaluation. By the mid-1990s, roughly two-thirds of the Cour's resources were devoted to the assessment of financial management and performance in the broadest sense (NAO 1996a, p. 65). Since 1996 the Cour has, under a new article in the Constitution, produced '*le rapport sur la sécurité sociale*' following its examination of the execution of the annual law on the ways and means of social security. From 1997 the annual public report has included a section on the impact of previous reports.

The Netherlands

The Algemene Rekenkamer was established in 1814, although the origins of state audit date from several centuries earlier (NAO 1996a, p. 142). Under the first Budget and Accounting Act, which became law in 1927, the Rekenkamer had the task of auditing the efficiency and/or effectiveness of public policy and expenditure (Leeuw and Engwirda 1993/4, p. 16). After the Second World War, attempts were made to reduce public expenditure in the Netherlands by improving the performance of government activities. The Algemene Rekenkamer began to conduct the forerunners of performance audits, in particular with emphasis on aspects of efficiency and the organization of the public service, issues that were of most interest to the States General (Algemene Rekenkamer 1989, p. 25).

In the mid-1950s discussion arose in the States General about the emphasis that should be placed by the Algemene Rekenkamer on performance audit, and the office was encouraged to carry out more audits of efficiency and effectiveness, examining the reasons behind government decisions and whether objectives had been achieved. It was also suggested that it draw attention to undesirable side-effects, conflicts with other goals, or the lack of available information at the time of decision-making (Algemene Rekenkamer 1989, pp. 26–9).

It was during the 1950s that performance audit assumed the status of an independent aspect of audit work within the Rekenkamer, and from the middle of the decade staff began to examine and report on policy goals. Despite this, changes were still under consideration. In 1956 the Minister of Finance appointed a committee to undertake a general review of the Budget and Accounting Act, with the aim of providing a statutory basis for developments that had been going on since the 1920s, including the role of performance audit. However, a new Act was not passed for twenty years, when powers to conduct performance audits were incorporated into the 1976 Government Accounts Act. This stipulated that the Rekenkamer pay attention to the 'efficiency and effectiveness of government management and of the organization and performance of the public service' (Leeuw and Engwirda 1993/4, p. 17). In addition, the Rekenkamer was to present information in its Annual Report that might enable parliament to assess government policy, and could be asked by parliament to conduct specific performance audits (Rekenkamer 1989, pp. 27–8).

Despite the new legislation, in the early 1980s only a small proportion of the Algemene Rekenkamer's work could be classified as performance audit, and it was only in the following years that 'a conscious effort [was made] in favour of the selection, planning and implementation of performance audit on an increasingly systematic basis' (Algemene Rekenkamer 1991, p. 35). As the number of examinations grew during the decade, the work was also developed in other ways. In particular, in 1985 the Rekenkamer reported on its first government-wide audit, looking at the organization of accounting divisions across government ministries. These broad audits grew in number during the mid to late 1980s, looking, for example, at the control of the budgetary process, and at the efficiency and effectiveness of the management of 722 central government subsidies (Leeuw 1991, p. 26).

In 1989 the remit of the Rekenkamer was extended to include inspection of welfare benefits and state-aided bodies, permitting performance audit in these areas. Article 59 of the Governmental Accounts Act also enabled the Rekenkamer to examine both the regularity and the performance aspects of corporate entities performing a function regulated by statute, or where the state owned more than 5 per cent of issued capital, or which received a state grant, loan, or subsidy. Under a further amendment to the Budget and Accounting Act, made in 1992, the Rekenkamer's role was specified in more detail as 'auditing the effectiveness and efficiency of management, which includes all possible aspects of the internal management at departments of the public service; auditing the effectiveness and efficiency of the organization; and auditing the effectiveness and efficiency of the policy implemented' (Leeuw and Engwirda 1993/4, p. 17). Greater consideration was given subsequently to the focus of the Rekenkamer's work, and in 1995 the board announced an office goal of producing studies examining the effectiveness of government activities (personal interviews).

The Rekenkamer's reports developed significantly during the late 1980s and 1990s. Traditionally, it produced a single annual report, and occasionally separate 'interim' reports. In the late 1980s the number of interim reports grew, and between 1990 and 1995 compendiums of performance audit reports were published each June and December. In 1996 the Rekenkamer broke with its tradition of issuing one large annual report containing details of all its audit activities, and now publishes an annual regularity report relating to all departments, and about thirty separate reports, one for each audit (Witteveen 1996, p. 28).

Sweden

An important forerunner of performance audit in Sweden was the work of the State Subject Auditors, whose role developed during the Second World War as a response to the need to control the activities of government agencies and ensure that they were sound, appropriate, and economical. The Riksrevisionsverket (RRV) was established in 1961, on the merger of the National Accounts Board and the State Subject Auditors. Its development in the 1960s was closely related to the development of the Programme Budgeting System (which grew up between 1965 and 1975), as well as to the modernization of the budget process and long-term planning within state agencies (Swedish National Audit Bureau 1993, p. 36). The growing interest in performance audit was one of the main arguments for establishing the RRV.

Performance auditing began to develop after the RRV was restructured in 1967, with the aim of giving it 'a strategic policy role as a force for renewal in government administration' (Swedish National Audit Bureau 1993, p. 36). Financial audit was taken out of the RRV's remit and decentralized to the agencies, so that the main activities of the RRV were performance audit and supporting and developing financial management. The RRV's role was designed as a part of the overall state financial administration system, comprising planning, budgeting, accounting, and auditing. The RRV's task was to examine how agencies reached the goals set by central government, with recommendations intended mainly to make agencies aware of the possibilities of more efficient resource utilization, made possible by better planning and follow-up. The aim was for the RRV to undertake regular audits (every five years was the original intention, but this was never implemented) of agency financial administration, objectives, plans, and outcomes, to identify weaknesses, and to make recommendations. These recommendations were usually submitted to the agency itself (Swedish National Audit Bureau 1993, pp. 36–7).

In the 1970s it became clear from public debate that there was a need for broader and deeper analysis in performance audit, to look at the conditions, role, and functions of agencies in the wider context. Many examinations had, in practice, already gone beyond internal questions and perspectives, and other audit approaches and methods were developed. By the end of the 1970s agency audits covered a much wider context, and this led to more extensive analyses and the need for new competences. The link to programme budgeting weakened, and perspectives from other disciplines, such as the political sciences and sociology, were introduced. Increasingly, audit reports were submitted to the government, in line with the view that problems could be dealt with only at central government level.

During the 1980s performance audit developed further as the pressure for change in the public sector grew. In 1983 the State Agency Management Commission was set up to look into the problems of the public sector, which was widely considered too complex and ineffective. Parts of the Commission's examination covered the role of RRV's performance audit work, and supported the RRV's new type of broad 'systems-orientated' audits which assisted government decision-making. There was a growing expectation that more effort should be put into analysing possible alternative approaches and their consequences, and making more explicit recommendations. The overall expectation was that performance auditors would play a more active part in the reform of the state administration.

In 1987 financial audit, which had been outside the RRV's remit for twenty years, was returned to the RRV, and for a while it grew in strength with the development of the results-based budgeting and full accruals accounting. In 1989 the RRV's performance audit mandate was extended to include the auditing of state-owned companies and state-maintained foundations. At the same time, a single Performance Audit Division was founded (to replace the three existing ones) to help consolidate and coordinate audit activities. Performance auditors tried to take a more active role in the work of bringing about change in government administration and examining those problems considered urgent.

Two years later, the Swedish name for performance audit activity was changed from (directly translated) 'management audit' to (directly translated) 'effectiveness audit'. Since 1993, performance auditors have also participated in the annual auditing of agencies' performance reports. In 1994 the government gave the RRV the task of identifying the scale of abuse of social benefits and allowances, and subsequently it has reported on early retirement pensions, unemployment insurance funds/unemployment cash allowances, housing benefit, sickness benefit, and parental allowances (Sandberg and Ivarsson 1996, p. 29).

United Kingdom

Value-for-money (VFM) work of some kind has been conducted in the United Kingdom for many years. One authoritative source (Normanton 1966, p. 105) argued that the examination of the economy and efficiency of government expenditure, rather than just its regularity, was a feature of the comptroller and auditor general's (C&AG's) work in the 1880s, supported by the Public Accounts Committee (PAC) in the House of Commons. Subsequently, examinations took place into many aspects of financial management, and 'VFM examinations', in their broadest sense, were an established element of work at the Exchequer and Audit Department (E&AD, the forerunner of the NAO) well before the Second World War (Dewar 1991, p. 198). This work grew after 1945, 'with a marked acceleration in scale and coverage from the early 1950s, as the great post-war surge in government activity and the corresponding expenditure programmes gathered weight' (D. Henley, quoted in Glynn 1985, p. 151). Between then and 1983, the E&AD published more than 1,000 reports of varying length on a wide range of subjects, including defence procurement, contract pricing, and agriculture schemes (Dewar 1991, p. 198).

Despite this, some still expressed concerns about the E&AD's approach. Normanton described its emphasis on regularity as 'not simply insufficient, but terribly inadequate in the epoch of heavy spending', noting that, in almost all Western European countries, national audit offices had been liberated from concentrating on regularity and so were making a growing contribution to the development of public administration and government as a whole. In the 1970s the E&AD's VFM work consisted mainly of the examination of large projects, numerous individual transactions, or computer interrogations. Some subjects naturally chose themselves, while others arose from financial audit work and individual intuition, but few arose from any comprehensive review or evaluation of departmental systems. Many staff regarded the work as 'point hunting' to provide material highlighting individual failures, with wider issues less important.

In 1978 an internal E&AD review (Exchequer and Audit Department 1978) resulted in a shift of resources from VFM work to financial audit, and for a while VFM work was reduced from two-thirds of the E&AD's effort to about one-third. Around the same time, however, consideration was given in a number of parliamentary committees to the role of the C&AG and the adequacy of state audit in the UK (Garrett 1986, pp. 422–3). The House of Commons Expenditure Committee reported in 1977 that, compared with other countries, the system of public audit in the UK was outdated, and suggested that the C&AG's audit be extended to cover the scrutiny of the efficiency and effectiveness of the bodies responsible for the accounts which it was already auditing. In 1981 a PAC examination of the role of the C&AG made a number of recommendations for the reform of the post, including the VFM remit.

At that time, the remit was subject to a number of restrictions. The C&AG did not have specific statutory authority to carry out VFM examinations, instead doing them with the support of the PAC (Dewar 1985, p. 12). His reports were published as part of departmental accounts or as memoranda to the PAC, with legislation precluding him from reporting at any time other than when the accounts were laid before the House. As a result, there were complaints about the timeliness of reports, as there were about finding reports, which were, effectively, forewords to published accounts spread throughout numerous official publications.

Pressure for change led eventually to the National Audit Act 1983, which gave VFM work a new statutory basis and impetus. The Act, which established the National Audit Office (NAO), specifically allowed the C&AG to examine the economy, efficiency, and effectiveness with which government departments and a range of other bodies had used their resources, although it prevented consideration of the merits of policy objectives, and excluded the C&AG from nationalized industries and a number of other bodies such as the BBC. It also allowed the C&AG to present reports on individual subjects to Parliament at any time the House was sitting.

During the 1980s and 1990s, VFM work grew steadily within the NAO, and by the end of 1997 the C&AG had provided Parliament with some 500 published reports, the annual total reaching around fifty. The stated focus was primarily intended to be aspects of economy, efficiency, and effectiveness, but also took in quality of service matters as a specific concern from the late 1980s and, increasingly, issues of corporate governance in the mid-1990s. Major government initiatives such as the privatization programme of the 1980s and early 1990s became a regular focus of attention from the late 1980s onwards, while the Private Finance Initiative and utility regulatory regimes attracted attention in the late 1990s.

Other important developments during the 1990s included the increased attention paid to presentational aspects of reporting. Graphics, photographs, and layout were improved, along with stand-alone summary and conclusions sections. More attention was paid to study design, and attempts were made to find a broader range of methods, particularly from the mid-1990s. Many of these developments were encouraged in response to outside comments, and from 1993 all reports were examined by specialist public administration academics, who assessed and advised on proficiency in areas such as methodology, presentation, and the conclusions and recommendations of individual reports.

The staffing of VFM work also underwent some change during the 1990s. Traditionally, E&AD and NAO staff had undertaken both financial audit and VFM work. From 1991, staff in the NAO chose to specialize in either financial or VFM audit, the aim being to encourage greater professionalism in the approach to both types of work. Study teams increasingly contracted in specialist consultancy assistance to help with their work, while specialists with operational research, evaluation, or economics skills, or with expertise in subjects such as health or defence, were recruited to the NAO's permanent staff to supplement the predominantly accounting background of most audit staff.

References

Aberbach, J., Putman, R., and Rockman, B. (1981) *Bureaucrats and politicians in western bureaucracies*, Cambridge, Mass.: Harvard University Press.

Ahlenius, I-B. (1997) 'Auditing and evaluation in Sweden', pp. 80–5 in E. Chelimsky and W. Shadish (eds.), *Evaluation for the 21st century: a handbook*, Thousand Oaks, Calif.: Sage.

—— and Jonsson, G. (1995) 'A new strategy for performance audits of social security systems', *International Journal of Government Accounting*, April, pp. 7–9.

Algemene Rekenkamer (1989) *Algemene Rekenkamer: past, present and future*, The Hague: Algemene Rekenkamer.

—— (1991) *Vigilant and resolute: the challenges facing the Netherlands Court of Audit*, The Hague: Algemene Rekenkamer.

—— (1995) *Tweede Kamer*, 1994/95, 24120 no. 3, The Hague: Algemene Rekenkamer.

—— (1996) *Financial relations with major companies (summary)* (English-language summary briefing note), The Hague: Algemene Rekenkamer, October.

—— (1997) *Manual on performance audits*, The Hague: Algemene Rekenkamer.

Anand, P. (1988) 'Monitoring and auditing value for money in the UK: the scope for quantitative analysis', *Financial Accountability and Management*, 4:4, Winter, pp. 235–70.

Banefelt, R. (1992) 'How do we choose audit areas and audit subjects?' in *RRV Yearbook 1992: Development and Trends*, Stockholm: Swedish National Audit Bureau.

Barzelay, M. (1996) 'Performance auditing and the new public management: changing roles and strategies of central audit institutions', pp. 15–56 in OECD, *Performance audit and the modernisation of government*, Paris: PUMA/OECD.

—— (1997) 'Central audit institutions and performance auditing: a comparative analysis of organisational strategies in the OECD', *Governance*, 10:3, July, pp. 235–60.

Bekke, H., Perry, J., and Toonen, T. (eds.) (1996) *Civil service systems in comparative perspective*, Bloomington: Indiana University Press.

Birchall, J., Pollitt, C., and Putman, K. (1997) *Opting out and the experience of self-management in education, housing and health care*, Swindon: Economic and Social Research Council.

Boston, J., Martin, J., Pallot, J., and Walsh, P. (1996) *Public management: the New Zealand model*, Auckland: Oxford University Press.

Bourn, J. (1994) 'National Audit Office: force for change', pp. 69–74 in N. Flynn (ed.), *Reader: change in the Civil Service*, London: Public Finance Foundation/CIPFA.

Bowerman, M. (1994) 'The National Audit Office and the Audit Commission in areas where their VFM responsibilities interface', *Financial Accountability and Management*, 10:1, pp. 47–67.

Buxton, M. and Hanney, S. (1995) 'How can payback from health services research be assessed?' *Journal of Health Services Research Policy* (pre-launch issue), October, pp. 10–18.

Carter, N., Klein, R., and Day, P. (1992) *How organisations measure success: the use of performance indicators in government*, London: Routledge.

Centre for Finnish Business and Policy Studies (1996) *Not revolution but re-evaluation: a report of political decision-making in Finland*, April, Helsinki (translated by the Ministry of Finance).

Chambers Encyclopaedic English Dictionary (1994), Edinburgh: Chambers.

Chancellor of the Duchy of Lancaster and Financial Secretary to the Treasury (1997a) *The governance of public bodies: a progress report*, Cm. 3557, London: the Stationery Office, February.

—— (1997b) *Next steps: agencies in government review 1996*, Cm. 3579, London: HMSO.

Chelimsky, E. (1985) 'Comparing and contrasting evaluation: some notes on their relationship', *Evaluation Review*, 9:4, pp. 483–503.

Clark, D. (1998) 'The modernisation of the French civil service: crisis, change and continuity', *Public Administration*, 76:1, Spring, pp. 97–111.

Committee of Public Accounts (1994) *Eighth Report: the proper conduct of public business*, London: HMSO.

Committee Wiegel (1993) *Towards core departments: choosing a high quality, flexible state service*, Fourth External Committee of the Special Committee Moot Points, 21 427, no. 52, The Hague: Second Chamber of the States General.

Contact Committee of Presidents of the SAIs of the European Union Ad Hoc Group on Auditing Standards (1998) *European implementing guidelines for the INTOSAI auditing standards*, EU Contact Committee.

Cour des Comptes (1995) *Rapport au Président de la République*, Paris: Cour des Comptes.

—— (1997a) *Les musées nationaux et les collections nationales d'oeuvres d'art*, Rapport public particulier, Février, Paris: Direction des journaux officiels.

—— (1997b) *Le Rapport public annuel, 1997*, Paris: Cour des Comptes.

de Montricher, M. (1996) 'France: in search of relevant changes', pp. 243–77 in J. Olsen and B. Guy Peters (eds.), *Lessons from experience: experiential learning in administrative reforms in eight democracies*, Oslo: Scandinavian University Press.

Descheemaeker, C. (1992) *La Cour des Comptes*, Paris: La Documentation Francaise.

Dewar, D. (1985) 'Value for money audit: the first 800 years', *Public Finance and Accountancy*, 30 August, pp. 10–12.

—— (1991) 'Current issues in auditing: the audit of central government', in *State audit and accountability: a book of readings*, Jerusalem: State Comptroller's Office.

Dowie, J. (1999) 'The "pathology" of decision making in clinical practice and a framework for evaluations', in H. Selbmann (ed.), *Guidelines for guidelines in health care*, Baden-Baden: Nomos-Verlag.

Duran, P., Monnier, E., and Smith, A. (1995) 'Evaluation à la francaise', *Evaluation*, 1:1, July, pp. 45–63.

Efficiency Unit (1988) *Improving management in government: the next steps* (the Ibbs report), London: Cabinet Office.

Evans, M. (1998) 'Public audit: a comment and clarification of CIPFA's views', *Financial Accountability and Management*, 14:1, February, pp. 71–5.

—— and Thornton, S. (1997) *What is the proper scope of public audit?* London: Public Finance Foundation.

Exchequer and Audit Department (1978) 'Management review of the Exchequer and Audit Department', unpublished report, Exchequer and Audit Department.

Farnham, D., Horton, S., Barlow, J., and Hondeghem, A. (eds.) (1996) *New public managers in Europe: public servants in transition*, Basingstoke: Macmillan Business.

Flynn, N. and Strehl, F. (eds.) (1996) *Public sector management in Europe*, London: Prentice Hall/Harvester Wheatsheaf.

Garrett, J. (1986) 'Developing state audit in Britain', *Public Administration*, 64:4, Winter, pp. 421–33.

General Accounting Office (GAO) (1994) *Government audit standards*, GAO/OCG-94-9, June, Washington, DC: Comptroller General of the United States.

Glynn, J. (1985) *Value for money auditing in the public sector*, London: Prentice-Hall International.

—— Gray, A., and Jenkins, B. (1992) 'Auditing the three Es: the challenge of effectiveness', *Public Policy and Administration*, 7:3, Winter, pp. 56–70.

Goldsworthy, D. (1996) 'The Highways Agency's bridge programme: lessons learned from a VFM study', paper prepared for the UK Evaluation Society annual conference, London, 19–20 September.

—— (1997) 'Achieving impact: the NAO's approach', paper prepared for the UK Evaluation Society annual conference, London, 8–9 December.

Gray, A., Jenkins, B., and Segsworth, B. (eds.) (1993) *Budgeting, auditing and evaluation: function and integration in seven governments*, New Brunswick, NJ: Transaction Books.

Gustafsson, L. (1987) 'Renewal of the public sector in Sweden', *Public Administration*, 65, pp. 179–92.

Hague, R. and Harrop, M. (1987) *Comparative government and politics: an introduction*, 2nd edn, Basingstoke: Macmillan.

Hencke, D. (1998) 'Jobcentres fiddled the figures', *Guardian*, 8 January, p. 2.

Hennessy, P. (1990) *Whitehall*, London: Fontana.

Hepworth, N. (1995) 'The role of performance audit', *Public Money and Management*, 15:4, October/December, pp. 39–43.

H. M. Treasury (1991), *Competing for quality: buying public services*, Cm 1730, London: HMSO.

—— (1996), 'The External Audit of Public Bodies', in CIPFA, *Adding Value?* London: CIPFA.

Hodges, R. (1997) 'Competition and efficiency after privatisation: the role of the NAO', *Public Money and Management*, 17:1, January/March, pp. 35–42.

Hogwood, B., Judge, D., and McVicar, M. (1998) 'Too much of a good thing? The pathology of accountability', paper prepared for the Political Studies Association annual conference, University of Keele, 7–9 April.

Hood, C. (1991) 'A public management for all seasons?' *Public Administration*, 69:1, Spring, pp. 3–19.

—— (1996a) 'Exploring variations in public management reform of the 1980s', pp. 268–87 in H. Bekke, J. Perry, and T. Toonem (eds.), *Civil service systems in comparative perspective*, Bloomington and Indianapolis: Indiana University Press.

—— (1996b) 'United Kingdom: from second-chance to near-miss learning', pp. 36–70 in J. Olsen and B. Guy Peters (eds.), *Lessons from experience: experiential learning in administrative reforms in eight democracies*, Oslo: Scandinavian University Press.

—— and Jackson, M. (1991) *Administrative argument*, Aldershot: Dartmouth.

INTOSAI (1992) *Auditing standards*, International Organisation of Supreme Audit Institutions.

Jones, G. (1993) *International trends in public administration*, LSE Public Policy Paper No. 7, London: London School of Economics.

Keating, M. (1983) 'Decentralisation in Mitterrand's France', *Public Administration*, 61:3, Autumn, pp. 237–51.

Keen, J. (1998) *From checking to observing: reflections on study design*, London: National Audit Office.

—— (1999) 'On the nature of audit judgements: the case of value for money studies', *Public Administration*.

Kelly, J. (1997) 'Watchdog orders end to computer systems row', *Financial Times*, 24 November, p. 7.

Kemp, P. (1997) 'Out with the auditors, in with the innovators', *Accountancy Age*, 16, October, p. 14.

Kerrison, S., Packwood, T., and Buxton, M. (1994) 'Monitoring medical audit', pp. 155–77 in R. Robinson and J. Le Grand (eds.), *Evaluating the NHS reforms*, London: King's Fund Institute.

Kickert, W. (1997) 'Public governance in the Netherlands: an alternative to Anglo-American "managerialism"', *Public Administration*, 75:4, Winter, pp. 731–52.

—— and t'Veld, R. (1995) 'National government, governance and administration', pp. 45–62 in W. Kickert and F. van Vught (eds.), *Public policy and administration sciences in the Netherlands*, London: Prentice-Hall/Harvester Wheatsheaf.

Kraan, A. and Rozendal, P. (1997) 'Using evaluations in performance auditing: the case of the Netherlands Court of Audit', paper presented to the European Evaluation Conference, Stockholm, 6–8 March.

Lamarque, D. (1997) 'Social policies to assist handicapped adults. Theme: how to conduct effectiveness audits', aide memoire for presentation at the Second Tokyo International Audit Forum, June.

Lane, J-E. (1995) 'The decline of the Swedish model', *Governance*, 8:4, October, pp. 579–90.

Leeuw, F. (1991) 'Characteristics of government-wide audits', pp. 25–36 in *Auditing at the Netherlands Court of Audit: case studies*, The Hague: Algemene Rekenkamer.

—— (1992) 'Performance auditing and policy evaluation: discussing similarities and dissimilarities', *Canadian Journal of Program Evaluation* 7:1, pp. 53–68.

—— (1996) 'Auditing and evaluation: bridging a gap: worlds to meet?' pp. 51–60 in C. Wisler (ed.), *Evaluation and auditing: prospects for convergence*, New Directions for Evaluation, no. 71, Fall.

—— and Engwirda, M. (1993/4) 'Effectiveness auditing in the Netherlands: history, charter and case studies', *EUROSAI 1993/94*, pp. 16–20.

Lijphart, A. (1984), *Democracies: Patterns of Majoritarian and Consensus Government in Twenty One Countries*, London: Yale University Press.

Lovell, A. (1996) 'Notions of accountability and state audit: a UK perspective', *Financial Accountability and Management*, 12:4, pp. 261–80.

—— (1998) 'Public audit: a clarification of CIPFA's views—a reply', *Financial Accountability and Management*, 14:1, February, pp. 77–84.

Luder, K. (1994) 'The "contingency model" reconsidered: experiences from Italy, Japan and Spain', pp. 1–16 in E. Bushor and K. Schedler (eds.), *Perspectives on performance measurement and public sector accounting*, Bern: Haupt.

Lumijarvi, I. and Salo, S. (1997) *Steering and auditing: public management reform and the new role of the Parliamentary actors*, Bern: Peter Lang.

McEldowney, J. (1994) 'The control of public expenditure', in J. Jeffrey and O. Dawn (eds.), *The changing constitution*, Oxford: Clarendon Press.

Ministère de la Fonction Publique (1994) *L'accueil dans les services publiques*, Paris: Ministère de la Fonction Publique.

Mol, N. (1995) 'Quality improvement in the Dutch Department of Defence', pp. 111–20 in C. Pollitt and G. Bouckaert (eds.), *Quality improvement in European public services: concepts, cases and commentary*, London: Sage.

Mosher, F. (1979) *The GAO: the quest for accountability in American government*, Boulder, Colo.: Westview Press.

Mul, R. (1996) 'Between government-bashing and consultancy: strategies of six Supreme Audit Institutions', unpublished paper, Netherlands School of Government.

—— and van Westing, B. (1996) 'Re-inventing a SAI: re-organizing the Netherlands Court of Audit', *International Journal of Government Auditing*, April, pp. 13–15.

Naschold, F. (1995) *The modernization of the public sector in Europe: a comparative perspective on the Scandinavian experience*, Helsinki: Ministry of Labour.

National Audit Office (NAO) (1986a) *Department of the Environment, Scottish Office and Welsh Office: Enterprise Zones*, HC 209, London: HMSO.

—— (1986b) *Ministry of Defence: management of work at research establishments*, HC 462, London: HMSO.

—— (c. 1987) *A framework for Value for Money Audits*, London: National Audit Office.

—— (1988) *Department of the Environment: derelict land grant*, HC 689, London: HMSO.

—— (1993a) *Qualitative techniques: their practical uses in VFM audit* (Unit A: investigative techniques guide no. 6), London: National Audit Office.

—— (1993b) *Study design* (Unit A: investigative techniques guide no. 5), London: National Audit Office.

—— (1993c) *Department of National Heritage, National Museums and Galleries; quality of service to the public*, HC 841, London: HMSO.

—— (1993d) *Sale of the Scottish Bus Group*, HC 884, July, London: HMSO.

—— (1993e) *The cost of decommissioning nuclear facilities*, HC 692, London: HMSO.

—— (1993f) *Accounting for inflation in defence procurement*, HC 54, London: HMSO.

—— (1994a) *Annual report, 1994*, London: National Audit Office.

—— (1994b) *Metropolitan Police Service: responding to calls from the public*, HC 753, London: HMSO.

—— (1994c) *Overseas Development Administration: management of programme aid*, HC 68, London: HMSO.

—— (1995a) *Annual report 1995*, London: National Audit Office.

—— (1995b) *The Meteorological Office: evaluation of performance*, HC 693, 25 August, London: HMSO.

—— (1995c) *Ministry of Defence: procurement lessons for the Common New Generation Frigate*, HC 692, London: HMSO.

—— (1995d) 'VFM standards', unpublished document.

—— (1996a) *State Audit in the European Union*, London: National Audit Office.

—— (1996b) *The work of the directors general of telecommunications, gas supply, water services and electricity supply*, HC 645, London: House of Commons, 24 July.

—— (1996c) *Annual report 1996*, London: National Audit Office.

—— (1996d) *Health of the nation: a progress report*, HC 656, London: HMSO.

—— (1996e) *Focus groups: how to apply the technique to VFM work*, London: National Audit Office.

—— (1997a) *Designing VFM studies: a guide*, London: National Audit Office.

—— (1997b) *Annual report 1997*, London: National Audit Office.

—— (1997c) *Value for money: handbook*, London: National Audit Office.

—— (1997d) 'Management of assets', *NAO Focus*, no. 5, September, London: National Audit Office.

—— (1997e) *Focus groups*, London: National Audit Office.

—— (1998a) *Annual report 1998*, London: National Audit Office.

—— (1998b) *Validation of performance measures: summary of key concepts*, London: National Audit Office.

Netherlands Court of Audit (1996) 'Financial relations with major companies' (English summary), The Hague: Algemene Rekenkamer.

Next Steps Team (1998) *Towards best practice: an evaluation of the first two years of the Public Sector Benchmarking Project, 1996–1998*, London: Cabinet Office (Office of Public Service).

Normanton, E. (1966) *The accountability and audit of government*, Manchester: Manchester University Press.

OECD (1993) *Managing with market-type mechanisms*, Paris: PUMA/OECD.

—— (1994) *Performance management in government: performance measurement and results-oriented management*, Paris: PUMA/OECD.

—— (1995) *Governance in transition: public management reforms in OECD countries*, Paris: PUMA/OECD.

—— (1996) *Performance auditing and the modernisation of government*, Paris: PUMA/OECD.

—— (1997a) *Trends in public sector pay in OECD countries, 1996*, Paris: PUMA/OECD.

—— (1997b) *In search of results: performance management practices*, Paris: PUMA/OECD.

Österberg, J. (1995) 'Svensk Förvaltningspolitik i Förändring: Utvecklingstendenser i Statlig Förvaltningspolitik 1982–1995' (The development of the Swedish politics of public administration), mimeo, University of Gothenberg School of Public Administration.

Pendlebury, M. and Schreim, O. (1990) 'UK auditors' attitudes to effectiveness auditing', *Financial Accountability and Management*, 6:3, Autumn, pp. 177–89.

Perkinen, L. (1997) 'Hallintopolitiikka ja toiminnantarkastuksen strategia: Valtionlouden tarkastusviraston suorittaman toiminnantarkastuksen muutos, 1985–95', Masters thesis, University of Helsinki Department of Political Science.

Pierre, J. (1995) 'Administrative reform in Sweden: the decline of executive capacity?' paper presented at the conference 'Administrative reform in Europe', Institut International d'Administration Publique, Paris, 15–16 June.

Pollitt, C. (1984) *Manipulating the machine: changing the pattern of ministerial departments, 1960–1983*, London: Allen & Unwin.

—— (1993) *Managerialism and the public services: cuts or cultural change?* 2nd edn., Oxford: Blackwell.

—— (1994) 'The citizen's charter: a preliminary analysis', *Public Money and Management*, 14:2, April/June, pp. 9–14.

Pollitt, C. (cont.) (1995) 'Justification by works or by faith? Evaluating the new public management', *Evaluation*, 1:2, pp. 135–57.

—— (1998) 'Managerialism re-visited', pp. 45–77 in B. Peters and D. Savoie (eds.), *Taking stock: assessing public sector reforms*, Montreal and Kingston: McGill-Queen's University Press.

—— and Bouckaert, G. (1996) *Improving the quality of public services: recent experience in Belgium and the UK*, Uxbridge: Centre for the Evaluation of Public Policy and Practice, Brunel University.

—— and —— (1999) *Public management reform: a comparative analysis*, Oxford: Oxford University Press, forthcoming.

—— and Summa, H. (1996) 'Performance audit and evaluation: similar tools, different relationships?', pp. 29–50 in C. Wisler (ed.), 'Evaluating and auditing: prospects for convergence', special issue of *New Directions for Evaluation*, no. 71, Fall, San Francisco: Jossey Bass.

—— and —— (1997a) 'Trajectories of reform: public management change in four countries', *Public Money and Management*, 17:1, January/March, pp. 1–13.

—— and —— (1997b), 'Reflexive watchdogs? How Supreme Audit Institutions account for themselves', *Public Administration*, 75:2, Summer, pp. 313–36.

—— and —— (1997c) 'Performance auditing: travelers' tales', pp. 86–108 in E. Chelimsky and W. Shadish (eds.), *Evaluation for the 21st century: a handbook*, Thousand Oaks, Calif.: Sage.

—— and —— (1998) 'Evaluation and the work of Supreme Audit Institutions', pp. 63–82 in M-C. Kessler, P. Lascoumes, M. Setbon, and J-C. Thoenig (eds.), *Evaluation des politiques publiques*, Paris: l'Harmattan.

—— Hanney, S., Packwood, T., Roberts, S., and Rothwell, S. (1997a) *Trajectories and options: an international perspective on Finnish public management reforms*, Helsinki: Ministry of Finance.

—— —— —— —— and —— (1997b), *Public management reforms: five country studies*, Helsinki: Ministry of Finance.

—— Birchall, J., and Putman, K. (1997c) *Opting out and the experience of self-management in education, housing and health care*, Swindon: Economic and Social Research Council.

—— —— and —— (1998) *Decentralising public management*, Basingstoke: Macmillan.

Power, M. (1995) *Audit and the decline of inspection*, London: Public Finance Foundation/CIPFA, November.

—— (1997) *The audit society*, Oxford: Oxford University Press.

Prime Minister (1991) *The Citizen's Charter: raising the standard*, Cm 1599, London: HMSO.

—— (1992) *The Citizen's Charter: first report 1992*, Cm 2101, London: HMSO.

Puoskari, P. (1996) *Transformation of the public sector*, Helsinki: Ministry of Finance.

Riksrevisionsverket (RRV) (1987) *20 ar med RRV*, Stockholm: Riksrevisionsverket.

—— (1993) *Den statliga forvaltningsrevisionen vid RRV*, Stockholm: Riksrevisionsverket.

—— (1996) *Housing benefit: a performance audit on an instrument of social and housing policy*, Stockholm: Riksrevisionsverket.

—— (1997a) *Annual report and accounts, 1995/96*, Stockholm: Riksrevisionsverket.

—— (1997b) *Report of the Auditor General to the Government, 1997*, Stockholm: Riksrevisionsverket.

Roberts, S. and Pollitt, C. (1994) 'Audit or evaluation? A National Audit Office VFM study', *Public Administration*, 72:4, Winter, pp. 527–49.

Robinson, A. (1988) 'The House of Commons and public money' in M. Ryle and P. Richards (eds.), *The Commons under scrutiny*, London: Routledge.

Rouban, L. (1995a) 'Public administration at the crossroads: the end of French specificity?' pp. 39–63 in J. Pierre (ed.), *Bureaucracy in the modern state*, Aldershot: Edward Elgar.

—— (1995b) 'The civil service culture and administrative reform', pp. 23–54 in B. Guy Peters and D. Savoie (eds.), *Governance in a changing environment*, Montreal: McGill-Queen's University Press.

Sandahl, R. (1991) *Resultatanalys*, Stockholm: Riksrevisionsverket.

Sandberg, B. and Ivarsson, S. (1996) 'Fraud and abuse of the welfare system in Sweden', *EUROSAI*, no. 3, pp. 29–32.

Segergren, I. (1992) 'Performance auditing: better results through open dialogue', in *RRV Yearbook: development and trends, 1992*, Stockholm: Swedish National Audit Bureau.

Sengupta, K. (1998) 'MPs call for new audit powers over Camelot', *Independent*, 6 February, p. 2.

Smith, T. (1993) 'How to get more value for money from the NAO', *Accountancy Age*, 14, October, p. 10.

State Audit Office of Finland (SAO) (1994a) *Annual report*, Helsinki: State Audit Office of Finland.

—— (1994b) *Vankeinhoidon henkiloston kaytdn tuloksellisuus, Esi tarkastus, 218/54/92; Tarkastuskertomus 218/54/94* (*Report on the performance audit in prison administration*, pre-study 1992; final report 1994), Helsinki: State Audit Office of Finland in Finnish).

—— (1996) *The State Audit Office of Finland: general introduction*, Helsinki: State Audit Office of Finland.

Summa, H. (1995), 'Old and new techniques for productivity promotion: from cheese-slicing to a quest for quality', pp. 155–65 in A. Halachmi and G. Bouckaert (eds), *Public productivity through quality and strategic management*, Amsterdam: IOS Press.

—— (1996) 'Giving up orthodoxy in performance measurement: from effectiveness to process measures in a case of Finnish prison administration', pp. 145–56 in A. Halachmi and D. Grant (eds.), *Re-engineering and performance measurement in criminal justice and social programmes*, Perth, Western Australia: Ministry of Justice.

Swedish National Audit Bureau (1992a) *Human resources management in a perspective of change*, Stockholm: Swedish National Audit Bureau.

—— (1992b) *Annual Yearbook 1992*, Stockholm: Swedish National Audit Office.

—— (1993) *Performance auditing at the Swedish National Audit Bureau*, Stockholm: Swedish National Audit Bureau.

Swedish National Audit Office (undated—mid-1990s) *The Swedish National Audit Office: a presentation*, Stockholm: Swedish National Audit Office.

—— (1995a) *Performance auditing at the Swedish National Office*, Stockholm: Swedish National Audit Office.

—— (1995b) *A strategy for performance auditing of social security systems*, Stockholm: Swedish National Audit Office.

—— (1996) *Handbook on performance auditing: theory and practice*, Stockholm: Swedish National Audit Office.

Swedish National Audit Office (cont.) (undated—c. 1997) *A presentation*, Stockholm: RRV.

Terry, F. (1996) 'The Private Finance Initiative: overdue reform of policy breakthrough?' *Public Money and Management*, 16:1, January/March, pp. 9–16.

Timmins, N. (1997) 'It's time for a good think', *Financial Times*, 14 November, p. 6.

Trosa, S. (1995a) 'Quality in the French public service', pp. 58–68 in C. Pollitt and G. Bouckaert (eds.), *Quality improvement in European public services: concepts, cases and commentary*, London: Sage.

—— (1995b) *Moderniser l'administration: comment font les autres?* Paris: Les editions d'Organization.

Tulip, S. (1997) 'The audit trail', *Supply Management*, 22 May, pp. 22–6.

University of Vermont (1997) *Managing for results: the key to more responsive government, Manual and facilitators guide*, Concord, Vt: University of Vermont Division of Continuing Education.

Valtiontalouden tarkastusvirasto (1992) *Toiminnantarkastuksen hallinta*, Helsinki: Valtiontalouden tarkastusvirasto.

—— (1993) *Tullivalvonta: tarkastuskertomus*, Helsinki: Valtiontalouden tarkastusvirasto.

—— (1994) *Keskushallinnon organisaatiouudistukset*, Helsinki: Valtiontalouden tarkastusvirasto.

—— (1995) *Kantokykyluokitusjarjestelma: Tarkastuskertomus*, Helsinki: Valtiontalouden tarkastusvirasto.

—— (1997) *Toimintasuunnitelma*, Helsinki: Valtiontalouden tarkastusvirasto.

—— (1998) 'Toiminnantarkastuksen laatukriteerit', unpublished internal report, Helsinki: Valtiontalouden tarkastusvirasto.

Weekes, T. (1996) 'Who guards the guardians?' National Audit Office special report in *Public Finance*, 19 April, pp. 13–19.

Weiss, C. (1987) 'Evaluating social programs: what have we learned?' *Society*, November/December, pp. 40–5.

Wighton, D. (1998) 'NHS rapped for delay to report', *Financial Times*, 8 January, p. 8.

Wilkins, P. (1995) 'Performing auditors? Assessing and reporting the performance of national audit offices: a three country comparison', *Australian Journal of Public Administration*, 54:4, December, pp. 421–30.

Witteveen, T. (1996) 'Relations between the Netherlands Court of Audit and Parliament: a Dutch perspective', *EUROSAI*, no. 3, pp. 26–8.

Wright, V. (1989) *The government and politics of France*, 3rd edn., London: Unwin Hyman.

Yin, R. (1994) *Case study research: design and methods*, 2nd edn., London: Sage.

Index

Page numbers in bold refer to figures and those in italic refer to tables.